Crafting the Republic

Crafting the Republic

Lima's Artisans and Nation Building
in Peru, 1821–1879

Iñigo L. García-Bryce

UNIVERSITY OF NEW MEXICO PRESS ❧ ALBUQUERQUE

First paperbound printing, 2008

13 12 11 10 09 08   1 2 3 4 5 6 7

Some material in chapter four appeared in an earlier version as the article
"Politics by Peaceful Means: Artisan Mutual Aid Societies in Mid-Nineteenth-Century
Lima, 1860–1879. *The Americas* 59:3 (January 2003): 325–45. Used with permission
of *The Americas*.

Paperbound ISBN: 978-0-8263-3393-3

LIBRARY OF CONGRESS CATALOGING-IN-PUBLICATION DATA

García-Bryce, Iñigo L., 1966–
   Crafting the republic : Lima's artisans and nation building in Peru, 1821-1879 /
Iñigo L. García-Bryce.
      p. cm.
   Revision of the author's thesis (doctoral—Stanford, 1999).
   Includes bibliographical references (p.) and index.
      ISBN 0-8263-3392-3 (cloth : alk. paper)
   1. Artisans—Peru—Lima—History—19th century.
   2. Artisans—Peru—Lima—Political activity—History—19th century.
   3. Artisans—Peru—Lima—Societies, etc.—History—19th century.
   4. Working class—Peru—Lima—Political activity—History—19th century.
   5. Working class—Peru—Lima—Societies, etc.—History—19th century.
   6. Social classes—Peru—History—19th century. I. Title.

      HD8350.L562G37 2004
      331.7'94—dc22

                                        2004015736

                                        ❧

                        Book design and composition by Kathleen Sparkes
                        This book was composited using the Minion Family
                              Body type is Minion 10.5/13.5
                           Display are Minion and Minion Display

❧

I dedicate this book,

con mucho amor,

to my wife,

Andrea Orzoff

❧

Contents

❧

Figures

❧

Preface

From the skilled car mechanics who can fix any motor, to the men and women who sell orange juice on the streets of the Centro de Lima and carve the orange peel into elaborate shapes, to the *vendedores ambulantes* on Avenida Abancay who can take apart a watch in a few seconds and change its battery while one stands there waiting, to the weavers of beautiful tapestries, Peru is a country of *artesanos*. Lima is abuzz with the energy of these men and women, who can be seen working on street corners or in small workshops or at market stands. It was they who inspired me to begin asking questions about artesanos and their role in Peruvian history.

My main regret in writing this book is that I cannot say more about the nineteenth-century *artesanas* who formed an integral part of the world I am describing. Women worked beside men in workshops as part of family enterprises and surely had things to say about politics. While the public discourse was undoubtedly a male one and norms of citizenship excluded women, I am certain that women wielded power and contributed to shape the public sphere in ways that I have been unable to explore based on the sources available. The absence of female voices from this book has nothing to do with the "enormous condescension of posterity" and everything to do with the limitations of my own research.

Historical questions begin with the present. Peru's present-day artesanos operate in an increasingly globalized world just as their nineteenth-century predecessors had begun to do. My interest in the nineteenth-century age of liberalism stems from questions about this new age of neoliberalism in which

ordinary Peruvians face the daunting task of surviving amid the stark economic realities of the twenty-first century. In just what ways today's artesanos
and artesanas are adjusting to and contributing to the shape Peruvian politics
and society, I cannot be sure. Herein lies the limitation of history: it must wait
for the dust to settle, and my own personal limitation in that I live far away
from Peru.

But my students assure me semester after semester that history holds
important lessons. As the saying goes, "History may not repeat itself, but it
rhymes." I therefore leave it to the reader to listen for those rhymes.

Acknowledgments

One of the best rewards for completing a book is being able to thank the many people in many places who contributed to make the endeavor possible. At every stage of this project, I had the good fortune to exchange ideas with and receive suggestions from mentors, friends and colleagues. I value all these contributions, ranging from casual conversations in hallways to careful criticism of drafts. These many voices have helped to improve this book. I take sole responsibility for its shortcomings.

Since sources lie at the heart of historical interpretation, I begin by thanking the archivists in Lima whose professionalism and generosity made working on this project a pleasure. I thank the staffs of the Archivo General de la Nación, the Biblioteca Nacional del Perú, the Archivo Histórico Municipal de Lima, the Archivo Histórico Militar del Perú, the Instituto Riva Agüero, the Archivo Arzobispal de Lima, the Archivo de la Beneficencia de Lima, and the Biblioteca Denegri Luna, and particularly Yolanda Auqui, Roycida Aguilar, Elinos Caravasi, Janet Illya and Elia Lazarte for their constant interest in my project.

I also extend a special thanks to the members of the Sociedad Fraternal de Artesanos who generously opened their private archive, and in particular to the late Miguel Tristán, who literally brought the past to life by engaging in the much-forgotten art of conversation. I thank my research assistant Richard Becerra for his help with the tedious task of data entry.

I am greatly indebted to two teachers who will sadly be unable to read their names here in the acknowledgements. Frederick Bowser introduced me to the formal study of Latin American history; John Wirth directed the dissertation that would later become this book. I appreciate the encouragement and guidance of both. At Stanford, I also thank Peter Stansky for the many lessons learned about history in his colloquia and Steve Haber for constantly challenging my ideas.

I thank Margaret Chowning for her unwavering support through some difficult years during the PhD and for encouraging me to use diverse method-ologies in this project. In Lima, Scarlett O'Phelan gave generously of her time to discuss my research as it developed, and invited me to present my work at the Taller Permanente de Historia. I thank Nils Jacobsen for his support and incisive comments. Vincent Peloso offered valuable criticism of various con-ference papers that would become parts of the book and has remained enthu-siastic about this project since we first met. I thank Chuck Walker for both his friendship and his extensive comments on the entire manuscript.

For their comments on all or parts of this manuscript, I express my gratitude to Cristobal Aljovín, Jamie Bronstein, Stuart Finkel, Steve Jurichich, John Nieto-Philips, Andrea Orzoff, Chris Schmidt-Nowara, Reiko Shinno, Natalia Sobrevilla, Martin Valadez, and Alexandra Weinstein.

For their valuable advice at various stages of this project, I thank Carlos Aguirre, Gabriella Chiaramonti, Jesús Cosamalón, Leo Garófalo, Paul Gootenberg, Mildred Lopez, Natalia Majluf, Carmen McEvoy, Cecilia Mendez, Ramón Mujica, the late Franklin Pease, and Teresa Vergara. Francisco Quiroz deserves a special mention for his generosity in sharing sources and bibliography, as does Walter Huamaní for his eagerness to share his bibliographical knowledge. For his assistance with graphics I thank Mark Milliorn.

At the University of New Mexico Press, foremost, I thank my editor David Holtby for his interest in this project and for seeing the publication process through from its inception. The staff at the press did a wonderful job: I thank Evelyn Schlatter, Glenda Madden, Kathy Sparkes and Justin Parks. Also a special thanks to my copyeditor, Karen Taschek, for her careful work on the manuscript.

Institutions, as well as individuals, have contributed to make this book possible. I thank the Andrew W. Mellon Foundation, the Weter Foundation, the Center for Latin American Studies at Stanford University, and the Research Minigrants Program at New Mexico State University.

During the early stages of this project, Bolivar House, Stanford's Center for Latin American Studies, provided a nurturing environment complete with calor humano and intellectual stimulation. I thank Evelyn Castañeda, Beth Frankland, the late Alicia Herasimchuk, Terry Karl, Jutta

Mohr, Kathleen Morrison, and Victoria Sanford for creating un ambiente acogedor; the members of the Andean Working Group—José Carlos Fajardo, Luis Millones, Carla Faini and Sara Rondinel—for creating un espacio andino; and the many visiting scholars at the Center—Romana Falcón, Adolfo Gilly, Carlos Marichal, Lorenzo Meier, José Murilo de Carvalho—for those serendipitous conversations in hallways that contributed valuable insights to this project. In particular, I thank José Carlos Fajardo, Manolo Hidalgo, Jutta Mohr, and Martín Valadez for their friendship.

At Cambridge University, I thank Elisa Sampson for her hospitality and companionship, as well as Celia Wu and David Brading for introducing me to the Latin American Studies community.

Without the support and good humor of family and friends this project would not have gone very far. My parents, Alexandra Weinstein and José García Bryce, offered constant love and support, as did my sister Ariadna and cuñado Diego Alonso and my cousins Mariana and Maricarmen de Toro. Steve Jurichich, Consuelo Perales, Victor Endo, Martín Majluf, Ramón Mujica, Claudia Balarín all deserve special mention, as do Eloisa Guzmán, Fermín Carbonel, Demetrio García, Alejandro Alarcón, Juán Medina and Amelia de la Cruz.

I reserve my deepest appreciation for my wife, partner, and colleague, Andrea Orzoff, without whose love, encouragement, tolerance, and valuable criticism, this book would never have been written.

Introduction

WHEN PERU COMMEMORATED THE FORTY-FIFTH ANNIVERSARY of its independence from Spain on July 28, 1866, the festivities took on an added significance as a celebration of republican values. Just a few months earlier, on May 2, Peruvian military forces had valiantly defended the city's port, Callao, from attack by a Spanish squadron and put an end to Spain's renewed imperial ambitions in both Peru and Chile. As far away as Buenos Aires, people celebrated what was seen as the victory of a young Spanish American republic against its former imperial master. After all, French troops continued to occupy Mexican soil as liberals fought against the monarchy of Emperor Maximilian.

The members of Lima's Sociedad de Artesanos (Artisan Society) stood proudly that day among the participants in the two-day independence festival. After assembling at one of the portals of the old colonial walls, the members of this artisan mutual aid society, together with various other patriotic associations, opened the celebrations by singing the national anthem at the foot of a tree of liberty, a symbol dating to the American and French revolutions. The groups then marched to Lima's central square to witness a display of fireworks and an elaborate re-creation using model ships of Peru's recent naval combat with Spain. During the course of the day's events, artisans were honored with two prizes, one for craftsmanship and one for bravery during the defense of the city's port from the Spaniards. At another point, the head of the Artisan Fire Brigade gave a patriotic speech and a young girl offered the Peruvian president, Mariano Ignacio Prado, a laurel wreath in the name of the city's artisans.

The presence of artisans in these patriotic celebrations reflects a tenacity among this sector of Lima's population in maintaining a social and political presence during a time of intense change in the young republic. The middle decades of the nineteenth century brought rapid transformations in Peru as liberal reformers sought to dismantle the remnants of the old colonial society and lay the foundations of a modern nation-state. A key figure in this transition was General Ramón Castilla, who oversaw a significant expansion of the state during his two presidential terms (1845–51 and 1855–62). Castilla abolished a number of institutions inherited from the colonial period and helped to lay the foundations for a modern Peruvian nation-state. His second presidency brought the abolition of both slavery and the *contribución indigena* (colonial Indian tax) as well as reforms in the area of public education, and the writing of a constitution (1860) that remained in place for sixty years (to this day, longer than any other in Peruvian history). The institutional changes were accompanied by an opening of the political arena as elections became meaningful contests and candidates increasingly turned to the popular classes for political support.

The growth of the state during this period was fueled by the windfall revenues derived from the exports of guano, a highly valued fertilizer in Europe and particularly England.[1] This period has thus come to be known in Peruvian historiography as the guano period. Some of the guano revenues contributed to transforming the old colonial city into a modern one. Lima could boast the first railroad in South America, joining the city to the port of Callao (begun in 1848). Soon the city's inhabitants would witness the installation of gas streetlights and iron plumbing and also the construction of a modern penitentiary, inaugurated in 1862. In 1869, squadrons of workers began to dismantle the old colonial city walls, whose materials were used to build the new Palacio de la Exposición, a modern set of pavilions that housed one of the country's first agricultural and industrial exhibitions in 1872. Progress had clearly reached the shores of Peru.

The reforms of the liberal age initially seemed to bring only adversity to Lima's artisans. During the early decades of the national period, from the 1820s to the 1840s, artisans had developed close ties to the government through their guilds and had been favored with protectionist policies. The shift during the 1840s and 1850s toward a government policy of economic liberalism brought a general lowering of tariff barriers and an influx of cheaper imported products that directly competed with national production.[2] With the definitive adoption of free-trade policies over the course of the 1850s, artisans saw their very livelihood threatened. As liberalism gained ground all over Latin America as a hegemonic ideology, liberal ideologues launched direct

FIG. 1. *Map of Peru, 1865 (Mariano Paz Soldán).*

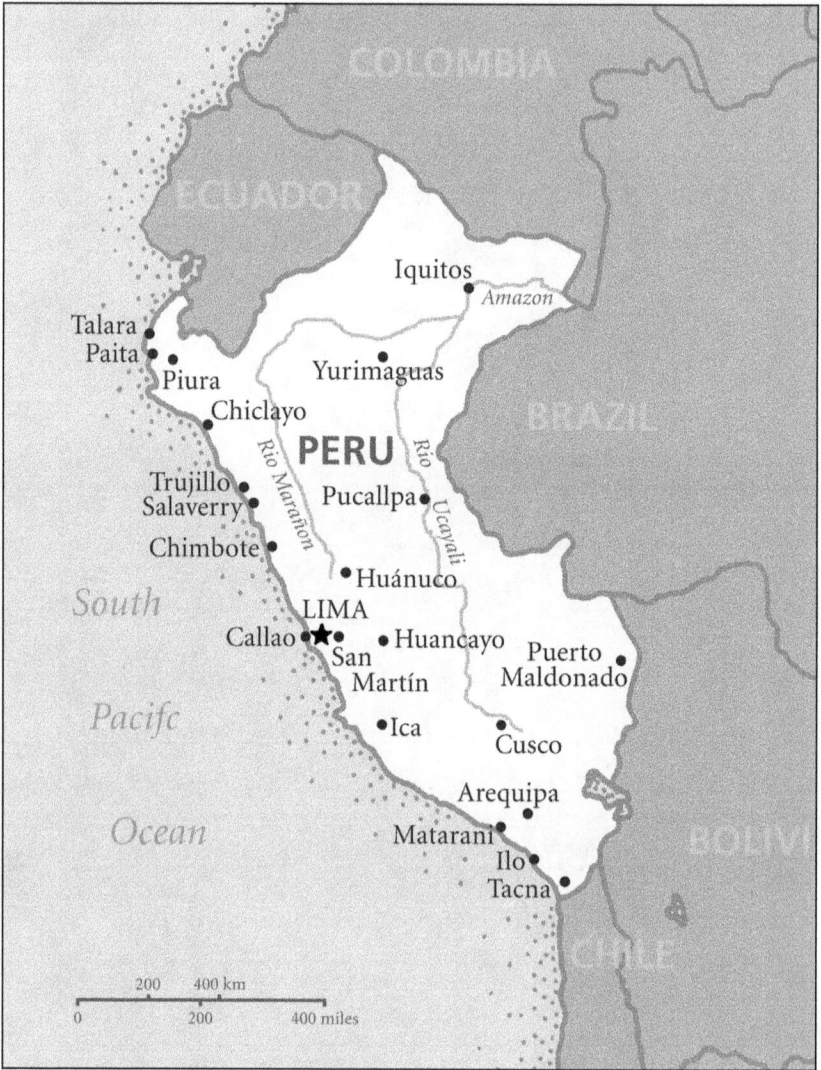

FIG. 2. *Present-day map of Peru.*

attacks on artisan guilds. Liberals considered the guilds yet another remnant of the old corporate society that needed to be destroyed in order to lay the foundations for a modern nation of individual citizens. Progressively weakened by their economic irrelevance and political ineffectiveness, the guilds were officially abolished in 1862.

Despite the lost battle with economic liberalism, artisans adapted to the new climate and remained important players on the political stage in mid-nineteenth-century Peru. In fact, historian Paul Gootenberg has termed the 1860s and 1870s a period of "renascence of artisan politics." This "renascence" revealed the presence of a distinct artisan sector that had succeeded in shedding its colonial identities and now embraced the language of liberal republicanism. Artisans established a political presence as an influential sector of the electorate that could not be ignored by elites. When Peru's first civilian political party, the Partido Civil, came to power in 1872, its leaders assiduously sought out artisans as supporters of the party.

This book tells the story of how artisans not only survived the vicissitudes of the liberal age, but also ensured a presence for themselves as citizens in the political arena of mid-nineteenth-century Peru. It argues that after the defeat of their guilds during the 1850s, artisans remained a politically vibrant social sector that succeeded in forging a new postcolonial identity: the artisan as hardworking republican citizen. Artisans borrowed from liberalism but also reinterpreted liberal ideas to carve a space for themselves within the emerging political arena. They claimed that their role as workers gave them a privileged position within the republic. By increasingly emphasizing their ties with other laborers, artisans also began to forge notions of a working class in Peru. The political culture of mid-nineteenth-century Peru was the creation not only of political elites, but also of ordinary citizens.

The events narrated bridge two consecutive political periods in the transition from colony to nation in Peru. The first, the period of caudillo (military) rule from 1821 to 1845, provides the background for understanding the formation of a distinct artisan identity. During this period, liberals laid the ideological foundations for the nation-state by writing constitutions while military caudillos sought to consolidate political power, and artisans emerged as a distinct social sector whose political identity was closely associated with the battle against economic liberalism. The second period covered is the epoch of liberal reforms from 1845 to 1879, also known as the guano period in Peruvian historiography. The economic stability afforded by guano exports allowed liberals to push for real reforms at many

different levels—legal, educational, economic. At this time, artisans participated in the institutional development of the nation-state, yet maintained
their independence as a distinct political group.

Artisans and the Liberal Polity

This study sheds new light on the complex relationship between liberal
nation building and popular politics in Latin America. I argue here that to
understand the "renascence of artisan politics" during the 1860s and 1870s,
it is necessary to explore the ways artisans faced the challenge of liberalism
during the heyday of liberal reforms. While many trades undoubtedly
suffered from the increased competition of imported products, artisans
nonetheless adapted to the changes brought about by liberal reformers and
succeeded in making various liberal institutions their own. Their opposition to economic liberalism didn't imply a rejection of liberalism's social
and political tenets. My research thus points to a greater proximity between
artisans and liberal reformers than was previously assumed.

This new artisan politics emerged as a result of the interaction between
artisans and liberal nation builders. Artisans' public, and sometimes violent, opposition to liberal free-trade policies made them an important
group to placate. Their openness toward liberal visions of politics and society also made them a natural constituency for liberal politicians. The hege-
mony of liberal ideas thus did not lead to the defeat of the artisanry. Rather,
artisans adapted to changing circumstances and were able to recast their
demands and stake a distinct position for themselves within the liberal polity.[3] For their part, liberal politicians embraced artisans as potential "good
liberal citizens."

While economic liberalism dealt a death blow to artisan guilds, liberal
political reforms opened doors for artisans to enter the emerging national
polity as citizens. With the liberal reforms of the 1850s, elections became more
meaningful loci for the definition of political contests and liberals sought to
bolster their political position by drawing on the support of artisans.[4] The
invitation was somewhat tentative—Peruvian liberals, like their counterparts
throughout Latin America, Europe, and the United States, were wary of the
abilities of the lower classes to exercise the rights of citizenship. In Peru, the
divide was compounded by a racial division: those at the bottom were also
the dark-skinned mestizos, mulatos, blacks, and Indians who had occupied
society's inferior ranks during the many centuries of colonial rule. Artisans,

being a racially heterogeneous group, were therefore suspect. Nonetheless, given artisans' association with the world of labor, liberals looked favorably upon them as potential citizens.

In turn, artisans borrowed key elements of liberal discourse that resonated with their own experiences and demands. By disengaging from the guilds, participating in liberal schools, and establishing their own voluntary associations, artisans made a deliberate transition away from the colonial institutions maligned by liberals as obstacles to progress. Furthermore, liberal political discourse provided a source of legitimacy for artisans as citizens whose labor proved vital to the young nation. Relying on the liberal emphasis on work as the cornerstone of national prosperity, artisans recast themselves as hardworking republican citizens of the new liberal polity. The association between Lima's artisans and national prosperity based on work seemed all the more poignant in the waning years of the guano period, at a time when critics pointed to the dangers of excessive reliance on guano exports. The image of the honest and hardworking artisan stood in stark contrast to that of the unproductive government employee inflating the ranks of the guano-based state bureaucracy. The association of artisans with the world of labor allowed them to legitimate their position as citizens.

While adapting to liberal institutions and discourse, artisans also developed their own understanding of their place within the nation. Throughout the period studied, artisans continued to organize both socially and politically as a group or sector—a form of organization rejected by liberal ideologues. A prominent feature of nineteenth-century liberal thought was a conception of the polity as based on individual actors with a common set of economic interests rather than special-interest groups. As historian James Sheehan writes about nineteenth-century German liberalism: "Liberals . . . customarily tried to obscure or absorb their conflicts over economic issues by defining themselves in terms of common attitudes and by insisting that whatever interests were present in their ranks were identical with the properly understood interests of society as a whole."[5] In the case of Peru, from the outset of the national period, artisans had challenged this conception by identifying as a sector with a set of common interests that did not necessarily harmonize with those of society. This sectoral identification clashed with the universalistic notions of citizenship propounded by liberals. Eventually, by the 1870s, artisans strayed even further from the liberal paradigm by beginning to define themselves and other workers as part of a working class, a process described in the last chapter of this study.

My work explores the complex relationship between elite and popular discourse. In fact, the influence of liberalism on artisan discourse during this period suggests the existence of a kind of popular or artisan liberalism. The liberalism of artisans was also distinguished from elite liberalism in that religious ideas remained central to artisan thought—the image of Christ as artisan appears in the artisan press of the 1870s. In this way, artisans gave their identity as citizens a historical dimension that linked them to what was perceived as a common past. Artisan ideas contrasted with the ahistorical nature of Latin American liberalism that sought to introduce the abstract notion of republican citizenship without attempting to create links to colonial traditions—liberalism actually sought to break away from colonial traditions altogether.

While the story told here begins with the hopeful transformations that occurred in the transition from colony to nation as artisans embraced the possibilities of citizenship, it ends with a period of economic depression that revealed the limited opportunities available for artisans within a society exposed to the vicissitudes of the world economy. The promise of political integration brought by liberals was not paralleled by real opportunities for social mobility—the guano model of growth proved its limitations as Lima was struck with depression during the 1870s. Things were only made worse with the outbreak of the War of the Pacific in 1879 and the subsequent invasion and occupation of the city of Lima by Chilean forces in 1881. The extension of an artisan identity to embrace all workers sadly coincided with a period during which depression was operating as an equalizing force and bringing the lives of artisans closer to those of other manual laborers.

The Issue of Race

The issue of race is central to an understanding of the social place of the artisanry. Historically artisans were characterized by their racial heterogeneity and in particular by the high proportion of Indians, blacks, and mestizos among them. The presence of blacks in the trades is particularly noteworthy in the case of the city of Lima.[6] The racial makeup of the artisan population, as reflected in an 1866 census of Lima, reveals a higher proportion of individuals of mixed race among artisans than among the rest of the population.[7] Based on a sampling of the city's shoemakers, carpenters, tailors, and tanners, I calculate the following proportions: 34 percent *zambo* (black with some white ancestry), 25 percent white, 13 percent mestizo

Racial Composition of Lima's Artisans, 1866

Negro 6%
Mulato 1%
Cholo 1%
Blanco 25%
Chino 2%
Indio 16%
Moreno 0%
Mestizo 13%
Pardo 2%
Zambo 34%

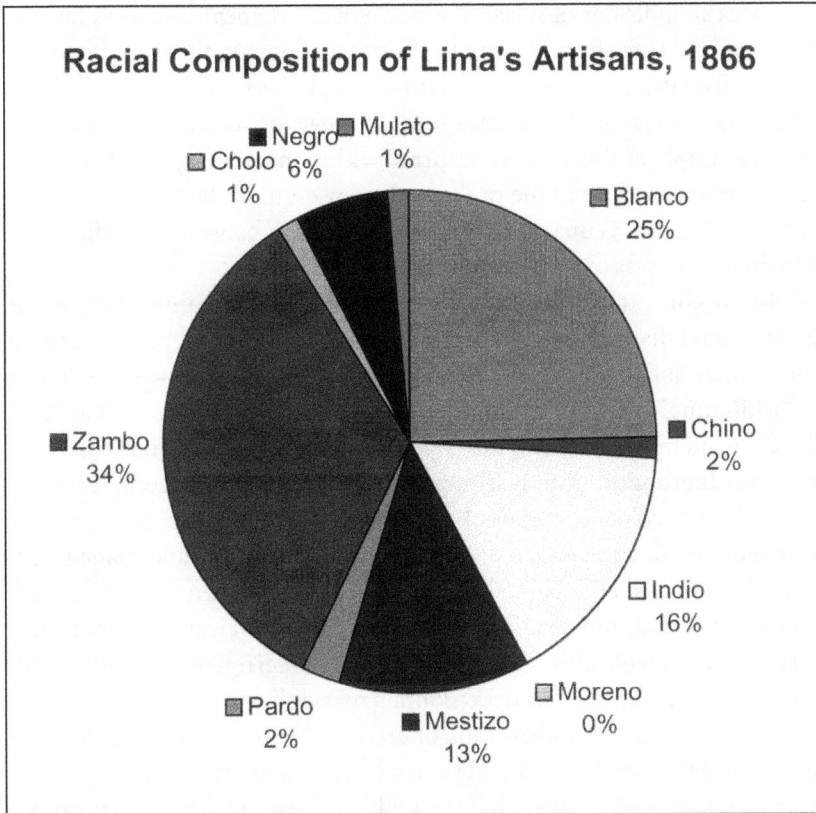

FIG. 3. *Racial composition of Lima's artisans, based on a sampling of shoemakers, carpenters, tailors, and tanners (1,126 individuals) from the 1866 city census (Archivo Histórico Municipal de Lima).*

(Indian and white), 16 percent Indian, 6 percent black, and 6 percent other less numerous categories denoting mixed races (see Figure 3). The proportions of blacks and zambos is particularly high in relation to the general proportion for the city of Lima of 9 percent.[8]

The complexities of race constitute a particularly significant factor in the events narrated in this book. The predominance of mestizos, blacks, and Indians among the artisan population continued into the republican period, as reflected in the 1866 census. On the one hand, in a society where racial categories had traditionally reinforced social hierarchies, race continued to weigh heavily as an indicator of social class and as a key element distinguishing the Europeanized elites from the rest of the population. On the other hand, the official dismantling of colonial hierarchies at the time of independence offered new social opportunities to individuals of mixed race. The most visible example of this process occurred within the military, where mestizo individuals moved up in the ranks, and a few even reached the presidency. President Agustín Gamarra (1829–33, 1839–41) was considered Indian, and Ramón Castilla was considered mestizo.

In the context of a society that continued to adhere informally to the strong racial distinctions established during the colonial period, artisan adoption of liberal ideas gains an added social significance—the possibility of "whitening" oneself. By defining themselves as "artisans" and as "citizens," the members of the trades were taking distance from guilds and religious brotherhoods, both institutions associated with the complex racial hierarchies of colonial culture. By claiming to be liberal citizens, artisans differentiated themselves from the visibly nonwhite *plebe* and made themselves into respectable citizens of the new liberal society identified with progress.[9] Within nineteenth-century Peru, liberals clearly distinguished between respectable citizens adhering to the modern tenets of individualism and citizenship and the dark-skinned masses.[10]

Adherence to liberalism thus offered an opportunity for artisans to leave old racial and social categories behind and define a position as respectable citizens. The possibility of taking distance from a racially based identity calls for some explanation. The concept of "social race," coined by Charles Wagley, offers some insight into this process: the term emphasizes the fact that despite the use of biological terminology, the process of categorization by race is based on a series of cultural assumptions that vary from region to region. During the national period, in the regions of Latin America with large indigenous populations, "emphasis has been placed mainly on criteria of social and cultural status, almost to the point of ignoring the criterion of physical appearance."[11]

The reading of liberal newspapers, attendance at liberal schools, and, perhaps most visibly, membership in mutual aid societies all constituted cultural markers that enhanced the status of artisans and placed them within the bounds of respectable society, as defined by liberal reformers.[12] The link to liberal discourse reinforced the position of artisans as a middle sector whose values stated values more closely resembled those of the elites than those of the plebe.

Defining a Class Identity:
A Middle Sector Between Plebe and Elite

A study of artisans and nation building raises questions about the emergence of class identities in nineteenth-century Peru and challenges existing conceptions of nineteenth-century Peruvian society. Who were Lima's artisans? What place did they occupy in the socioeconomic structure of the city? How were they perceived, and how did they perceive themselves in mid-nineteenth-century Lima? During this period, artisans formed part of what I will call the middle sectors, situated socioeconomically between elites whose wealth was based primarily on landholdings and large-scale commercial enterprises and the poorest sectors of society, which included servants, slaves (until 1854), day laborers, and the unemployed—referred to as *plebe* (plebeians) in Peruvian historiography.[13] The term *middle sector* encompasses a range of professions such as shopkeepers, lawyers, doctors, notaries, and students, of which artisans can be placed at the lower end. Numerically, artisans constituted a small fraction of the total urban population. The 1876 census for Lima calculates artisans at about 5 percent of the city' population, or about 5,000 artisans for a city of 100,156.

My interpretation of artisans thus challenges the two-tiered view of Latin American society that does not fully take into account the presence of middle sectors between elite and plebe. I argue that the political revolutions that brought nation-states into existence also resulted in significant social changes. I therefore call into question the notion of "traditional modernization" presented by Fernando Trazegnies, according to which, despite economic changes during the national period, the colonial social structure remained intact.[14]

While artisans can be broadly defined as those individuals who worked with their hands to transform raw materials into manufactured products, they also constituted a heterogeneous sector. The most numerous trades were shoemakers, tailors, and carpenters. Some trades traditionally carried more prestige than others—silversmiths, for example, had been at the top of the hierarchy during the colonial period. A carpenter making luxury furniture for members of the elite would probably have looked down on a shoemaker or tanner. Quoting from a contemporary source in nineteenth-century Mexico, Torcuato di Tella describes the clear hierarchies that existed among the popular sectors: "But the Mexican populace 'had its hierarchies, its nobility, its aristocracy. . . . A barber looks down on a mason's *peon* with as much disdain as the richest speculator on a junior clerk."[15] Similar attitudes could be found in Lima. During much of the nineteenth century, artisans continued to be distinguished from unskilled workers such as domestic servants or day laborers.

The term *middle sectors* also has political connotations in Latin American historiography stemming from the use of the category by historian John Johnson. The term was applied primarily to twentieth-century Latin America by Johnson, who identified the middle sectors as a progressive social group pushing for social change and democratization.[16] Johnson finds antecedents for the middle sectors in the nineteenth century, and his original definition of the term included primarily people in the liberal professions, the bureaucracy, the military, the arts: "They [the middle sectors] were teachers and bureaucrats, lawyers, notaries, newspaper men, publishers, and artists. These functions tended to identify them with the elites and to dissociate them from the laboring groups."[17] The absence of laborers in the definition points to the fact that Johnson was subscribing to the classic political model in which the popular sectors remained outside of politics over the course of the nineteenth century.

Johnson's category can be expanded to include artisans without doing violence to his original definition. Johnson pointed to six characteristics of the middle sectors: their urban nature, the fact that they had above-average education and believed strongly in public education, their belief in the need for industrialization, their nationalism, their support of the state as an agent of social and economic change, and their support of organized political parties.[18] Lima's artisans conform to all of these criteria, and while their level of education certainly did not compare to that of the classic members of the middle sectors according to Johnson, their levels of literacy were well above those of the majority of the population: artisans' literacy rates were 80 percent, compared to 42 percent for the general population.[19]

Why use the term *middle sector* rather than *middle class*? I consider the very imprecision of the term *middle sectors* to be appropriate to this period of transition from colonial social terms that combined corporate and racial categories to modern social terminology of social classes. I do not use the loose definition of artisans as a middle sector to avoid the issue of class—rather I use it to emphasize the fluid identity of artisans during this period. Artisans did not specifically identify as a middle class; rather, toward the end of the period studied, they came increasingly to identify as a working class. While liberal intellectuals may have occasionally defined artisans as a middle class, artisans themselves did not use this term in their political discourse. I thus follow the culturalist approach in placing weight on the process of self-definition as a class.[20] As Katznelson writes about the process of transition from guild to class identification in Europe: "Working people, for the first time, altered their vocabularies and world views to speak and think of themselves as workers, rather than just as members of this or that trade."[21]

My analysis of the process of class formation follows E. P. Thompson's seminal study of the English working class. Thompson's contribution to the study of class lies in his departure from the notion of class as a fixed category and his presentation of class as a historical phenomenon involving individuals who gain an understanding of themselves as a class. According to him, "Class happens when some men, as a result of common experiences (inherited or shared) feel and articulate the identity of their interests as between themselves and as against other men whose interests are different from (and usually opposed to) theirs."[22] Class ceases to be an exogenous category in the tradition of classic Marxist studies, and the focus shifts to the ways workers became aware of themselves as a class and began to act in "class ways." Members of the working class are historical actors rather than passive subjects of economic forces. However, Thompson remains faithful to certain Marxist tenets, most notably the idea of class conflict and of a consequently radical working class. The working class does not necessarily adopt a radical ideology, as critics of Thompson have indicated. For example, Geoffrey Crossick has pointed to the middle-class aspirations of London artisans during the second half of the nineteenth century.[23]

When artisans did begin to define themselves in class terms, they identified as part of the working class, yet a working class that aspired to liberal rather than revolutionary values. During the 1860s and 1870s, artisans contributed to define working-class culture in its early stages. The artisan press of the 1870s, analyzed in the last chapter of this book, reflects a growing identification of artisans with the idea of a working class. The press also reveals the strong influence of liberalism on artisan ideas. The artisan press borrowed heavily from liberal notions of citizenship, emphasizing the importance of education. Workers were presented as performing activities vital to the building of a modern nation. In many ways the working-class values were portrayed as akin to the values of "middle class" respectability championed by liberals, values that included hard work, thrift, and a frugal lifestyle opposed to the baroque "excesses" of popular culture.[24]

The broad notion of middle sectors also implies a conscious relationship to those above and those below. In his definition of the term *middle classes* for twentieth-century Peru, Francois Bourricaud explicitly states, "The denomination 'middle' indicates that those who apply it to themselves, or to whom it is applied, are primarily concerned with their relationship towards those above or below them. Being neither at the top nor at the bottom, they define themselves negatively: they do not belong to the governing class, yet are distinguished from the masses."[25] Or as Michael Mann claims in his study of Europe during the nineteenth century, "Artisans possessed an ambiguous class position between propertied 'people' and propertyless 'populace.'"[26]

In the case of artisans, the very ambiguity of their position could also work to their advantage. Artisans belonging to mutual aid societies, attending liberal schools, and participating in the political process could aspire to be respectable national citizens. Yet at certain times they had also participated alongside poorer popular sectors associated with political violence. There were numerous instances of violence perpetrated by crowds in Lima. In 1858, artisans participated in a protest against the importation of carpentry goods that ended violently with crowds dumping cargoes of imported goods into the ocean.[27] Again in 1872 artisans could be counted among the crowds that resisted a military coup and executed its perpetrators, the Gutierrez brothers. The bodies were hung from the tower of Lima's cathedral.[28] While artisans consciously attempted to distance themselves from any association with the plebe, the fact that they had participated in episodes of political violence can be seen as a source of potential political strength: elites understood the political dangers of alienating artisans.

Nation and Citizenship in Nineteenth-Century Peru and Latin America

This study of Lima's artisans sheds light on the role of the urban middle sectors in the process of nation building in nineteenth-century Latin America. In doing so, it contributes to the latest historiography that challenges long-standing views of nineteenth-century Latin American politics and society. The most recent generation of Latin American historians has expanded our understanding of this period by examining the role of the popular sectors in nation building. The result has been a more nuanced view of the nineteenth-century polity. Yet few studies have examined the urban middle sectors; most have focused on the peasantry. The present study not only places artisans more fully on the historical map; it also argues that artisans help to provide a deeper understanding of the liberal polity and offer a more complex model of nineteenth-century Latin American society than the usual two-tiered division into elites and popular sectors.

Historians increasingly challenge an earlier view of the nineteenth-century polity as a space exclusively dominated by Creole elites and military leaders, with little room for popular political participation of any kind.[29] According to this earlier view, the liberalism of Latin American elites could be seen primarily as an ideology that excluded broad sectors of the population. Or in the words of Peruvian historian Alberto Flores Galindo, the nineteenth-century polity was a "republic without citizens."[30] Continuity outweighed change: modern Latin America had inherited a static corporatist and hierarchical political culture from the colonial period. According to this conception, a deeply ingrained Catholic political culture conflicted with modern political ideologies such as liberalism.[31]

By introducing the notion of political culture into the study of Latin America, recent historiography has made a significant contribution to revise such long-standing views. Influenced by the methodology of the "new cultural history," Latin American historians have highlighted the importance of political practices and language in shaping people's conception of the world they inhabited and made such language and practices a valid subject of historical inquiry.[32] The work of Jürgen Habermas has further influenced the study of the public sphere in nineteenth-century Latin America and the efforts to understand the emergence of new forms of political sociability.[33] Recent studies of the early national period in both Peru and Argentina emphasize the importance of republican discourse in shaping the polity.[34] In her study of nineteenth-century Peruvian politics, Carmen McEvoy argues that political elites during the 1870s extended new forms of democratic sociability to the middle sectors of the population. Likewise, in a study of Buenos Aires politics during this period, Hilda Sábato points to the emergence of a vibrant civil society that included elections, citizen associations, and other forms of political participation.[35] Such a view appears in a number of other studies throughout the region.[36]

Historians have thus begun to steer away from earlier conceptions of a "republic without citizens." A series of studies have highlighted the ways popular political participation contributed to shape the nineteenth-century process of nation building in Latin America.[37] In a recent study of Cusco politics during the early republican period, Charles Walker expresses the view of many recent studies by claiming that "Indians and other lower-class groups also participated in these discussions, and in doing so, they contested the narrow notions of citizenship and political rights propagated by elite groups."[38] In the case of Mexico, Richard Andrew Warren has argued for the impact of popular participation on politics in post-independence Mexico. According to Warren, the political behavior of the popular sectors affected the building of a political system in Mexico: "The urban underclass' enthusiastic participation in the political system was a major factor in stimulating a reassessment of Mexico's political direction by moderates and conservatives."[39] These urban poor, Warren argues, were a force in favor of political change.

Yet within this new historiography, the vision of an exclusionary liberal polity has remained. This may have much to do with the fact that a primary subject of historical inquiry has been the indigenous peasantry. Given the clash between liberal individualism and peasant corporate identities, the studies of peasants while providing a vision "from below" have also reinforced the notion of liberalism as an exclusionary ideology. The most influential work on the subject is that of Florencia Mallon. In a comparative study of peasant discourses in Mexico and Peru, Mallon argues for a distinct form of peasant nationalism. She sets elite and popular discourses at odds with each other by referring to "counterhegemonic liberalism" and by using such terms as "communitarian liberalism," which she defines as "an especially radical and decentered form of Liberalism."[40]

The view from the city appears somewhat different. Within the setting of nineteenth-century Lima, artisans contribute to offer an alternative view of liberalism by questioning the notion of the liberal polity as exclusionary. In a hierarchical society, liberals put forth the radical notion of equality, and social groups such as artisans sought to put this ideal into practice. As part of the urban middle sectors, artisans were in contact with liberal intellectuals and politicians and sought to establish a footing in the liberal polity rather than challenge it entirely. For their part, despite their moralizing discourse, liberals encouraged artisans to become citizens. The political engagement of artisans thus reinforces recent views on the importance of constitutions, elections, and notions of popular sovereignty in determining the rules of the political game. A study of urban artisans will contribute a few missing pieces to the jigsaw puzzle and help to improve the situation described by historian Peloso in the following terms: "We lack a satisfactory model (or models) for understanding the influence of liberalism in the formation of nineteenth-century Latin American states."[41]

The Study of Artisans in the Atlantic World

By placing artisans in the context of wide-sweeping changes associated with the age of liberalism, this book contributes to the general historiography of artisans in the Atlantic world. Artisans throughout this vast region have been studied primarily in relation to the broad social, economic, and political transformations of the modern age. The central questions asked have involved the role of artisans in transformations that include interrelated events such as the Industrial and French revolutions, the American Revolution, and the Latin American independence movements. Lima's artisans were a part of this general process of change during the nineteenth-century, and the ways they adapted to these changes can help to answer questions about the general history of working peoples in this Atlantic world, broadly conceived.

By studying artisans in the context of the age of liberalism, this book challenges two major patterns that have shaped the historiography of artisans in the Atlantic world. The first is the tendency to view artisans as holdovers from an earlier preindustrial age. In Latin American historiography, artisans often appear primarily as defenders of colonial guilds and economic privileges against the threats posed by the emergence of free-trade regimes.[42] In British historiography, E. P. Thompson's classic study of the English working class falls into this category. Thompson sees artisans as the defenders of a "moral economy" that is being challenged by the capitalist developments of nineteenth-century England. This view has led to a sometimes idealized conception of the preindustrial artisan past. The dichotomy can be taken to an extreme in which the role of the monetary economy for preindustrial artisans is minimized. E. J. Hobsbawm, for example, writes, "In short, the trade was not so much a way of making money, but rather the income it provided was the recognition by society and its constituted authorities of the value of decent work."[43] This paradigm has also influenced U.S. labor history. While he takes distance from this formulation, Bruce Laurie also characterizes the preindustrial era as "the happy epoch [that] was about to end."[44]

This dichotomy has been called into question by the work of Michael Sonenscher. By examining the world of eighteenth-century artisans in France, Sonenscher challenges the notion of a fixed artisan culture linked to guilds and to a "moral economy." Rather, he argues, artisans operated within a larger economic framework, often independently of the guilds. He argues that "the antithesis between competitive individualism and collective association that was made so frequently during the early nineteenth century was less a judgment upon the noxious effects of unregulated markets than it was a response to the absence of any formal injunctions compelling artisans to associate as they had done before the Revolution."[45]

The second pattern in the study of artisans involves seeing nineteenth-century artisans primarily as precursors of the modern labor movement of the late nineteenth and early twentieth century. This historiography has studied artisans in relation to the process of working-class formation and the related question of class consciousness. With the advent of the "new labor history," labor historians extended their inquiries beyond the realm of organized labor movements to seek the roots of class and class consciousness in the preindustrial world of labor. Often journeymen are considered precursors to the propertyless proletariat of the nineteenth century. The Marxist influence on the study of artisans has led historians to establish links between artisans and radical politics. In fulfilling E. P. Thompson's call to rescue the common man "from the enormous condescension of posterity," historians have characteristically rescued artisans under a particular political sign: that of radicalism. William Sewell's classic study *Work and Revolution in France: The Language of Labor from the Old Regime to 1848* traces a radical working-class consciousness back to the "corporate idiom" of prerevolutionary France.[46] Sean Wilentz's study of New York artisans also seeks the roots of modern class consciousness in an "artisan republicanism" whose roots can be traced to a preindustrial egalitarianism and rejection of market individualism.[47]

In Latin American history, this trend has led to an examination of artisans particularly during times of political protest. The attempt to see artisans as precursors of later labor movements has also led to a paucity of studies on mutual aid societies—the conciliatory politics of these societies are seen as antithetical to the politically more combative unions that developed later.[48]

By studying artisans not as holdovers from an earlier age or as precursors of a later one, I provide an understanding of artisans in their proper historical context—that of the liberal age. The establishment of republican discourse and institutions created opportunities for political participation that had been absent in the premodern setting. Lima's artisans began to experiment with the language and institutions of liberalism to create a place for themselves as legitimate political actors in the nineteenth-century political arena. In doing so, they followed trends identified more broadly by historians of the United States. Studies of artisans in Philadelphia and New York artisans confirm the idea that the political revolutions of the Atlantic world opened up opportunities for urban artisans—both Olton and Rock in their respective studies argue that artisans sought to improve the inferior social status they had held during the colonial period to carve a place for themselves in the young republic.[49]

Chapter Descriptions

This book is divided into five chapters. Chapter one, "The Artisan in Colonial Society: Guilds, Brotherhoods, and Bourbon Reforms," traces the formation of an artisan identity back to the Bourbon reforms of the late colonial period. By placing artisans in the context of the institutional history of the colonial period and examining the changing relationship with the colonial state toward the end of the eighteenth century, this chapter sets the stage for events in the national period. The chapter traces the history of the primary artisan institutions, the guild and the religious brotherhood (*cofradía*). It also discusses the process of Bourbon reforms, which involved both administrative and ideological changes in colonial society. The Bourbon reforms affected artisans by bringing them under greater control of the state and were the basis for the rupture of colonial corporate identities and the strengthening of a sectoral artisan identity. These reforms stand as a clear antecedent to nineteenth-century liberal reforms.

Chapter two, "Artisans and Guilds in the Transition to the Liberal Age, 1821–1860," discusses the entry of artisans into national politics and traces the relationship between artisans, the state, and liberal ideologues during the period of caudillismo. Artisans entered the political arena on the side of the protectionist bloc in the debates over commercial policy between protectionists and free traders. During this period, artisans engaged in politics through their guilds and were tied to the webs of patronage that kept caudillos in power. With the advent of the guano period and the shift toward free-trade policies, artisans faced the limitations of the guilds in furthering their political goals. In the battles against economic liberalism, both in the national congress and through the press, artisans began to develop a sectoral identity that transcended individual guild identities.

While liberal intellectuals and the liberal state attacked the guilds and rejected the notion of offering artisans special economic privileges, they reached out to artisans as potential citizens of a modern nation. Chapter three, "The Making of Productive Citizens: Artisan Schools and National Expositions, 1860–1879," specifically addresses the liberal project of artisan education and the organization of National Exhibitions that included displays of artisan products and awarded artisan prizes. I argue that these efforts must be understood within the broader liberal project of reforming the plebe, considered uncivilized and prone to idleness and drunkenness. The involvement of artisans in the productive process led liberals to consider artisans as more redeemable than the plebe. The artisan would embody the liberal ideal of the thrifty, hardworking, sober, and civic-minded citizen.

Chapter four, "Mutual Aid Societies and Artisan Respectability, 1860–1879," examines artisan adaptation to the liberal polity through the formation of mutual aid societies. The efforts from above by liberal intellectuals to "educate the masses" described in chapter three contributed to create a space for a transformation in the image of the popular sectors. Yet the shift in the image of the artisan and the active presence of artisans in the political sphere during the second half of the nineteenth century were the result not of elite fabrication or manipulation: artisans themselves contributed to establish a new institutional foothold through the formation of mutual aid societies. These societies enabled artisans to gain respectability during the period of liberal reforms and to pursue economic, social, and political goals. The mutual aid society offered artisans financial assistance during times of hardship and allowed artisans to differentiate themselves socially from the plebe. Despite their expressly apolitical nature, artisan mutual aid societies enabled artisans to establish important social ties with the political establishment. However, although the adoption of voluntary associations pointed to artisan adaptation to liberal paradigms, artisans did not subscribe to universalistic notions of citizenship but rather continued to identify as a separate sector with a common set of interests. Mutual aid societies thus reinforced a concrete identity as "artisans" rather than the abstract liberal ideal of "citizens."

Chapter five, "'Artisan Liberalism' and the Beginnings of a Working Class, 1860–1879," examines artisan and worker newspapers and argues that artisans during the 1870s began to identify as a working class. This period was one of economic downturn that threatened artisans' livelihood. By engaging in politics as an interest group rather than as individual citizens, artisans challenged the liberal model of the polity. Class and nation come together in the political culture of the period: artisans presented themselves as pivotal both to national prosperity and to the formation of a working class. The identification of artisans with a working class must be understood in the context of the economic downturn of the 1870s, the tail end of the guano boom, that dampened artisans' prospects for upward mobility. The public outcries of artisans over the cost of living in Lima reflects the economic problems during this period. The higher cost of living contributed to create a pressure of downward mobility. While it is difficult to ascertain the degree of representativeness of the ideas to be found in the artisan newspaper *El Artesano* and the printers' newspaper *El Obrero*, it is fair to say that the economic pressures of the 1870s would most likely have impoverished artisans and have facilitated the identification of artisans with other workers.

The notion of the artisan as a centerpiece of the emerging polity was a new idea without antecedents in colonial times. The centrality of labor to national prosperity was a central tenet of liberalism throughout the Atlantic world. Reinhard Bendix describes the way the notion of a growing role of the people comes to the fore in England, where "the idea gains acceptance that the people's rights as citizens have been denied unjustly because as working people they have rights by virtue of their contribution to the nation's wealth."[50] Hence a worldwide theme of modernity played itself out as Lima's artisans claimed a greater role for themselves within the emerging nation.

At the heart of my book is the issue of the relationship between nation building and social and political change in Peruvian society. Lima's nineteenth-century artisans demonstrate the ways the middle sectors adopted and reinterpreted elite liberalism to carve a place for themselves within a polity broadly defined along liberal lines. Ideas of political equality became a strong rallying point for individuals seeking social mobility and political inclusion. The events narrated here suggest the need to reconsider the classic notion of an exclusionary liberal polity. In fact, the polity was defined in a sufficiently inclusionary manner as to allow artisans to participate as citizens. Artisans even succeeded in sending one of their own, Cusco carpenter Francisco González, to Congress as a representative in 1876.

Not all could gain entry into the public sphere: rural Indians who continued to speak the indigenous languages Quechua and Aymara and retained corporate traditions remained excluded by liberal discourse. Urban artisans, on the other hand, could more easily conform to the liberal view of citizenship. Corporate traditions had never been strong among them: they showed a willingness, by the middle of the nineteenth century, to adopt liberal voluntary associations and participate in liberal educational institutions. Most importantly, artisans participated in politics on their own terms not merely as pawns in an elite-driven process, but as independent actors. In the process they developed their own view of their role within the nation.

CHAPTER ONE

The Artisan in Colonial Society:

Guilds, Brotherhoods, and

Bourbon Reforms

A DISCUSSION OF THE ROLE OF ARTISANS in colonial society constitutes a necessary prelude to nineteenth-century events, both for the continuities and the changes between these two periods. Lima's artisans during the early national period inherited institutions and cultural attitudes shaped during the three centuries of Spanish colonialism. Despite a remarkable pre-Hispanic tradition of craftsmanship, Spanish rule broke earlier patterns and established new institutions intended to incorporate native populations into a Hispanized way of life. The two main artisan institutions of the colonial period—the guild and the religious brotherhood (cofradía)—were originally transferred from Spain in the sixteenth century. The guild sought to regulate economic activity by limiting the scope of the trades to guild members. Religious brotherhoods provided a link to Catholic institutional life and also a rich social network that supported artisans in times of hardship. Both of these institutions gave artisans a recognizable public place as a distinct corporate group within the complex hierarchies of colonial society.

Sixteenth-century Spaniards brought with them to the Americas not only their trades and the institutions associated with the trades, but also the prevailing Spanish attitudes that considered the trades to be demeaning and thus unbefitting to those of noble status.[1] Burkholder argues that "the noble attitude toward manual labor received reinforcement in the colonies. In 1552 the crown prohibited stone-masons, tailors, potters, and other 'low persons'

who worked as artisans (*oficios mecánicos*) from serving as provincial officials (*corregidores*)."[2] Artisans were thus considered to be part of the lower
orders of society and were barred from any claims to *hidalguía* (petty nobility).[3] By the eighteenth century many Indian artisans had even adopted
Spanish values against manual labor and sought to avoid trades that involved hard labor such as blacksmith, stonecutter, and mason.[4] These attitudes would not come under attack until the late-eighteenth-century process
of Bourbon reforms and persisted well into the modern period.

Within the lower orders, however, artisans occupied a middle sector
between the elite and the very poor. Despite the stigma attached to manual
labor, for many people the trades constituted an important vehicle of social
mobility. In a society with strong racial prejudices, the trades offered economic and social opportunities to Indians, blacks, and *castas* (people of
mixed race). As apprentices, these individuals could develop skills as tailors
and carpenters, as blacksmiths and silversmiths, as shoemakers and tanners.
Eventually some of them were able to establish their own workshops.
Within the parameters of a hierarchical society, the trades allowed the non-
European lower orders a degree of mobility.

Over the course of the colonial period, a significant number of Indians
established themselves as artisans in the city of Lima, and some set up their
own workshops.[5] There is even evidence of some Indian artisans being
addressed with the title *don* (which tended to be a prerogative of the Hispanic
world).[6] By one calculation, Lima had 323 Indian tailors, 129 Indian shoemakers, and eighty silk weavers in the year 1612.[7] According to Karen Spalding:

> These people were in their appearance and habits very like the
> members of European society among whom they lived and
> worked. They, and even their women, wore European-style rather
> than Indian-style clothing. They participated fully in the European
> money economy, tending to invest their earnings in urban proper-
> ty—stores or houses that were rented out for income—rather than
> in land for cultivation. They spent their money on luxury clothing
> or jewelry, and saved, like their European counterparts, buy buy-
> ing objects of gold and silver.[8]

Frederick Bowser's classic study of the African population in early colonial
Lima demonstrates the degree of participation of African slaves and their
descendents in the trades. Blacks were to be found working as carpenters,

shipwrights, joiners, caulkers, blacksmiths, tile makers, tanners, tailors, and shoemakers.[9]

The nineteenth-century political role of artisans also has colonial precedents. Evidence from the eighteenth century indicates that certain artisans, particularly the prominent silversmiths, were in a position to act politically. According to Scarlett O'Phelan, the participation of silversmiths in an uprising in the southern Andes in 1739 was more than coincidental, and she points to the links of both guilds and religious brotherhoods to the Church as important factors in this uprising. Silversmiths also figured prominently in what was known as the Cusco "Silversmith Conspiracy" in 1780, part of the general discontent in the southern Andes with the increased taxes brought by the Bourbon reforms. According to O'Phelan, "In both instances, the evidence suggests that institutions such as the Guilds were breeding grounds for plotting revolt against the government during the colonial period."[10] In other cases Indian artisans in Lima were directly involved in the leadership of various revolts.[11] While instances that appear in the extant historiography refer to cases of revolt, further study is needed on the long-term political role of artisans in the colonial city.

The reforms of the trades associated with nineteenth-century liberalism can also be traced back to the colonial period. During the last fifty years of the colonial period, the process of Bourbon reforms introduced liberal ideas and brought about a number of social changes that continued during the nineteenth century. The Enlightenment in Spain initiated a critique and various attempts at reforming existing corporate institutions. The most prominent figures in the Spanish Enlightenment, such as Pedro Rodriguez Campomanes and Melchor de Jovellanos, attacked artisan guilds and made specific proposals to reform the guilds and to give the state a greater role in regulating the artisan sector. Such reforms were implemented among Lima's guilds. An understanding of the place of artisans within colonial society and of the eighteenth-century reforms thus offers necessary background for the discussion of nineteenth-century developments.

Artisans and Their Guilds in Colonial Society

In the sixteenth century, at the outset of the colonial period, Spanish artisans brought their trades with them to the New World. In fact, many of the conquistadores themselves practiced a skilled trade, and according to Lyman Johnson, "Artisans were probably the largest single occupational group during the early [colonial] period."[12] As colonial society grew, the increasing demands of new towns and cities in the Americas soon exceeded the capabilities of Spanish artisans, and increasingly blacks and Indians were drawn into the urban trades, not only as assistants to Spanish masters, but also as artisans in their own right. The attempts by Spaniards to regulate and control the trades were constantly threatened by the vital role of the mixed-race populations in the production process.

To regulate the functioning of the trades, sixteenth-century Spanish artisans established guilds. In its formal structure and functions, the guild in Spanish America resembled its European counterpart. Guilds served primarily as regulatory institutions for internal control of the various trades. In theory, only master artisans examined by the guild were licensed to open workshops in the city. The trades were divided according to internal hierarchies into master artisans, journeymen (*oficiales*), and apprentices. The relationship between masters and apprentices can best be characterized as paternalistic. Apprentices learned the trade while living in the master's household. The maintenance of both household and workshop also followed the model common to much of early modern Europe.

Like the Spanish guilds, Spanish American guilds from the earliest times remained subject to supervision by municipal authorities. The colonial municipality, the *cabildo,* often participated in the appointment of guild authorities. In theory, the process of examining artisans in the various trades would begin with a petition to the cabildo and would take place under the supervision of the municipal authorities: "The examination took place in the presence of the mayor of the city (or a representative) and the municipal scribe. The presence of this authority was intended to imbue the act with the necessary seriousness and solemnity, as well as to reinforce a sense of control over artisans."[13] The municipality often succeeded in imposing price controls on the output of artisans in various trades.[14]

Despite similarities in structure to European guilds, the Spanish American guilds remained much weaker than their European counterparts. Various factors contributed to weakening the economic power of guilds in Spanish America. The protection of Spanish products and the presence of contraband restricted the ability of artisans to control colonial markets. The use of slaves as apprentices undermined the traditional master-apprentice relationship. And the presence of a large number of non-Europeans in the trades limited the power of the guilds to control labor.

In his study of Lima's colonial guilds, Francisco Quiroz argues that the trades functioned somewhat in the shadow of official guild regulations. Official requirements such as examinations were often ignored, and unexamined artisans were able to practice the trade merely on the strength of their reputation.[15] The ability to work outside the guild system offered artisans belonging to the castas a possibility of economic success.[16] In fact, Quiroz argues, guilds had little economic clout in colonial society and their power to exclude nonguild members from the trades was limited: "The guild in Lima had barely any economic functions and had limited power to exclude non-guild members from the crafts. In practice, the guild in colonial Lima cannot even be considered to have served strictly speaking as a guild. The crafts were `free.' There was no real persecution ... against those artisans who sold their products outside the guild."[17]

Nonetheless, the guilds did seek to reinforce the hierarchies of Spanish American colonial society by formally attempting to maintain the trades as the exclusive preserve of Spaniards. While non-Spaniards had originally worked primarily as helpers to Spanish artisans, the growing racially mixed population soon threatened Spanish dominance of the trades. According to Quiroz, "Thus, a group of skilled journeymen in the various trades began to appear in the city and posed a serious threat to Spanish master artisans."[18] Guilds continued to attempt to exclude individuals of mixed race from their ranks. For example, the rules of the Guild of Spanish Tailors prohibited master artisans from teaching their trade to slaves and excluded blacks and zambos from membership in its brotherhood.[19] The attempts at exclusion by race often occurred at times of increased competition.

Some of the early artisan guilds were divided according to race. For example, separate tailor guilds grouped Spaniards and Indians: the Gremio de Sastres Españoles (Guild of Spanish Tailors) and the Gremio de Sastres Naturales (Guild of Indian Tailors). In certain cases, Indian artisans succeeded in using the separate legislation to their benefit by escaping the regulations of the Spanish guilds. Francisco Quiroz presents the case of the Spanish tailors' guild attempting to impose regulations on Indian tailors who were competing with them. The Indian tailors took refuge in their separate status, claiming not to be subject to the jurisdiction of the Spanish guild.[20] Most guilds had ceased to identify on the basis of race by the eighteenth century.[21] Yet some racial distinctions within the guilds survived into the early part of the nineteenth century: as late as 1809 distinctions can still be found in the official documentation between Spanish and Indian tailors and between Spanish and Indian hatters.[22]

For the most part, however, the realities of the colonial economy and society worked against the Spanish ideal of separateness. Throughout the colonial period, attempts by Spaniards to limit the participation of Indians, blacks, and castas in the trades were unsuccessful. The increasing demands of the colonial economy meant that ever-growing numbers of non-Europeans entered the production process and thus undermined the racially segregated nature of guilds. Spanish artisans could not keep up with demand and so had trouble convincing colonial authorities to fully support their attempts at exclusion.[23] In fact, as Lyman Johnson notes, guilds often ended up functioning as mechanisms for the integration of Indians and populations of mixed race: "Although white racism was a powerful force in colonial society, many of the early guilds permitted Indians to enter without restriction, and within a short period Indian master craftsmen were found among the painters, sculptors, silk weavers, glove makers, and many other artisan groups."[24]

The rapid pace of miscegenation in colonial society and the complexities of racial identification also worked against racial segregation in the guilds. The Spanish crown's efforts to maintain a society with separate realms for Spaniards and Indians (Republica de Españoles/República de Indios) were quickly undermined; miscegenation led to the emergence of a growing population of castas that fit neither of the original categories. The categories themselves, "Spaniard," "Indian," quickly ceased to have a purely ethnic content and became categories with strong economic, social, and cultural components.[25] Thus, a successful mestizo artisan, for example, could probably make his way into a guild nominally intended only for Spaniards.

Its economic weaknesses notwithstanding, the guild remained an important social institution that gave artisans a recognized status in society. The guild gave artisans a defined corporate existence in relation to the colonial state. As corporations, guilds had a legal existence that allowed them to own property and engage in numerous economic transactions. In his study of Mexican guilds, Castro Gutierrez points to the advantages of such a corporate organization for artisans: "The Spanish state preferred to relate not to individuals but rather to corporations. . . . Guild membership gave the artisan a social and political recognition that he could rarely have achieved on his own, and made him part of a stable, hierarchical organization with established and familiar patterns of conduct."[26]

Initially not all artisans formed guilds. During the sixteenth century, tailors, carpenters, shoemakers, and hatters founded guilds in the city of Lima. By the early seventeenth century twelve trades had been organized into guilds. It wasn't until the eighteenth century, under the prompting of colonial authorities seeking greater control over artisans, that the remaining trades were organized into guilds. Guilds also appeared in the other major colonial cities, such as Mexico City and Guatemala.

Public festivals offer an indication of the corporate nature of various trades in colonial society. Guilds partook of both civic and religious celebrations, and some of the wealthier guilds contributed to finance special celebrations. For example, in Lima in 1659 various artisan guilds paid homage to the king of Spain:

> Friday, December 29, the silversmiths held their celebration, together with some other guilds, and they brought out nine carriages and each symbolized a kingdom, and they offered the prince the treasures of each kingdom. And likenesses of all of the grandees of Spain came out, well dressed and with great elegance, and also all of His Majesty's guard, Germans and Spaniards, with the captains of the guard. And it all was very sightly. There was a bullfight that afternoon and they jabbed four bulls that emerged like grandees of Castile; it was a joyful afternoon with much to see.[27]

The ability of guilds to finance such festivities enhanced the prestige of its members in the eyes of the public.[28]

Often public festivals became a means of enhancing the social standing of a particular guild in relation to others. The trades enjoyed differing degrees of social prestige, depending primarily on the value of the raw materials worked.[29] Thus gold- and silversmiths were considered more prestigious than shoemakers and carpenters. Lyman Johnson writes: "It is clear that the prominent participation in civic life by organized craftsmen helped to fix their place in the urban social structure. In some cases, artisans, particularly silversmiths, were actually given precedence over merchants and other wealthier groups in municipal celebrations."[30] The importance of the guilds in the celebration of Corpus Christi in colonial Mexico has been studied by Linda Curcio-Nagy, who pointed to the issue of rivalry among guilds.[31] During the sixteenth century, such rivalry took the form of quests to achieve a more central role in the procession. In the following century "guilds attempted to win public favor by the sumptuousness of their processions, by tossing to spectators small coins minted with their insignia, and by including bullfights as part of the festivities.... A unique guild contribution to Corpus Christi was the patronage of sermons, which required the panegyrist to include references to the sponsoring guild."[32]

The corporate identity associated with the guilds is particularly significant in the light of the high number of castas among artisans, a phenomenon true not only for Peru, but also for Mexico and Guatemala.[33] As James Lockhart writes: "The crafts were the very domain of the castas."[34] The possibility of acquiring a corporate identity in relation to the guild offered castas an opportunity for upward mobility: "It would not be an exaggeration, in fact, to say that this corporate identity often superseded such individual characteristics as ethnicity and even wealth."[35] Despite the prejudices against manual labor inherited from Spain, artisans in colonial society enjoyed a certain degree of prestige that put them at the upper echelons of the urban popular sectors. The fact that artisans practiced a craft separated them from the lower classes made up of servants, slaves, and the unemployed—a group that has been referred to as *"la plebe"* in recent Peruvian historiography.[36] The status as artisan could give a person of African descent an otherwise unattainable social status. In reference to the early colonial period, Frederick Bowser writes: "In a society where educational opportunity, membership in the prestigious professions, and bureaucratic position was denied to all but the lightest and luckiest of African descent, the crafts promised financial security and some standing in the community."[37]

The Religious Brotherhood (Cofradía)

While guilds functioned intermittently and never really dominated the trades in Spanish America, another institution, the religious brotherhood (cofradía), had a much greater impact on the daily lives of artisans. Like the guilds, cofradías had their origins in the European medieval period. They came to be closely associated with Christian popular devotional practices. In Spanish America, brotherhoods originally played an important role in integrating the Indian population into Spanish religious life. While guilds functioned primarily as regulatory institutions in relation to the world of work, brotherhoods were lay religious institutions with two sets of functions: the cult of a particular saint and the provision of mutual assistance for its members. Although brotherhoods were subject to some Church supervision, they enjoyed a certain degree of independence.

The brotherhood offered its members assistance during times of illness and, perhaps more importantly, the opportunity for a dignified funeral. In the strongly religious culture of colonial society, the cult of a saint and the assurance of a dignified burial provided important forms of security. According to Lyman Johnson, "This final function was of real importance in the devout Catholic societies of Spanish and Portuguese America. It meant that every member, regardless of his material circumstances and social origins, was buried with great dignity and provided with memorial masses."[38] Brotherhoods offered their members burials that included such features as music, candles, and ornaments, all indicative of social prestige. Often they would compete in offering more attractive benefits, such as a burial with the same kind of music and degree of solemnity as that of a priest.[39] For Indians, blacks, and castas, brotherhood membership reinforced the position in the upper echelons of the popular classes and separated them from the plebe.

Within each brotherhood, authorities elected on a yearly basis were in charge of the finances of the brotherhood and of the other main function of this institution: the celebration of festivities for the patron saint. As Olinda Celestino and Albert Meyers write: "Religious brotherhoods organized an imposing celebration on the day dedicated to their patron. They participated with great ostentation in all of the processions and public festivals, both civil and religious, as the luxury and ostentation they displayed to the public constituted a source of prestige and social standing."[40] Such festivities were of great importance both for the spiritual welfare of the brotherhood members and as a sign of social prestige. The saints venerated by the various brotherhoods were situated in a chapel in one of the city's many churches.

Together with their important religious role, brotherhoods helped to reinforce group social identities within the hierarchical social order of the colonial period. Many brotherhoods restricted membership to individuals of a given race. Indians, blacks, and castas participated actively in brotherhoods, many of which maintained their racial identity throughout the colonial period. Referring to black brotherhoods, Bowser writes that "these brotherhoods . . . no doubt gave those blacks and mulattoes who were fortunate enough to belong some sense of spiritual well-being and standing in the larger community."[41] Lima's original brotherhoods were divided among those of Spaniards, Indians and blacks, and mulattos.[42] The nature of the brotherhood tended to vary according to the social sector. Those associated with the upper echelons of colonial society concentrated on performing

religious and social duties, while the poorer brotherhoods played an important role in offering mutual aid to their members.

Artisans often established their own brotherhoods, and devotion to a
particular saint could be associated with a specific trade. In contrast to
their elite counterparts, these brotherhoods associated with the trades
were considered "minor brotherhoods." For example, "the Saint Eloy brotherhood was considered a 'Minor Brotherhood of the gold and silversmiths established at the Church of San Agustín.'"[43] Some artisan
brotherhoods dated to the early colonial period. The tailors' brotherhood,
established in the Church of San Francisco, dated to 1573. The shoemakers' brotherhood of San Crispín in the Cathedral dated to the sixteenth
century.[44] The Indian silversmiths worshiped the Gloriosa Santa Ana; the
Indian shoemakers, San Crispín and San Crispiniano; the Spanish silversmiths, San Eloy; the hatters, Santa Rosa; the blacksmiths, San Lorenzo;
the Indian tailors, San Agatón; and the chair makers, San Joaquín.
Brotherhoods prospered over the course of the colonial period. Celestino
and Meyers note an increase in the number of artisan brotherhoods during the late colonial period. The wealthiest brotherhood remained that of
the Spanish silversmiths. In his study of worker organizations during
colonial and national periods, Temoche Benites points out that among the
silversmiths "relations between the gremio and the *cofradía* were close and
both possessed significant wealth since its members practiced the trade of
making sacred ornaments out of silver and also objects for the use of
Spanish families."[45] In 1792 the prestigious San Eloy brotherhood of gold
and silversmiths had 1,725 members.[46] Despite the association with a
specific trade, membership in these brotherhoods was not always limited
exclusively to artisans.

In some cases, artisans seem to have used the brotherhood as a kind of
guild. According to Quiroz, Indian artisans tended to identify more strongly
with the brotherhood than they did with the guild. "Sometimes the guild and
the *cofradía* were mistaken for one another, and the name of each used inter-
changeably. The Indian button-makers presented their legal petitions in the
name of the brotherhoods of *Nuestra Señora de Desamparados* and the *Señor
del Triunfo*, the shoemakers appeared as members of the brotherhood of
Saint Lazarus, the chair-makers as the brothers of Saint Joaquin, etc."[47] Other
guilds linked to brotherhoods were the Gremio de Petateros (Guild of Straw
Craftsmen), associated with Nuestra Señora Santa Ana, and the Gremio de
Sastres Españoles (Guild of Spanish Tailors), linked to Nuestra Señora de la

Agonía in the now-vanished Church of Desamparados. The guild of button makers worshiped Nuestra Señora del Triunfo.[48]

The participation of brotherhoods in religious festivals reinforced a sense of communal civic consciousness.[49] Lockhart writes that "lay brotherhoods in fact became social clubs, giving cohesion to residential, occupational, or class groupings."[50] Clara García Ayluardo adds: "Devotional activities fostered a spirit of ethnic or group identity. The sense of involvement and commitment, particularly in a prominent brotherhood, enhanced the status of its members."[51] Competitiveness between the different brotherhoods was not uncommon and could sometimes lead to incidents of violence. In his portrait of daily life, Jean Descola describes these rivalries as follows: "Each *hermandad* [brotherhood] was anxious that its Virgin should be distinguished from that of the others by the richness of its vestments on days when it was carried in procession and bloody brawls frequently broke out between the members of the various rival confraternities."[52]

Artisans and Eighteenth-Century Bourbon Reforms

The Bourbon reforms during the late colonial period introduced a series of changes that modified the social role of artisans in Spanish America. To begin with, the corporate culture in which artisans had participated, both through the guild and the brotherhood, now came under attack. The new economic thinking of the Spanish Enlightenment challenged this corporate culture and placed greater emphasis on the individual as a source of wealth. The intellectual changes associated with the reforms thus foreshadowed nineteenth-century liberalism.

These new ideas coincided with the strengthening of the absolutist state. As the Bourbon dynasty attempted to modernize Spain, the colonies were exposed to an increasingly active monarchy seeking to centralize power and increase colonial revenue. The strengthening of the state had a direct effect on the world of colonial artisans as the monarchy attempted to regulate the guilds more tightly. Thus, paradoxically, while reformers in Spain challenged the institutions of a corporate society, in the colonial setting they attempted to strengthen a traditional institution in the name of greater state control.

Faced with the declining power of Spain in the European context, Spanish thinkers influenced by the Enlightenment sought to strengthen Spain's economic power according to the new ideas of the epoch. The eighteenth century ushered in a shift away from the mercantilist notion that wealth derived from bullion to the liberal idea that a nation's wealth was based on production: "Like a number of his contemporaries, Jovellanos believed that a new historical period was beginning in which traditional values would make way for economic power. We have remarked the interests of members of the elite in economic problems."[53] Ideas of economic liberalism and free trade were cautiously introduced by a monarchy seeking to establish absolute power. The Comercio Libre decrees of 1778, for example, now allowed for greater trade among different regions within the empire. The expulsion of the Jesuits from the empire in 1767 reflected the monarchy's new assertion of control and attack on the power of corporate groups in society.

As a result of the process of reform, the corporate social order came under attack and hence also the Spanish guilds. The corporate nature of artisan organizations made them a direct subject of Spanish enlightened thought and reform. The artisan guild came under fire as an institution that stood as an obstacle to the kind of economic development necessary for Spain to compete with other European nations. According to the new economic thinking, Spanish industry needed to be free in order to compete with its rivals in northern Europe. In Spain, the monarchy set up a number of factories for the production of a variety of products ranging from textiles to pottery and swords.[54] It was hoped that by eliminating many of the restrictive aspects of the guilds and following the ideas of *industria libre* (free industry), Spain would prosper.

In their writings, Spain's most prominent thinkers and political reformers attacked the guilds. Pedro Rodriguez de Campomanes, who served as adviser in the regime of Charles III, suggested weakening the guilds in his 1775 *Discurso sobre la educación popular de artesanos y su fomento* (Speech on promoting the popular education of artisans). This work stressed the need to train artisans by teaching them the most recent technical procedures. Campomanes envisioned the formation of a prosperous artisan class that would supersede the guilds.[55] The implementation of these ideas led to a lifting of a number of restrictions on production. The innovations that contributed to break local guild monopolies included the provision of training for children at schools, the extension of labor to women, and the opening of the guilds to craftsmen from various parts of Spain and even from abroad.[56]

The new economic philosophy brought a shift toward a greater involvement of the state in economic affairs. In Spain, the monarchy eliminated certain price controls and broke guild-master monopolies by lifting some of the restrictions on entry into the guilds. For example, anybody who had passed the examinations would now be allowed to practice a trade. Political theorists of the period envisioned a much more central role for the state in the process of training artisans. The emphasis on popular education can be considered a part of the transition toward greater dependence on the state, as the skills particular to artisans would no longer remain the domain of guilds and the apprenticeship system but rather would move into the realm of supervision by the state.

The attack on the guilds did not by extension imply an attack on artisans. In fact, artisans began to be portrayed as a basis for future economic prosperity based on industry. Spanish enlightened reformers lauded artisans for their potentially important role in generating economic prosperity and attempted to combat many of the traditional prejudices against the artisan in Spanish society. Writers criticized excessive luxury, and the wealthy came under attack.[57] The monarchy even attempted to legislate against the stigma attached to manual labor. In 1783, according to Richard Herr, "the occupations of tanner, smith, tailor, shoemaker, carpenter, 'and others of this kind' were specifically declared honorable and compatible with the rank of nobility, and those who followed them were declared eligible for municipal offices."[58] He continues: "If craftsmen were deprived of their exclusive privileges, they had the satisfaction of being told by the king (if not by the hidalgos) that they were more valuable citizens than idle nobles."[59] The notion of an artisan class that transcended corporate identities and with a role in furthering the prosperity of the nation was thus put forth during this period.

In Spanish America, the emphasis on industrial development as a source of wealth took a decidedly secondary place with respect to the Bourbon monarchy's plan to increase its fiscal revenue. Over the course of the colonial period, in its attempt to protect Spanish industry, the monarchy had followed a policy of discouraging industries in the colonies that might compete with their Spanish counterparts. The strengthening of the absolutist state and the goal of increasing Spanish prosperity translated into a policy of tighter fiscal control in Spanish America. In order to increase the revenue flowing into the royal coffers, the monarchy implemented a series of reforms that strengthened local government and bureaucracies.

Paradoxically, in Spanish America the age of Bourbon reforms and *industria libre* led to a strengthening of the guilds as the state attempted to exert greater control over artisans.[60] The attack on corporate privilege that was a crucial element of the reforming efforts lost some of its edge in the case of colonial artisans, given the weakness of the guild system. As Lyman Johnson writes: "The general weakness of the artisan sector in Spanish America provoked a number of reform efforts in the eighteenth century. . . . These reform efforts were generally conservative in intent, seeking to create or reinvigorate artisan guilds."[61] During the late eighteenth century, Spanish American artisans experienced a tightening of state control over the guild and more stringent fiscal demands. The state mandated that all artisans belong to guilds. According to a new municipal code, *Nuevo reglamento de policía* of 1786, "a shop or store could not open for business without a license from the *ayuntamiento* (municipal council), which had to keep a separate book in its archives for each guild. The election of alcaldes (guild officials) was to be held in the residence of the senior alcalde ordinario at the beginning of each year. Should a guild lack a set of rules for its government, one had to be drafted immediately by the procurator-general and approved by the cabildo and the intendant."[62]

The administrative changes implemented during this period sought to increase colonial revenue. From the point of view of the Bourbon state, the reorganization of the guilds would make these institutions useful for the purposes of controlling production and implementing taxes. The general increase in the sales tax (*alcabala*), which caused hardship and led to revolts in the southern Andes, had a direct effect on artisans.[63] In 1780, the crown mandated that artisans register with their guilds to facilitate collection of the alcabala.[64] The reforms also attempted to regulate and tax the materials used by artisans in an attempt to guard against contraband. A 1776 ordinance, for example, "prohibited the Guild of silversmiths and goldsmiths to work on silver and gold that had not been previously tested, taxed and stamped."[65] In 1778, Viceroy Guirior imposed stringent regulations on Lima's silversmiths, including rules on apprenticeship terms, purchase of raw materials, and sale of finished products.[66]

The interests of the state sometimes dovetailed with those of master artisans seeking to exert greater control over their guilds. The late-eighteenth-century attempts to reorganize the guilds followed a long period of laxness during which guilds had become weakened. Even prior to the full-fledged reform efforts, master artisans had sought to impose a more stringent control on the trades. Competition from nonguild members continued to concern guild members throughout the colonial period. Artisans in various different trades responded to the calls for guild reorganization. According to Quiroz, "During the [1770s] groups of master artisans began to make more frequent demands and throughout the city master artisans asked the authorities to help them impose 'order' in their respective trades."[67] The reinforcement of official rules among guild members occurred in a number of trades, including leather curriers, chair makers, blacksmiths, coach makers, hatters, and coopers. Some new guilds were established by straw craftsmen (*petateros*) and string makers (*cuerderos*).

As occurred with many of the reform efforts in Spanish America, the stringency of the measures meant that implementation fell short of stated goals. While the reforms had a limited impact, they led to the strengthening of certain guilds and brought artisans in various trades into closer contact with municipal authorities.[68] During the 1780s, the colonial authorities implemented regulations affecting all the city guilds. In 1785 the municipal authorities were given power to supervise artisan production within the city. Artisan guilds were required to keep their documentation up-to-date, and every workshop was to register in order to operate.

Inevitably, the strengthening of the guilds during this period often brought the issue of race once again to the forefront. Artisans attempted to reinforce the regulatory functions of the guild by making demands such as limiting the marketing of products to guild members and restricting the entry of castas into the trade. Lima's chocolate makers demanded support from the authorities to restrict the entry of castas, shoemakers attempted to restrict competition from artisans working outside the guild, and a number of guilds (including passementerie makers, Spanish tailors, silk weavers, bonnet makers, button makers, and embroiderers) attempted to reestablish the system of examinations in their respective trades.[69] Yet in most of these cases, the authorities failed to second the exclusionary efforts, which would probably have been difficult to enforce given the traditional weakness of the guild.

For all the state-led efforts to regulate the guilds in Spanish America, the traditional economic weakness of these institutions persisted. In addition to the issue of slave labor, which undermined guild power, other economic factors contributed to work against the possibility of a guild-based regulatory system. In the more complex economy of the late colonial period, successful artisan entrepreneurs undermined the power of the guilds. As Lyman Johnson writes: "Generally speaking, the most successful artisans of the late colonial period were individuals who had put some distance between themselves and their trades. In the expanding colonial marketplace, access to credit and a flexible, inexpensive labor force were more important predictors of material success than were the individual skills and corporate institutions associated with traditional artisan life."[70] Francisco Quiroz has recently explored incipient industrial production in Lima during this period and demonstrated the existence of "mass production," which brings into question the traditional notion of a guild-regulated artisan workshop.[71]

Certain guilds escaped this general trend. Silversmiths traditionally remained influential throughout the colonial period, although their power would decline in the nineteenth century. Over the course of the eighteenth century, the bakers' guild developed into an extremely power-ful group and continued to be influential well into the nineteenth century. The bakers' guild was further strengthened by the fact that it grouped individuals involved in production and commercialization.[72] The strength of the guild was due to its links to major commercial interests, such as wheat-importing merchants.

The reformist efforts of the Bourbons were all-encompassing, and eco-nomic reforms went hand in hand with attempts to reform social mores.[73] The attack on corporations brought an attack on many of the social cus-toms associated with these entities. Reformers displayed a particular con-cern with discipline and order both in the workplace and in daily affairs. Popular religion became a favorite target of Bourbon reformers, who con-demned a number of religious practices such as processions and the cult of saint relics as superstitious. The criticism of popular religious practices spans the eighteenth century in Spain.[74] In particular, reformers were con-cerned with festivities considered to be unnecessary and wasteful. According to Clara García Ayluardo: "It was precisely this uncontrolled sen-timent and lavish display of baroque piety that eighteenth-century reform ministers found objectionable."[75]

The prominent role of religious brotherhoods in such religious festivi-ties made them a target of the reforms. In Lima, the number of brother-hoods had increased over the course of the colonial period. Attempts to limit the duration and scope of festivities during saint day celebrations abound in eighteenth-century Lima. Archbishop Barroeta y Angel (1751–58) played a pioneering role in attempting to reform popular culture prior to the full-fledged efforts at reform later in the century.[76] The Bourbon attacks against the brotherhoods aimed both to increase the power of the monar-chy with respect to corporations and to curb, according to García Ayluardo, "unbridled piety that could result in disturbances."[77]

Concerns with regulating the outward form of festivities were followed by more stringent rulings against the brotherhoods that sought to limit their assets. Toward the end of the eighteenth century the crown even legislated to abolish brotherhoods altogether. A royal decree in 1798 forced brotherhoods to sell their properties.[78] The Bourbon attempts to abolish the brotherhood were unsuccessful, given the institution's strong popular roots, but brotherhoods entered the national period weakened by the Bourbon reforms and by the ascendance of liberal ideology.

Conclusions

The guild and the brotherhood gave the artisan a defined place within the hierarchical and corporate order of colonial society. While long-standing prejudices against manual labor barred artisans from reaching the upper echelons of society, the trades nonetheless played a crucial role in allowing for a degree of social mobility for those at the bottom: Indians, blacks, and castas. In particular, for the individuals of mixed race, who made up the increasing population of castas, the artisan trades offered a recognized social and legal status that contrasted with the otherwise uncertain position of the castas in colonial society.

In numerous ways, the eighteenth-century Bourbon reforms challenged the corporate ideal and contributed to define a new social role for the artisan. The reforms set in motion a process of liberalization that began to redefine the relationship between state and society. Spanish Enlightenment thinkers introduced ideas of political economy and initiated a shift in the understanding of the origins of wealth. Mercantilist ideas gradually gave way to the notion that the wealth of nations stemmed from the labor of its inhabitants.[79]

While the Bourbon authorities sought to reorganize the guilds for their own fiscal purposes, artisans also sought concessions and attempted to further their interests by attempting to obtain the support of colonial authorities to increase the regulatory powers of the guilds.[80] For the most part, such requests went unheeded. No longer the corporate institutions of the early colonial period, the eighteenth-century guilds now acted as a link between artisans and a stronger colonial state seeking to increase its fiscal revenue. The persistence of the guild during the early republican period both as a fiscal mechanism and as a locus for artisan demands of the state was a direct legacy of the late colonial period. As Thomas Kruggeler writes:

"The newly independent Peruvian state was confronted with a guild system that had gained institutional strength during the past decades only because of the intervention of colonial authorities."[81]

The transition to nationhood following independence from Spain (formally declared in 1821 and achieved in practice in 1824) added a new dimension to the relationship between artisans and the state. Unlike the colonial regime, the early republican state needed to establish a basis of legitimate authority in keeping with new republican principles. The colonial state had primarily sought to tax and regulate the guilds but remained unresponsive to the demands for increasing their regulatory powers. As we shall see in the following chapter, the caudillos who governed Peru during the decades immediately following independence sought the political support of artisans and proved somewhat responsive to their economic interests.

In the national context, artisans began to act politically by making a series of demands on the new national state. In the process of participating in national politics, artisans discovered the limitations of the guild and developed new institutional ties to the emerging Peruvian state. Through their political participation, artisans thus contributed to the process of liberal nation building by leaving behind the corporate institutions of the colonial period. Yet as will be discussed in chapters 4 and 5, elements of the old corporate identity persisted as artisans developed a modern political identity in nineteenth-century Peru. The initial relationship between artisans, the early national state, and liberal elites will be the subject of the next chapter.

CHAPTER TWO

Artisans and Guilds in the Transition to a Liberal Age, 1821–1860

*Between innovation and retrieval lay a set of connections
between craft and politics spelled out in the banners, speeches,
and street dramas. At one level, the ceremonies announced
the artisans' determination to be part of the body politics—
no longer " meer mechanicks," no longer part of the vague
lower and middling sort of the revolutionary mobs, but
proud craftsmen, appearing for all to see on important civic
occasions, marching in orderly formation up and down lower
Broadway with the regalia and tools of their crafts.*

—Sean Wilentz, *Chants Democratic*

DURING THE TRANSITION FROM COLONY
TO independent republic in Peru, Lima's artisans emerged as distinct political actors in the national political arena. This chapter bridges two successive periods in Peru's early national history. The first is the period of caudillismo, from independence in 1821 to 1845, a time of political instability during which caudillos dominated the political process. The second is the period of consolidation of the liberal state over the course of the 1850s. Historian Jorge Basadre has referred to the early period as that of the "formation of nationality."[1] While the importance of the military is paramount during this epoch, historians have increasingly noted the inclusive nature of caudillo politics. During the second period, the 1840s and 1850s, the state was able

to grow and modernize relying on the massive revenues from the guano trade. This period has commonly been referred to in Peruvian history as that of "Fictitious Prosperity" (Prosperidad Falaz).

Over the course of both of these periods, Lima's artisans began to play a visible role in the process of building a new national state. During this period of caudillismo, artisans developed close ties to the state through the surviving colonial guilds. Caudillos used these institutions to perform some of the new functions of the early national state, including military recruitment and taxation. In return for their role in supporting caudillos, artisans could count on the continuation of protectionist policies that shielded their products from foreign competition. Artisans thus figured prominently in the patronage networks that supported caudillos.

During the second period, that of the consolidation of the liberal state, artisans found themselves in a new economic environment hostile to their interests. The close relationship between artisans and protectionist caudillos began to change over the course of the 1840s as economic liberalism gained ground. As in many cases in nineteenth-century Latin America, the spread of economic liberalism went hand in hand with the emergence of a strong centralized state. The consolidation of the liberal state under General Ramón Castilla during the 1840s and 1850s occurred thanks to the windfall revenues from the guano trade that made the Peruvian state financially solvent for the first time since the wars of independence.

Artisans resisted the lowering of tariffs and increased influx of foreign products that competed with national goods. They turned to the state that had once protected them for solutions. They also sought to influence public opinion, speaking out vociferously in favor of protectionist policies and casting themselves as the *hijos del país* (sons of the country), the true representatives of the Peruvian nation.[2] Artisans fought the battle against free-trade policies through petitions to the national congress and through the press. As early as 1828, they petitioned Congress for high tariffs to protect national products from foreign competition. With the consolidation of the liberal state during the 1840s and 1850s, artisans increasingly attacked state policies of free trade that eroded their interests. Whereas initially they had embraced the guilds, they now distanced themselves from these institutions, which increasingly came under attack by liberal ideologues.

This chapter describes how over the course of the period from 1821 to the 1850s, artisans began to forge a distinct political identity. From the earliest years of the republic, as part of the patronage networks of caudillos, artisans found that they possessed some political clout through their guilds. Their links to the state through the guilds also reinforced the social position of artisans as separate from the plebe. Artisans began to redefine their identity in the context of republican politics by speaking out in the public sphere. They did not simply become passive recipients of state patronage—rather, artisans became a social group with a clearly voiced position in the debates over commercial policy. As state protectionism gave way to free trade during the 1850s, the caudillo patronage networks dissolved and artisans found themselves increasingly having to fight their political battles on their own, sometimes even turning to violence. While economic liberalism harmed artisans' interests, it also further contributed to forging the artisanry as a political group independent of the state.

Caudillos and Popular Politics

The establishment of an independent nation-state during the 1820s altered the colonial polity in fundamental ways by modifying the rules of the political game and by bringing new social groups, primarily Creoles and mestizos, into politics.[3] The establishment of a constitutional republic in Peru during the 1820s followed a long period of wars that involved significant portions of the population. The 1824 battle of Ayacucho put an end to over three centuries of Spanish rule. Within the national scenario, artisans, like other social groups, entered an entirely new political process whose dynamics differed markedly from those of colonial politics. From the point of view of political leaders and ideologues, a primary concern during this period was the issue of establishing a legitimate state in the absence of the Spanish monarchy. During the decades following independence from Spain, political life was dominated by the presence of the caudillos, who made use of their military power and prestige to establish themselves as national leaders. The period has thus come to be known as the epoch of caudillismo.

The upheavals of postindependence politics created new opportunities for social mobility. The restrictions that had kept the highest administrative posts during the colonial period in the hands of Spaniards disappeared in the new national setting, ushering Creole elites into political power. While Creoles dominated the political process, the appearance of mestizos at the highest levels of government constituted a significant break with the past. The possibilities for social mobility for mestizos brought about by independence are perhaps best appreciated in the case of the military. According to Basadre, "Militarism ... played a democratic role by elevating Indians and mestizos, providing the only means of social ascension possible in such a society."[4] Two presidents during this period were of Indian or mestizo origin, respectively. Agustín Gamarra, who governed from 1829 to 1833 and from 1839 to 1841, was of Indian origins, a native of the Andean city of Cusco.[5] In fact, Gamarra's opponents openly denigrated his Indian origins. General Ramón Castilla (1845–51 and 1855–62), a mestizo, is credited by historians with having brought political stability to Peru at the outset of the guano period. While the predominance of Creoles in politics is clear, the presence of mestizos in politics attests to the relative openness of this early national period.

Given the violent nature of caudillo political struggles, it is perhaps not surprising that the classic view of this period has minimized the role of republican politics. The political ascendance of caudillos has been explained as a result of their reliance on military power and traditional patronage networks.[6] Recent historiography on Peru has questioned this view of caudillismo and posited a more complex view of the political process. Revisionist studies, such as that by Cristobal Aljovín, emphasize the degree to which caudillos were bound by constitutions that set political parameters: "Revolutionaries did not intend to build a dictatorship. They sought a solution for a stable republic. In the aftermath of coups, they followed a constitutional ritual of congressional convocation and presidential elections in order to legitimize their power. They needed the 'approval' of the people."[7] Notions of popular sovereignty became important ideological referents in the political process, and hence political leaders sought the support of the urban populace to establish their legitimacy. The impact of constitutions on the political rules of the game has been noted more generally for Latin America during this period.[8] According to Charles Walker, the civil wars between caudillos "involved intense debate in the press and in public forums about the postindependence state, particularly the questions of political stability and the role of the lower classes."[9]

This view of the postindependence polity suggests that popular participation played a more significant political role than had previously been assumed. The legitimacy of caudillos depended, among other factors, on their ability to seek a broad basis of support among the population. Historians have pointed to the democratic features of a period during which caudillos needed to create a wide base of support in order to consolidate their political power. In fact, this period of militarism opened up channels of political participation during the first decades of national life, particularly in the urban setting. Recent studies have confirmed the political importance of the urban populace, both in Peru and other parts of Latin America.[10]

The greater relevance of popular political participation following independence must also be understood against the backdrop of the economic devastation that acted as a leveling force during this period. According to Gootenberg, "Universal poverty in the post-Independence era diminished social distances, making politics more egalitarian."[11] The late-colonial elite was particularly affected by the impoverishment.[12] Numerous agricultural estates had been destroyed during the wars of independence, and a large number of Spaniards who occupied bureaucratic posts fled the country.

Artisan Guilds and the National State: Taxation and Militias

In the process of recruiting popular support, successive caudillos found artisan guilds to be particularly valuable. From the earliest times after independence, these institutions began to play a role as instruments of the government in exercising a degree of social control. The persistence of the guild was a direct result of the institutional weakness of the early national state. The newly established national state made use of existing guilds to serve as tax collection mechanisms among artisans. As Gootenberg writes: "The Peruvian state had a strong vested interest in propping up the guilds, even when they were disintegrating on their own, essentially for tax purposes."[13] The fiscal importance of guilds harkens back to the late colonial period, when the Bourbon reforms strengthened the guilds for taxation purposes. The state also relied on the guilds to help with recruitment to the National Guard and to fulfill a number of other functions. Guilds served "as a means of enforcing contracts and settling economic disputes" prior to the adoption of the civil code in 1852.[14] Guilds also served educational purposes through the apprenticeship system.[15]

Soon after independence, some guild regulations reflected their new functions on behalf of the state within the national context. The guilds adopted the moralizing language of liberal reformism in referring to their own social functions. The ordinances of the shoemakers' guild for 1827, for example, equate the evasion of military service with vice. Ordinance 11 attempted to ensure that all artisans within workshops were subjected to both taxes and military service and read: "No master artisan shall have hidden *oficiales* [journeymen] at work because of the damage done to the state, depriving it of the patente tax, both first and second class, and the damage to the guild, since such hiding does harm to the reciprocal tasks within the workshop, resulting in an excuse to not march in the civic militias and leading to a life of vice."[16] The ordinances mentioned the involvement of the guild in both taxation and military recruitment, together with the traditional guild functions, ranging from the mechanics of internal elections to apprenticeship terms.

The fact that caudillos sought to include artisans in their patronage networks meant that artisans enjoyed some political influence during this period. As Gootenberg writes: "With the institutional fluidity of the state (which precluded other methods of social control) and the absence of formal political parties, craftsmen came to exert their new pull in republican politics and were valued for their ability to mobilize forces for the paramilitary or electoral exploits so crucial to caudillos."[17] During the 1830s artisans openly supported caudillos such as Salaverry and Gamarra and received benefits in return through the implementation of protectionist policies.[18]

The fiscal contribution of artisans proved all the more significant during the decades immediately following independence, given the early national state's constant fiscal crisis. The nations of Latin America waged their wars of independence with scant external financial support and thus had to rely primarily on internal revenues. In 1821, artisans were among the many sectors of society called upon to make emergency contributions to the armies led by General José de San Martín. In 1823, for example, when the personal contributions and the silver taken from churches fell short of the 300,000 pesos being collected by the state to fight the independence wars, contributions were exacted from various city guilds. The silversmith guild remained the wealthiest at this point and was expected to make the highest contribution, of 1,000 pesos. The next-largest contributor among the guilds was the tallow-chandler guild, required to pay 500 pesos.[19]

Following the final defeat of Spanish forces at the battle of Ayacucho in 1824, the guilds were assigned a fixed institutional role within the fiscal apparatus of the Peruvian state. A decree on August 11, 1826, created the *patente* tax.[20] Collected from individual artisans by the guild masters, the patente was a license fee based on an artisan's estimated income.[21] The tax was based on a division of the taxpayers into four income brackets: "first class," "second class," third class," and "fourth class." While the guild served as the vehicle for collecting the taxes, the patente was not a corporate based tax but rather a tax that depended on the individual income of each artisan.

Although the patente provided only a small percentage of the state's total revenue, according to Gootenberg, it "was considered to be the ideal 'Republican' means to raise revenue, even if dependent on the guilds."[22] Historian Emilio Romero has argued for a connection between taxation and republicanism during the early national period. From 1827 to 1842, prior to the influx of guano revenues, the government relied primarily on internal sources of revenue. Of this period, Romero writes: "A tax-paying consciousness arose that was indispensable to the creation of a national budget, a task begun by José Larrea y Loredo [an early finance minister]. Despite the routine criticisms of the period between the battle of Ayacucho and the appearance of guano... this was a virile time of republican beginnings within a democratic framework."[23] The patente was occasionally subject to the vagaries of caudillo politics, as in 1835, when the liberal Salaverry briefly took over the presidency and temporarily abolished the tax.[24] National artisans were not the only ones to pay the patente; the state relied on it to integrate foreign artisans into the domestic tax structure.[25]

Some artisans enjoyed a very direct form of state patronage through contracts for supplying the military. The size of many of these military contracts would have called for the employment of artisans on a fairly large scale. For example, the tanner Mariano Agreda had numerous contracts, some quite sizable, with the army. Agreda owned his workshop, on San José Street (later renamed Zárate Street). Despite the magnitude of many of the contracts, Agreda did not die a wealthy man and in his will, dated 1859, left only his workshop, valued at about 400 pesos, fifty saddles, and various outstanding loans, some to fellow artisans.[26]

One of Agreda's contracts with the army for the year 1842 is for 23,925 pesos worth of military equipment and includes the production of a number of leather goods, such as cartridge belts, rifle sheaths, and leather backpacks.[27] As Kruggeler has concluded in his study of Cusco artisans, fulfilling such large orders must necessarily have drawn on the labor of other artisans in a number of the city's workshops. For example, a number of tailors in the Andean city of Cusco produced uniforms for the military following an 1829 government decree mandating that uniforms for both armed forces and police use government cloth.[28] Kruggeler has pointed out that fulfilling these orders would have involved either working in conjunction with other guild members or hiring workers outside the guild system.[29]

The absence of sources allowing us to reconstruct the ways an individual artisan such as Mariano Agreda perceived his place within national society necessarily confine this subject to the realm of speculation. But it is difficult to imagine that the changes affecting Lima society with the advent of independence would not have altered the ways an artisan such as Agreda understood his role in the nation. To some degree, his identity would continue to be defined by membership in the religious and corporate institutions inherited from the colonial period: he was a member of an Indian brotherhood, the Cofradia de Nuestra Señora Rosario de Peruanos, in which he held the prestigious position of *mayordomo*. Yet as a member of the tanner's guild, he was subject to the new patente tax, and in the year 1833 he was one of the officials (*diputados*) for the guild in charge of collecting that tax.[30] His links to the state through military contracts and his new role as tax collector for the national state created allegiances of a different kind. The military supplies to be produced by Agreda were for the army fighting against an invading Bolivian army in late 1841 and early 1842. The fighting was concentrated in the southern part of Peru, particularly in the department of Puno. Whatever Agreda's personal views on the war may have been, he now saw himself tied to a military effort on a national scale that created allegiances beyond the narrow confines of specific brotherhoods or guilds.[31]

The number of artisans working on military contracts during this period was probably substantial. Documentation on the subject ranges from requests for a few artisans to work on government orders to fairly large orders of the magnitude of those received by the tanner Agreda. An 1821 document responds to a request for five tailors (Jose Matayana, Matías García, Hilario Zavala, Raymundo Salas, and Martín Detal)[32] to be sent from the town of Sayan (situated in the Andes, east of Lima) by indicating that four of them will begin walking on the following day while the fifth is away in another town.[33] A much larger request is made in 1823 by Agustín Gamarra (at the time fighting against the Spanish armies) for 100 tailors to make uniforms for his battalion.[34]

In addition to the economic benefits for national artisans of supplying the military, the guilds during the early national period provided further links between artisans and the military. Artisan participation in the military can be traced back to the late colonial period, with heavy artisan involvement in city militias.[35] Following the reorganization of the colonial militias under the rule of King Carlos III (1759–88), artisans appeared as successful participants, some attaining the ranks of officers.[36]

In the context of constant military mobilization both during the wars of independence and during subsequent political battles among caudillos, the role of the guilds in military recruitment gave artisans some political power. In 1821, for example, San Martín faced a crisis in the recruitment of militias when he failed to implement policies to protect artisans from the influx of foreign manufactured products.[37] Over the course of the first decades of national life, militias underwent a transformation and became part of the National Guard, created on February 24, 1834.[38] An 1839 decree by President Gamarra made guilds an integral part of the National Guard by ordering that "alcaldes" of the guilds ensure that nobody be allowed to work unless enlisted in the National Guard. The penalty for not enrolling in the National Guard was service in the army.[39] A law in 1842 abolished legal privileges (*fueros*) associated with the National Guard,[40] which eventually was extended to enlist all citizens.[41]

The Persistence of Guild Politics: the Bakers' Guild

These early decades of the national period brought a gradual transition in the situation of artisans with respect to the national state. On the one hand, within the emerging institutional structure of the nation-state, artisans were treated as individual citizens responsible for paying taxes and for serving in the military. On the other hand, this new relationship continued to be mediated by a traditional organization with corporate echoes, the guild. As guild members, artisans sought special privileges for their trades in the form of tariffs to protect them from competition from foreign manufactures.

Guilds had never been particularly strong as economic institutions and remained relatively powerless over the course of the colonial period with respect to their Spanish counterparts. In fact, guilds did not meet with any regularity in colonial Lima to elect their officials. During times of increased competition, a guild might attempt to enforce its exclusionary powers but usually did so with little success. The weakness of the guild persisted into the early national period. As Kruggeler writes, "The major reason why Latin American governments did not launch strong campaigns against the guild system immediately was that guilds were never strong or powerful urban institutions, neither in the colonial period nor during the first decades following independence."[42]

In the new national setting, guilds were affected by free trade. Guild documents reflect the changing pressures on guilds and an increasing appeal to the state for the solution of economic woes. No longer concerned with issues of internal competition from nonguild members—a primary concern of colonial guilds—the republican guilds faced the problems of a more unregulated environment at a time when free trade and freedom of industry (*libertad de industria*) became enshrined in the constitution. The adoption of libertad de industria in the constitution threatened the logic of the guild system.[43] For example, a commission investigating the situation of the cigar makers concluded the guild members were at a disadvantage as a result of the free trade in tobacco. Even private individuals "who previously went to the cigar stores to buy tobacco, now work it in their homes and as a result the guild members have a smaller production."[44] The commission recommended a reduction in taxes.

The transition toward economic liberalism occurred gradually during the first decades following independence. The 1826 *Reglamento de comercio* (Regulations on Commerce) supported free trade for certain products that would encourage national production, such as tools for agriculture and industry, but at the same time protected national carpenters, shoemakers, tailors, and other artisans with an 85 percent tax on competing goods.[45] While protectionist trade policy dominated during these decades, the alternations in power between caudillos with different constituencies led to shifts between greater and lesser degrees of protectionism. In 1835, the brief takeover of the government by the conservative caudillo Salaverry resulted in extreme protectionist measures, including total prohibition on the importation of a series of manufactured goods.[46] At this point, for the most part, the tariff structure favored Lima's artisans: "A finished piece of locally made clothing, for example, might enjoy tariffs of 50–90 percent; the imported cloth it was sewn from entered at 25 percent; and the tailor's tools came in duty-free."[47]

The history of the tariff over the course of the first four decades of the national period consists of three distinct stages: high tariffs between the years 1830 and 1834, a progressive liberalization of the tariff between 1834 and 1844, and finally the establishment of liberal tariffs between 1844 and 1861.[48] Economic liberalism was not necessarily detrimental to all artisans. According to Gootenberg, the manufacturing sector in fact experienced a limited recovery during the latter period, the outset of the guano boom: "The guano boom, with its tremendous impetus in demand (contributing to political consolidation) led to a slow recovery."[49] This suggests that while the guilds continued to oppose liberalization, individual artisans may have been able to prosper under the general economic expansion during the guano boom.

FIG. 4.
The Baker
(El Panadero),
*watercolor, Pancho
Fierro, 1840, Museo
de Arte de Lima.*

Yet the transition was uneven, and during episodes of intense protection-ism certain guilds attempted to reassert some of their powers. The shoemak-ers' guild, for example, sought to reinforce its own internal rules following a period during which the guild had been inactive "because the Constitution expressly forbade guilds and declared that industry should be free."[50] The guild sought to regulate traditional issues such as apprenticeships, quality of products, and entry into the trade. Tracing their guild back to 1572, the shoe-makers justified their renewed attempt to establish a system of examinations by appealing to an edict given in the city of Arequipa. The new demands included an attempt to establish more stringent norms such as the assurance that master artisans go through an examination process and that "journey-men" be able to leave their master if they received improper treatment. Yet the

same time, the guild regulations suggest an adjustment to the liberal requirements of industria libre in the elimination of examination fees that would
reduce a barrier to enter the trade.[51]

The case of the bakers' guild provides an exception to the pattern of
weakness of the guilds and an illustration of the persistence of what might
be termed "old guild politics" during the early national period—an attempt
by artisans of a single trade to control marketing and production. The issue
of the price of bread had been a traditional concern for authorities in Lima.
Following his declaration of Peruvian independence in 1821, General San
Martín, as Protector of Peru, made inquiries regarding the weight and the
quality of bread in Lima.[52] During the early national period, the municipality attempted to enforce restrictions on the weight and price of bread sold
in the city. Yet the bakers' guild proved to be quite powerful and made a
number of attempts throughout the early decades of the national period to
keep control of the trade.

Debates involving bakers can be found both in guild documents and in
the Lima press. Two sets of contentious issues arose: one between guild and
nonguild members about the restrictions imposed by the guild; the second,
the long-standing disputes between the guild and municipal authorities
about issues such as the quality and marketing of bread in Lima. The accusations against the guild made use of the prevailing liberal notion of libertad de industria, sanctioned by the early national constitutions. Guild
members protected themselves against these attacks by arguing for the
compatibility of the guild with the republican form of government.

The power of the bakers' guild can be attributed to its traditional links
to large merchant interests and to the nature of the product, which precluded competition from abroad. As Flores Galindo has shown for the late colonial period, bakeries were often owned by powerful merchants.[53] One baker
owned not only a bakery, but also two mills and various other businesses.
Quiroz reaches a similar conclusion for the early national period: "Their
ties to merchants gave them additional strength."[54]

The power of bakers was further increased by the informal role of bakeries as prisons. During the late colonial period, bakeries constituted one of
the main loci for prisoners to serve their sentences.[55] Bakers could count on
the labor of prisoners who had committed misdemeanors but were expected
to feed and clothe these workers. Bakers were not supervised, and thus conditions for the prisoners working in the bakeries were often dismal; according
to Galindo, "Certain employees, whip in hand, maintained a steady rhythm of

work so that bakeries came to resemble galleys."[56] Such cruelty in punishment was considered acceptable during the colonial period and continued into the early national period.[57]

The bakers' guild continued to foster a corporate identity and attempted to gain increasing powers during this period. In 1824 a group of forty-four bakers met informally to attempt to set limits on the marketing of bread. They agreed on such issues as eliminating bread sellers (*repartidores de pan*), prohibiting bakers from lowering prices—the norm was the sale of four loaves of bread per real, and bakers attempted to impose limits on those who sold more loaves for the same price—eliminating the so-called *vendaje* or *pan de regalo* or *yapa,* a free loaf of bread given away with a particular purchase.[58] Among the accusations against those selling more loaves of bread per real was that they were using lower-quality wheat (*tocadas*). In coming years, the guild continued to strengthen its stance, both attempting to defend its position with respect to municipal authorities and taking action against nonguild members. As Quiroz states, the guild became a powerful cohesive mechanism for bakers: "Now bakers began to see the guild as an entity that represented their interests and fostered cohesion and gave them an ability to pursue their interests that was unparalleled in the city's productive sector during those years."[59]

Over the course of the next decades, the guild fought frequently with the municipality. Guild members asserted their position, at times bypassing municipal authority and attempting to directly influence the government. In 1839, the bakers' guild managed to have its rules approved by the government in exchange for a monetary contribution to the Public Welfare Office (*Beneficencia*). Subsequent legislation undermined the guild's authority, and in 1847 the bakers unsuccessfully tried to reestablish their authority by offering to pay for the paving of Lima's streets. A similar attempt was made in 1849 when the bakers offered to build a new marketplace.[60] Such offers indicate the presence of powerful merchant interests behind Lima's bakeries.

The guild suffered constant attacks in the press. The newspaper *El Comercio* published numerous complaints against the guilds, accusing them of monopolistic practices and of interfering with free trade. In 1839 *El Comercio* wrote "In bakeries, as in all corporations, a corporate spirit is at odds with the rest of the population and takes advantage of the smallest oversight of its inspectors to evade their supervision. . . . The people, on the other hand, resist the monopoly that hinders competition and they feel the absence of the only force capable of regulating legitimate earnings."[61] Quiroz has argued that the bakers' guild generated a negative image for all artisans during this period: "The bakers came to stand for the republican guild in Lima.... The complaints against 'those speculators' were launched against artisans in general. The bakers came to be identified with all artisans: artisan = guild = antipopular privilege. The newspapers are full of letters against the bakers. It was undoubtedly the most hated guild in the city."[62]

While the case of Lima's bakers reveals the persistent strength of a traditional guild, it also demonstrates the degree to which ideas of economic liberalism had permeated social discourse and become a real weapon in local politics. In 1830, the head (alcalde) of the guild in 1830, Juan Pérez y Blanco, was accused by a baker by the name of Gomez Mantilla, who had faced sanctions he considered unfair from Perez y Blanco, of abusing his power to impose fines and confiscate bread not considered of the appropriate weight. In his own defense, the baker wielded two sets of arguments. The first involved the arbitrary behavior of the alcalde; the second was against the guild itself. In his petition to the municipality he referred to the bakers' guild as "a remnant of arbitrary power that stands in opposition to the principles of liberalism and philanthropy professed by Peru."[63] The guild was accused of imposing a monopoly.

A man by the name of Colmenares rose to the guild's defense, but even he had to acknowledge both the nation's constitution and the principle of libertad de industria: "The existence of the guild is not in my opinion contrary to the constitution. While the constitution allows for freedom of industry it does not prohibit those in the same trade to agree upon conditions that will guarantee order and a more favorable regime."[64] Colmenares attempted to assert authority through an appeal to tradition by pointing to the antiquity of the bakers' guild. The claim is somewhat ironic, given the fact that the history of the guild from the earliest colonial period was one of constant struggle with the municipal authorities, who sought to hold the bakers to certain standards of quality.[65]

In his attacks, Gomez Mantilla also made use of nationalist arguments, accusing the head of the guild of being a Spaniard. Gomez Mantilla had himself been a lieutenant colonel fighting against Spain in the wars of independence, and thus his patriotism was unquestioned. He had turned to the bread business, as he himself claimed, "in order to provide honorable subsistence for my family."[66] He questioned the authority of Blanco since he was a Spaniard and cited "the solemn oath I made to the Fatherland that I would not take orders from my enemies."[67] While the municipality ignored

FIG. 5.
The Water Carrier
(El Aguador),
*watercolor, Pancho
Fierro, 1840, Museo
de Arte de Lima.*

the arguments against the guild and affirmed that the guild was "not opposed to libertad de la industria," it responded to the attacks against the head of the guild and ordered that another person be elected to take his place, both because of his arbitrary behavior and because "he lacked . . . the rights of citizenship, without which he cannot make his fortune in the republic."[68] The municipal response attests to the power of the appeal to nationalism during this period.

The situation of the bakers was strengthened both by the guild's links to powerful commercial interests and by the nature of the product itself: bread production was sheltered from the possibility of foreign competition. Another guild, although less powerful than the bakers, was also sheltered by the nature of its activity and continued to maintain its cohesion well into the nineteenth century: the *aguadores* (water carriers). While aguadores cannot be considered artisans, given the nature of their work, the persistence of their organization demonstrates both the resilience of guilds and the process whereby guilds came to be negatively regarded in nineteenth-century Lima. The guild of aguadores engaged in long battles with authorities over complaints by the public that guild members charged too much for the service of carrying water from the city fountains to homes. The aguadores were accused of monopoly and were considered "the most infamous guild in Lima for artificially raising prices (and per-petuating a host of other abuses on the consumer) in an age when Lima households depended on five fountains for the water supply."[69] The power of the guild would eventually dwindle with the construction of a network of water pipes, during the second half of the century, that rendered their service obsolete.

In contrast to the bakers and water carriers, shoemakers, tailors, and other artisans faced a more daunting set of challenges: increased competi-tion from abroad. The guild proved powerless in this scenario. To face the increasing influx of imported goods during this period, artisans began to act politically as a bloc rather than through their particular guilds. The term *guild* itself gradually underwent changes in usage and came to refer not only to a legal organization, but also more loosely to a group of workers in the same trade, a connotation it continues to have today in everyday usage. By increasingly pursuing their interests as "artisans" rather than as individ-ual guild members, tailors, shoemakers, carpenters, cigar makers, and other artisans began to forge a new political identity in nineteenth-century Peru. In the context of national politics, artisans echoed many of the old corpo-rate demands for special privileges. Yet at the same time, they also became adept at making their demands through distinctly republican institutions such as the national congress and the press.

Artisans in the Public Sphere

By the 1840s, artisans had begun to act deliberately in the public sphere, attempting to affect public opinion. By participating in the debates over commercial policy, artisans stepped directly into the broader arena of national politics and sought to influence the government by providing arguments in support of their position. In his study of German history, James Sheehan writes:

> To think and act politically people have to make a connection
> between their personal condition and their public affairs. This
> connection is at once intellectual and institutional. It requires a set
> of ideas through which men and women can see how the immedi-
> ate realities of their lives fit into a larger world and a set of institu-
> tions with which they can co-ordinate and sustain their efforts to
> influence this world.[70]

With the progressive turn toward policies of free trade during the 1840s
and 1850s, certain groups of artisans appear to have made this crucial connection between their personal condition and public affairs. These artisans also discovered the limitations of the existing institutional setting of
guilds and began to act in an entirely new scenario and to take their petitions to Congress.

In 1849, while bakers continued to attempt to impose restrictions on
their trade, artisans for various different guilds joined forces and fought a
very different kind of political battle.[71] Joining the debates over commercial
policy, artisans named a representative, cigar maker José María García, to go
before Congress and argue for protectionism.[72] While the battle over trade
policy would soon be lost by artisans, the position of García and the artisans illustrates the degree to which artisans had begun to act politically as a
single bloc, beyond guild-based identities.

In his address to Congress on October 18, 1849, García claimed to speak
in the name of the city's artisans. In contrast to the demands made by the
bakers, García's speech represented a clear departure from the demands limited to a specific guild. Although *El Comercio* titled its article on the event
"Presentation Prepared by the Guilds for the Congress" (*Representación que
han elaborado los gremios ante las cámaras*) and although reference is made
to the guilds in the speech, García claimed to speak in the name of all the
city's artisans: "Don José María García, *maestro mayor* [Grand Master] of the
cigar-makers' guild, on behalf of myself and of the artisans of the capital city,
address the national congress with all due respect to say…"[73] The claim is
significant because it represented a move away from the corporate identity
of the guilds toward a new social and political identity embracing all of the
city's artisans.

The actions of artisans in Congress occurred within a changing political setting as liberal reformers began to expand institutional channels for
popular political participation. The guano age brought prosperity and

political reforms: the liberal project included the expansion of formal citizenship and thus an opening of the formal public sphere. In 1847, a law was passed allowing Indians and mestizos to vote.[74] During the elections of 1850, all three candidates—Vivanco, Echenique, and Elias—sought the support of artisans. This period offered artisans a greater foothold as citizens rather than strictly as guild members within patronage networks. The fact that they were sought out by politicians during times of elections contributed to reinforce the political role of artisans within the nation.

Within the more open liberal polity emerging during the 1850s, artisans remained a distinct constituency with a political identity based on their sectoral interests. In his address to the national congress, cigar maker García referred to artisans both as *"la clase industriosa"* (the industrious class) and "hijos del país." By voicing the demands of artisans, cigar maker García was bringing them into public affairs and casting them not as guild members but as a social sector with a set of common economic interests. While he praised independence as a "splendid conquest," García pointed to the detrimental impact of free trade on artisans: "The decree of unlimited free trade did not consider the fact that a large portion of the inhabitants of the republic who lived from a difficult industry and from the arts would be mortally wounded."[75] Not only did García define a common artisan identity within the nation beyond the individual guilds, but he even equated the plight of Peruvian artisans to that of artisans in other nations. Like Peruvian artisans, he noted, artisans in foreign countries had been destroyed by industrialization. As for solutions, García made a case for the specificities of the Peruvian scenario, claiming that it would do no good to apply theories from other nations: "It is a profound misconception that free trade constitutes the most powerful lever to achieve progress and happiness for any state without taking into account its exceptional circumstances, such as ours."[76]

While Congress responded favorably to the 1849 plea by artisans with protectionist measures—the Ley de Artesanos of December 21, 1849, instituted tariffs of 90 percent—the triumph proved short-lived.[77] During the next few years, the liberal bloc in Peruvian politics, backed by merchants both national and foreign, was able to set a new course of liberal economic policy. By 1851 the artisan position had been defeated and economic liberalism reigned supreme. Yet despite their defeat, artisans remained on the stage and would continue to figure as political actors over the course of the next decades.

The Protests of 1858

The next major appearance of artisans on the political scene took the form of a violent protest. In December 1858 a crowd of artisans in Lima's port Callao protested the arrival of a shipment of imported doors and windows from the United States. The imported goods were to be used in the construction of train stations for railways joining Lima to its port and to a nearby town. Informed of the shipment, carpenters and other artisans gathered at the shore and attempted to prevent the unloading. The prefect of the area intervened, and for the moment the goods remained offshore. During the following days the carpenters' guild presented a legal petition and a commission of artisans presented a complaint to the president, General Castilla, demanding protection for Peruvian artisans from competition from foreign goods. The president replied in broad terms, claiming that he was sympathetic to the cause of national artisans. In the following days, when artisans saw that the unloading of the imported goods continued, they eventually took events into their own hands and prevented further unloading by breaking the doors and windows and throwing them into the Pacific Ocean. The president himself led troops to the port to pacify the angry crowds. The protest was dispersed, but in the process a number of protesters were arrested, one person was killed, and five were injured. Following the repressive response, artisans continued to pursue their interests through legal channels. The carpenters' guild presented a legal petition to the prefect. A commission of artisans approached the president, and a request was made by the guilds to Congress. About 300 artisans entered the congressional building and sat through the sessions, pressuring for the passing of the laws they were demanding.[78]

The role of artisans as active political participants in crowds was not a new phenomenon.[79] When in 1834 the military followers of Gamarra blocked the election of the liberal Orbegoso and proclaimed their own candidate, Bermudez, as president, among the political actors of the period were the crowds of Lima. Basadre points out that there were artisans among them[80] and also makes a humorous reference to the proverbial political activism of artisans in Arequipa: "When the cathedral bell clanged, the artisans of Arequipa were noteworthy for abandoning their workshops and hurling themselves out into the streets, weapons in hand with a single question on their lips: whom do we fight for?"[81]

The greater artisan combativeness of the 1850s must also be seen as part of a broader trend set in motion by the 1848 European revolutions. In some cases, ideas may have traveled very directly with the many foreign artisans arriving in Peru during this period. Gootenberg points out that by 1848, 18 percent of Peru's tax-paying artisans were foreigners.[82] Furthermore, as Natalia Sobrevilla shows, the 1848 events received ample coverage in Lima's press and influenced political rhetoric and rituals in Peru—new forms of political mobilization in Lima, such as the banquet, appeared during this period.[83]

The events of December 1858 further emphasized the exhaustion of the guilds as a political weapon. Quiroz has argued that by the time of the violent protests in December 1858, artisans no longer counted on the guilds to organize this protest: "They had an organization that transcended the guilds and had defined plans of action. Beyond the influence of other factors—such as the participation of the plebe—it was essentially an artisan response, devised and directed by artisans."[84] This episode represented a final blow to the guilds and a realization of the need to move to a new type of organization. Gootenberg claims that by this point the "guilds felt intensely 'betrayed' by their traditional patrons and by the political system."[85] Not only did the state adopt free-trade commercial policies, but it also gradually ceased to purchase from national artisans. By 1867, for example, the purchase of military uniforms had expanded to include contracts with foreign firms such as Lawrence Philipps and Sons, based in London.[86]

The events of 1858 also signal an increasing appeal by artisans to broader public opinion via the press. Artisans continued to forge a new identity as actors within the emerging public sphere. A number of announcements signed by artisans appeared in the city newspapers. Even the petition submitted by the carpenters' guild strengthened its demands by presenting them in broader terms than those of the guild. Following the arrival of the ship with the load of imported carpentry goods, the carpenters' guild presented a legal petition to the prefect of the port of Callao asking that the shipment not be unloaded. The carpenters signing the petition were under the impression that the imported doors, windows, screens, and other carpentry goods were to be used to build houses. The petition indicated that the importation of these goods had caused alarm among artisans. While the petition was presented in the name of the carpenters' guild, it portrayed them as part of "the people" who upheld national institutions and "who deserve the consideration of the government thanks to the services they have provided with such abnegation to uphold the institutions of public order."[87] The petition included two sheets of signatures, probably including artisans in other trades.[88]

In subsequent weeks the campaign was pursued both in Congress and in the press. A series of announcements in *El Comercio* made a much broader appeal in the name not of carpenters alone but of the guilds and of artisans in general. The announcements that appeared in *El Comercio* during December reveal that artisans were skilled at presenting themselves to public opinion. In their public discourse they portrayed themselves as peaceful, patriotic, republican, and hardworking citizens. A newspaper announcement claiming to speak in the name of "the true artisans" attributed the violent protest to people outside the guilds and reaffirmed the desire of these artisans to pursue their demands peacefully. The announcement reaffirmed republican values: "Artisans who need peace and work, who aspire to guarantees and order, who have no ambitious pretensions and who respect constitutional authorities could only have done great damage to themselves by turning to disorder and tumult rather than to law and to Congress."[89] Artisans thus took care to differentiate themselves from the mob and to present themselves as patriotic citizens: "As honest artisans, we are enemies of disorder and we seek peace, in whose shadows the arts will prosper. As citizens we have constituted a compact phalanx to uphold institutions and we have proudly spilled our blood for them, opposing with our dead bodies a hurdle to despotism on the memorable day of April 22."[90]

The announcements also avoided the presentation of these demands as particular to artisans and equated the interest of artisans to those of both "the people" and "the working class." The cause of protectionism was said to affect not only artisans but "the people." In this article "the people" is equated to a patient suffering grave ills: "In the current circumstances, the patient is the people: the caretakers of the people will hasten to save it, because it is not plausible that they should see him die of misery."[91] Another announcement spoke in the name of the working class and called for unity with other workers, including those performing the most menial tasks, such as *cargadores* (carriers): "May we be driven by a single will and a spirit of progress under the auspices of the government, of good faith and of justice; keeping in harmony with the miserable water carriers, cargadores, farmers and with all industrial workers who groan and deplore their bitter misery and the poverty of their fellow citizens."[92] This theme would be further developed in coming decades, as discussed in chapter 5.

The government countered artisan demands with two sets of arguments: one based on economic theory, the other pragmatic. The first set of arguments emphasized the transition away from a society where corporations were entitled to special privileges. Artisans could not be entitled to special privileges. If artisans were to receive protection, then so must other groups, and the results would ultimately be detrimental, given the rise in prices. The second set of arguments was pragmatic: the total protection of artisan production would be detrimental as it would contribute to the proliferation of contraband.

The government was not completely blind to artisan demands and took the requests of artisans sufficiently seriously to order a special commission to investigate the problems affecting this sector. The resulting 1859 congressional report acknowledged the difficult situation of artisans faced with competition from abroad and referred to this as an "alarming economic phenomenon" that was besetting the republic for the first time:

> If one takes into account the fact that a growing number of artifacts similar to the ones made in our fatherland are imported, and that these [articles] are not only more perfect than our own but are also in greater demand as they can be offered to the consumer the moment he needs them and at a price almost twenty-five percent lower, and if in addition one takes into account the fact that the situation of our artisans makes it impossible for them to diminish their labor costs, one will find the origin of the alarming phenomenon that for the first time has appeared in the Republic and has complicated the evils of the present situation.[93]

While the report was addressed to the guilds, the kinds of solutions proposed mark a clear departure from earlier protectionist policies. The report indicated that the tariff had "done all that could be lawfully required" to protect the interests of artisans.[94]

The report promised that the state would help artisans in new ways by opening banks, providing technical training, and offering prizes as incentives for production. The age of liberalism had arrived, and the notion that tariffs could contribute to stimulate national production had been entirely abandoned at this point.

The Guild Under Fire

Despite their active participation in national politics, artisans remained in a situation of institutional uncertainty over the course of the first four decades of the national period. The main artisan institution, the guild, remained at odds with the liberal ideals upon which the nation was founded. While artisans derived benefits from the protectionist policies of caudillos, they continued to be associated with a corporate institution considered detrimental to the formation of a society of individual citizens. As liberalism gained a greater foothold in Peru toward the middle of the nineteenth century, the guilds became a direct object of attack by liberal pamphleteers. Attacks ended with their eventual abolishment by the state in 1862.

During the 1840s and 1850s, with the liberalization of tariffs, artisan guilds faced both the vicissitudes of increased foreign competition and the direct attack of liberal ideologues. Globally this was a period of enthusiasm for liberal free trade, referred to as the "Age of Capital" by Eric Hobsbawm.[95] The attacks against the guilds come from what has been termed Peru's second generation of liberals, a group considered more radical in its adherence to liberal ideals than the first generation of "founding fathers." During the period of caudillismo, a first generation of liberals had laid the blueprint for the republican form of government, defending the notion of popular sovereignty and ideas of individualism as the basis for society. In the political debates of the early period, liberals defended a strong legislative power against the arguments of conservatives (*autoritarios*) who advocated the need for a strong executive.

Liberals had remained inimical to the whole style of caudillo politics, in which the guilds participated during the early national period. In 1832, one of the most vocal liberal ideologues, a priest turned politician, Francisco de Paula González Vigil, denounced one of the early caudillos, President Gamarra, in Congress for unconstitutional acts. Vigil would write extensively over the next few decades defending the separation of church and state and advocating the need for voluntary associations as a way of building a liberal republic. Yet while the violence of caudillo politics limited the possibilities of building liberal institutions, the relative stability brought by Castilla during the 1840s created a more propitious environment for liberal institutional reforms.

In many respects, the position of mid-nineteenth-century liberals on the artisan guilds echoed the view of Spain's liberal eighteenth-century reformers.[96] Yet theirs was a radical liberalism. According to Frank Safford, the liberal politicians that emerged in the 1840s considered that the first generation of liberals "had failed in its mission to liberalize Spanish American society. Like the liberals of the 1820s, the reformers of 1845–70 affirmed essentially individualist conceptions of state, society and economy. . . . But they tended to be more absolute in their individualism, more fervent in their libertarian rhetoric. They called not merely for individual freedoms but for an absolute freedom of conscience, of the press, of education and of commerce."[97]

The most direct attack on the guilds came from a young lawyer, José Simeón Tejeda, from the Southern department of Arequipa. On August 6, 1852, at a lecture (later published) titled *Emancipación de la industria* (The Emancipation of Industry) and given upon his acceptance into the Academia Lauretana de Ciencias y Artes, Simeón Tejeda attacked a recent proposal in the city of Arequipa to regulate the guilds. The speech, according to Gootenberg, "was prominently displayed and quoted in Lima dailies."[98] Simeón Tejeda argued that industry must be free from any kind of government control and criticized the guilds for maintaining the "feudal" hierarchy of masters, "oficiales," and apprentices. He criticized the examination system, arguing that the public must be the arbiter of the quality of works produced by artisans. The proposals to restrict labor seemed unthinkable "in the nineteenth century, the enlightened century, the century of liberty."[99] Simeón Tejeda certainly exaggerated the powers of the guild, given the traditional weakness of this institution to enforce its regulatory powers.

Tejeda's speech centered on the issue of the social value of work. Tejeda, in fact, classified industry as a "social force." The restrictions on work placed by the guilds were thus detrimental to society as a whole. For example, he criticized the requirement that a man be married before he could become a master artisan as "economically absurd" since only by first being able to work would a man then be able to support a family. Likewise the requirement that apprentices be acquainted with Christian doctrine and be vaccinated he also deemed absurd since it was precisely by laboring in a workshop that an individual would be able to acquire such things. And he also argued that criminals should not be prevented from working, as the work would keep them from crime. He thus saw work as a panacea, imparting the virtues of Christianity and solving social problems such as crime.

Simeón Tejeda painted the picture of an ideal society in which workers could create wealth in the absence of government interference. The poorest class in society would be solely dedicated to labor with little concern for political matters:

Give the poorest class, that class whose only property is the use
of its hands, give it the security to acquire the sustenance and the
wealth that work and industry can bring without government

interference, and you shall see how little concern it shows for internal politics. It will only put its work aside when it sees its dignity trampled on, to reconquer it with the strength of its arm.[100]

This idyllic image of the laboring poor can also be seen as a wishful reaffirmation of peaceful values among a people who had occasionally engaged in political violence.

Six years after Tejeda's speech, a more comprehensive assessment of the entire situation of artisans from the liberal point of view was written by José Silva Santisteban. Following the protests of December 1858, Silva Santisteban wrote a pamphlet that condemned the uprising, attacked the guilds and the protectionist policies they espoused, presented his diagnosis of the problems affecting Lima's artisans, and finally proposed a series of solutions. The direct response of this work to the issues raised by artisans makes it a valuable source for understanding the place of artisans within the broader liberal nation-building project.

Silva Santisteban's pamphlet reflected the liberal fear of social disorder. The fear of popular insurrection is clear in his pamphlet: "Yet the danger has not completely disappeared, the fire controlled by the energetic action of the government still burns hidden among the ashes, and needs only agitation and fuel to turn into a devouring fire. The people have tried their strength: the slogan on the raised flag is a popular principle that fascinates and dazzles the crowd."[101] Silva Santisteban stood on the side of the government; the pamphlet was dedicated to President Ramón Castilla, who had squelched the uprising with force. In discussing the issue of free trade, Silva Santisteban even referred to the classic liberal dichotomy of "civilization vs. barbarism," presented in the classic work *Facundo* (1845), by the Argentine liberal Domingo Faustino Sarmiento. Silva Santisteban equated monopolists with barbarism and free trade with civilization.[102]

While approving the use of force, Silva Santisteban believed that the only way to avoid further violence was to reach the minds of the people. Therein lay the purpose of his pamphlet. His writings were based on the assumption that workers had certain rights, but that they were being misled by "enemies of the fatherland." His pamphlet intended to convince the masses to follow the path of reason: "Such is the objective of this work: to instruct and convince the masses gone astray. . . . Let us not be under any illusions, for as long as reason does not enter the conscience of the workers who consider their rights to have been harmed, tranquility will be deceptive, like the calm that precedes a storm."[103] Significantly, he made special reference to artisans as a group that would be responsive to reason: "If the good sense of artisans has been perverted and sidetracked by a wrong idea or by senseless offers, it will docilely be put back on track by the power of reason and truth, which is stronger than the instinct driven by brute force."[104]

In analyzing the revolt, Silva Santisteban carefully noted the differences between the Peruvian and the European situation and called the events in Lima "a sad parody of 1848." The 1848 Paris revolution had been staged in the name of the right to work. The major social problem in Europe stemmed from the impoverishment of workers resulting from industrialization. He even considered France and England "sick" nations, given their enormous impoverished proletariat. While defending a liberal solution, Silva Santisteban carefully presented his ideas in a way that would prevent him from being labeled as a socialist by conservative thinkers.[105] The solution to the problems of society lay in following the principles of political economy. The social problems of Europe stemmed from the lack of connection between political economy and morality. Yet he at all times reaffirmed the need to abide by the principles of political economy and in referring to the European revolutions wrote "and more than once they have endangered the sacred dogmas of property and evoked the terrifying specter of communism."[106] In presenting the general economic principles for his argument, Simeón Tejeda first criticized mercantilism and then praised the ideas of Adam Smith: "The industrial system, established by Adam Smith, reduces all wealth to work: even agriculture can only produce through human action; the wealth of the individual and of society are but accumulated work."[107]

Having offered a diagnosis of the European situation, Silva Santisteban then presented an economic analysis of the problems besetting Lima's artisans. He made two sets of claims: first, that Lima's artisans could not satisfy demand in the city; second, that wages were too high. He argued that Lima did not have a sufficient number of artisans to meet the city's demand and therefore the difference needed to be made up with imported products. Silva Santisteban claimed that the increase of demand in the city of Lima extended beyond the elite to all social classes, part of "a population of one hundred thousand inhabitants, where the number of buildings increases day by day, where the use of fine furniture and the frequent change of clothing has become widespread among all social classes."[108] Second, he argued that wages were too high and gave the example of the aguadores, who he claimed earned considerable wages by performing unskilled labor.

On the macroeconomic level, Silva Santisteban thus set forth the classic notion in economic liberalism that nations must take advantage of their comparative advantage. For the moment, Peru was best suited to remain an agricultural and mining rather than a manufacturing country. While unable to compete with machine-made European goods, Peru should dedicate its resources to agricultural production: "Rather than teach our workers a precarious trade, let us employ them to cultivate cotton, indigo, cochineal; let us spend our public funds on docks, ports and roads and let foreigners bring us the most fashionable shoes and clothes, for although it is good to be able to make them, it is always better to be able to pay for them."[109]

Silva Santisteban's assessment of the problems relating to imports revealed the tensions in the liberal view of artisans. On the one hand, artisans were presented as potential hardworking citizens; on the other, they remained part of the lazy masses that needed to be reformed. He offered six related causes for the malaise of Lima's artisans, all of them relating to deficiencies shown by Peruvian workers. Artisans were unfamiliar with notions of political economy and therefore didn't understand the need for importation of manufactures. They didn't receive an adequate artistic education and therefore the goods they produced "lack the finish and elegance of European products and reflect the lack of schooling and bear the stamp of roughness and empiricism."[110] They were "immoral," which amounted to their being unreliable—they could not be counted on to deliver their products in a timely fashion. Peruvian artisans lacked capital and hence wasted time by always having to fill individual orders rather than being able to sell from inventory. Artisans lacked good work habits, and finally, he argued, they lacked the ability to save money. He clearly revealed his liberal bias against national artisans by highlighting the superiority of foreigners, such as Italians, who established successful small businesses in Peru.[111] His explanations for the problems facing artisans reflected some of the main elements of the liberal nation-building project as well as some of the central prejudices of Latin American liberals.

Silva Santisteban insisted that the protests did not reflect deeper social problems but rather could be attributed to political causes. Unlike European artisans displaced by industry, Lima's artisans, he claimed, had plenty of work. Furthermore, if work should be lacking, they could always turn to farming—the ideal form of national development for Latin American liberals. Rather, the protests stemmed more specifically from the promises made to artisans at election clubs by politicians offering to ban the importation of manufactured products in exchange for the votes of artisans. This argument confirms the idea that artisans were an important political constituency and that politicians relied on them both to obtain access to office through elections and as a source of legitimacy.

In proposing remedies to the problems faced by many artisans, Silva Santisteban recognized the need to offer artisans some form of assistance rather than leaving them entirely at the mercy of the economic winds of the times. Although he considered any form of protectionism anathema, Silva Santisteban advocated the need to promote technical training through special schools and to provide capital for artisans through banks. The congressional report drawn up following the disturbances offered a similar set of solutions.

Conclusion

By the 1850s, artisan guilds were obviously powerless to protect their members against the effects of the large-scale process of greater commercial ties with foreign nations and the importation of foreign products. During the early decades following independence the guilds had succeeded in their requests for protectionist policies as part of a web of patronage of military caudillos. With the advent of free trade, the guilds found themselves having to defend their interests in Congress. The effort required moving beyond guild affiliation and naming a common representative to speak in the interests of all artisans to Congress. By eventually requesting that the state be involved directly in the education of artisans, guild members were tacitly acknowledging the institutional limitations of guilds and of the apprenticeship system to prepare artisans to face the new economic situation.

In this new economic environment of the guano period, artisans left behind the methods of the guilds and engaged in a series of new political tactics. From the earliest years of the national period artisans had learned to petition Congress as a block. Now artisans also became adept at appealing to public opinion on their own behalf and defending their interests in the press. Affecting public opinion became all the more urgent given the attacks against the guilds and the negative perception caused by the bakers' and water carrier guilds, which damaged the reputation of artisans. Finally, artisans also turned to violent protest as a means of political action. Through all these means, artisans left behind the corporate identities associated with colonial guilds and forged a new identity as artisans. This new identity combined universalistic notions of citizenship with the special claim to being artisans who deserved special treatment for their central role in the productive process.

Despite liberal attacks and the official abolition of this institution in 1862, the guild did not die out completely and lived on well into the nineteenth century. But membership declined substantially, and by the 1870s, guilds had ceased to figure in national politics and had once again come under the control of a strengthened municipal government. Among the guilds that remained active were the water carriers, the shrimp fishermen (although not considered artisans), and the chocolate makers.[112] Some new guilds even came into existence; for example, photographers formed a guild of their own.

Although the patronage networks that had originally linked artisans to caudillos declined with the advent of economic liberalism, the national government's reliance on the guild system continued for almost half a century. Even after their official abolition in 1862, the guilds continued to serve fiscal purposes. It appears that the 1862 abolition was not fully enforced, and in 1873 the Municipality of Lima was calling upon the guilds to appear and elect their representatives.[113] As late as 1887, the guild of shrimp fishermen (*gremio de camaroneros*) was being required to present its internal rules.[114] The state continued to rely on the guilds for fiscal purposes, and in 1879, as the country prepared for war with the invading Chilean army, the government turned to the remaining guilds, among other social institutions, for contributions to support the urban guard (*guardia urbana*).[115]

By the 1860s and 1870s, the demands made by guilds were restricted to internal problems and issues such as lower taxation.[116] They no longer operated as institutions channeling artisan political participation. During the second half of the century, artisans regrouped in an entirely new kind of organization to protect their interests: the mutual aid society. By forming mutual aid societies, artisans embraced liberal ideology, divorced themselves from the obsolete guilds, and sought new forms of integration into the liberal order.

CHAPTER THREE

The Making of Productive Citizens:

Artisan Schools and National

Expositions, 1860–1879

> *La culture populaire, par l'étendue et l'organisation de l'école*
> *primaire et par la création des écoles professionnelles (escuelas*
> *de artes y oficios) fut le centre de la grande transformation.*
> *On donnait une forte assise à l'égalité politique par*
> *l'expansion triomphale de la culture populaire. On peut*
> *même dire qu'un idéal de démocratie laïque et civile*
> *s'esquissait dans ces années trop courtes d'une période active.*

—Francisco García Calderón, *Le Pérou Contemporain*

Introduction

In 1864, Domingo Sarmiento, the prominent Argentine liberal intellectual and later president of Argentina, delivered one of the inaugural speeches at Lima's newly founded and state-funded School of Arts and Trades.[1] In his speech, Sarmiento criticized the traditional reliance on precious metals that had characterized the Hispanic world, which stood in stark contrast to the productive creation of wealth based on labor in Anglo-Saxon societies. He cited the legendary fame of Peru as the land of Inca riches and the reputation of Lima as a magnificent colonial city rivaling even its Spanish counterpart Seville. Lima continued to retain its bygone elegance and courtly manners. Yet the pre-Hispanic and colonial riches of gold and silver had not translated into present-day prosperity, and Peru was no better off than any neighboring countries.

What was missing in Latin America, Sarmiento argued that day, were schools for the training of productive citizens: "What was and is still lacking and what Spain lacked (hence the unproductive nature of the discovery of the new world) was the development, through education, of the abilities of the greatest number for the creation and increase of wealth."[2] Sarmiento contrasted the poverty of the Hispanic heritage with the richness of the Anglo-Saxon heritage and mentioned that recent settlements of the Anglo-Saxon world such as San Francisco and Melbourne had already established more schools than any of the Spanish American republics.

This chapter examines some of the institutions created by Peruvian liberals and by the liberal state to integrate artisans into the nation-building project. Like Sarmiento's, their vision of progress would lead to the formation of a modern nation in the model of Western Europe or the United States. In their efforts to create a nation of productive citizens, liberals considered artisans as a valuable sector of the population potentially receptive to the liberal creed. While for the most part, liberals viewed the popular sectors as idle and in need of reform, artisans, because of their independence and condition as laborers, seemed particularly redeemable to liberals. Within the general liberal project of establishing a system of secular education, artisans received particular consideration, with the creation of special schools for technical training. During the 1860s and 1870s a number of schools for artisans were established by the state, by the municipality, and by elite intellectuals. Although in some small measure these schools satisfied the demands made by artisans themselves for a technical education, they clearly reflected the priorities of liberals to instill artisans with the moral values deemed appropriate for the formation of productive citizens. The conception of citizenship thus had a clearly cultural dimension.[3]

Given the liberal view of export-led development, the efforts to promote artisans and encourage national industry cannot be seen as an attempt to create an industrial nation. Peruvian liberals had read their Adam Smith and were beginning to accept the role of Peru as an exporter of primary products within the international division of labor. The availability of cheaper imported manufactured products meant that Peru would necessarily have to accept its role as an agricultural and mining country. In his assessment of Peru's economic, social, and political situation following the 1858 riots, Silva Santisteban stated this in no uncertain terms: "Let us not fool ourselves: Peru is not a manufacturing country nor will it be for a long time.... Because the power of machinery is unknown, the skill and elements for work are lacking; because it cannot sustain competition with foreign manufactures, Peru is essentially an agricultural and mining country."[4] This is not to say that industrialist ideas had been discarded. As Paul Gootenberg has shown, a number of elite thinkers continued to promote ideas of industrialization.[5]

The restricted role of artisans in liberal economic thought appeared most visibly in the national expositions organized by the state in 1869 and 1872. The idea of such industrial and fine arts expositions can be traced back to eighteenth-century France and England and in particular to the famous 1851 Crystal Palace exposition in London. These fairs celebrated the products of a nation and emphasized the centrality of production, both agricultural and industrial, as the foundation of progress.[6] Both exhibitions, held in Peru at the tail end of the guano period, paid some tribute to national artisans by displaying their products and awarding them prizes. Nonetheless, artisans played a limited role within the overall structure of the exhibitions, which reflected the importance granted by elites to agriculture and mining over industry as driving forces of the national economy. Despite the existence of isolated industrial projects over the course of the century, industry took a back seat.

Why, given the liberal view of national development and the small size of the artisan population, did liberals take artisans into account at all? The answers must be sought primarily in the realm of politics. The political mobilization of artisans in defense of their interests dated to the early stages of the national period. The 1858 riot proved that urban artisans constituted a potentially volatile group and could pose a threat to the security of the capital city. Gootenberg claims that the artisan protests of 1858 played an instrumental role in accelerating the establishment of the School of Arts and Trades, a state school for artisans. On the one hand, the school satisfied artisan demands for the state to promote technical training. On the other, it constituted an ideal vehicle for social control.

The various schools for artisans established during this period reflect a broader effort at "moralization" to turn artisans into the ideal hardworking citizens of a liberal republic. Liberals did not advocate leaving artisans entirely to the whims of the free market. Rather, they responded to the need for technical training for artisans so that their products could compete with foreign ones. The establishment of such schools demonstrates that liberals recognized that some aspects of the guild—its educational functions—were useful and needed to be continued through the schools. These schools and other efforts

FIG. 6. *Lima's unpaved Main Square (Plaza de Armas)*,
    1860 (Estudio Courret).

to support artisans must be examined within the context of the broader liberal nation-building project of creating citizens with republican values.

Liberals established a strong connection between work and national
progress. Given their economic role as independent producers, artisans
stood closer to the liberal ideal of hardworking citizens than other sectors of
the urban poor. The various schools for artisans demonstrate that liberal
overtures were not empty gestures but were oriented to integrate artisans
and make them into citizens of the republic. Whatever the racist under-
tones of the liberal project, liberals considered artisans as workers who
could be educated and moralized to become reliable citizens. The efforts
should be understood in the context of the liberal reforming project that
saw education as a means of creating citizens and as one way of instilling
work habits in a population considered naturally idle.

The important role of artisans for liberals becomes evident when one
contrasts the view of artisans to the liberal view of Peru's Indian population.
Liberals held a dismal view of Peru's Indians, who constituted the majority of
the country's population. As Carlos Aguirre claims: "The creation of the

FIG. 7. *A sign of changing times, Lima's Main Square (Plaza de Armas), paved and adorned with statues, 1872 (Estudio Courret).*

image of Indians, blacks, and other nonwhite people as naturally resistant to hard work had a centuries-long history.... Rather than posing the problem in moral or religious terms (laziness and idleness as sin or proof of demoralization), it was now depicted as an impediment to progress and a proof of the lack of commitment to the 'true' needs of the Peruvian nation."[7]

Although this chapter will focus on the liberal point of view, it is important to keep in mind that education had different implications for liberal ideologues and politicians than it did for artisans—a subject to be developed in chapter four. From the point of view of liberals, education had a moral dimension. Schools would contribute to instill habits such as thrift and punctuality, considered the hallmark of civilized nations. As William French wrote about Mexico: "Morality served as a symbolic shorthand around which concepts of citizenship, work, and race were clustered, allowing members of *sociedad culta* to mark off the respectable from the dangerous lower classes while, at the same time, providing themselves with a means of class and self-identification."[8] For the artisan, education thus provided an opportunity to draw closer to the elite and differentiate himself from the mass of people, the plebe.

Education and the Making of National Citizens

With their attack on corporate privilege, liberal reformers ushered in a new conception of the polity in nineteenth-century Peru, one based on the participation of individual citizens. A cornerstone of the liberal conception of the nation was education, and part of the task undertaken by liberals was to foster notions of citizenship through education. Harkening back to the Enlightenment, the emphasis on education constituted a common feature of nineteenth-century European political thought. Referring to nineteenth-century England, Louis James wrote: "Jeremy Bentham and the Utilitarians... believed that the only block to progress was human ignorance, and that through education the ills of society could be done away with. This had widespread impact, in particular through its influence on Robert Owen (1771–1858), northern mill-owner and father of English socialism.... It is impossible, however, to identify the faith in progress through the spread of education with any particular philosophical group."9

Education constituted a prime instrument of social reform for Latin American liberal nation builders. Latin American liberals had to grapple with the problem of how to make principles of individualism and equality take hold in a profoundly hierarchical society where race reinforced social hierarchies. Having founded republics based on constitutional principles, liberals now faced the problem of turning the inhabitants of those republics into citizens in the liberal mold. The importance of education to Peruvian nation builders was reflected in successive constitutions that established literacy as the basis for citizenship.

Recent scholarship has called attention to the broad definitions of citizenship established at the outset of the national period in Spanish America. Ideologues wrote constitutions that included most of the male population as citizens. As Hilda Sábato wrote: "Throughout Iberoamerica nations began with relatively broad conception of citizenship, introduced following Independence, and that was closer to the citoyen of revolutionary France than to Locke's property-holding citizen."10 Later in the century, attempts would be made to restrict citizenship.

A tension existed between the liberal ideal of an educated citizenry and the reality of widespread illiteracy. As Safford wrote: "Political elites were worried that the ignorance of the mass of the people, as well as their lack of experience in self-government, might make impossible the foundation of republican governments."11 Some of the early Peruvian constitutions reflect a recognition of the gap between ideal and reality. The Peruvian constitution of 1823 established literacy as one of the requirements for citizenship but waived this particular requirement until 1840.[12] The writers of the constitution optimistically assumed that in the interim, schools would multiply and proceed to educate former imperial subjects to become national citizens.

The initial waiving of the educational requirement also reflects a realistic recognition on the part of the early state of its limited resources to provide schooling on a mass level. Although the constitution of 1839 guaranteed free primary-school education for all citizens, the state lacked the infrastructure to provide such education. During this period, the efforts at reform in education were channeled primarily into secondary and university education in the cities.[13]

The financial solvency that accompanied the advent of the guano boom allowed for greater state involvement in national education. The first effort to organize a nationwide educational system came during the guano period, when President Castilla issued the Reglamento General de Instrucción Pública (General Ruling on Public Education) on June 14, 1850.[14] The state thus took over a crucial function that had previously been the domain of the Church. A further step in the direction of secularization occurred during the 1870s under President Manuel Pardo. Pardo expanded state schools in rural communities and opened new faculties in administrative and political science at Lima's San Marcos University. Such efforts at secularization challenged the long-standing dominance of the Church in the field of education.

The general program for a national secular education included specific proposals for artisan schools. The ideas of establishing artisan schools date to the period of Bourbon reforms and to the outset of the republican period.[15] General San Martín had called for the creation of a national network of schools of arts and trades. One such school was to be founded in the capital of every department. The state's various rulings on education made special provisions for the training of artisans. The Reglamento of 1855 decreed that "the schools of arts and trades, aimed at perfecting artisan education, were intended both to offer a careful education and to offer theoretical and practical education in blacksmithing, carpentry, tailoring, shoemaking and other common arts."[16] Yet the project would not materialize until a decade later, when Castilla inaugurated the School of Arts and Trades in Lima in 1864. This school represented the most visible effort on the part of the national state to promote artisan education and production.

From Guilds to Artisan Schools

Echoing the 1855 legislation on the subject, artisans following the 1858 protests included the creation of schools of arts and trades among their demands. The need for such schools also appears in the writings of liberals and in the congressional report following the 1858 protests. An article in *El Comercio* signed by "Lima's artisans" made the following demands:

> The fortunes of Peru will benefit with the establishment of
> schools of arts and trades where its youth can receive instruction,
> acquire habits of morality, economy and work; with the creation
> of financing and savings banks; with the formulation of rules
> to specify the rights and duties of artisans; with repression by
> the authorities against the tendencies toward idleness among
> "oficiales" and apprentices and, in summary, with institutions to
> reconcile the interests of the community with those of artisans.[17]

While it is difficult to attribute the signature "Lima's artisans" to specific individuals, the request reflects the fact that artisans had begun to present their demands in the political language of liberalism. Gone is any reference to the corporate structure of the guilds. Although guilds had functioned imperfectly in colonial Spanish America, nominally they had remained the institutions in charge of administering exams and providing a modicum of regulation among apprentices. Artisans now recognized a clear role for the state in lieu of the guilds and acknowledged the need for the state to create institutions such as schools and banks that would promote artisan production. They also called for specific "institutions" to reconcile the interests of artisans with those of the community, an implicit recognition of the fact that artisans could no longer claim special privileges and needed to seek integration at the institutional level into a broader national community.

In another newspaper article, artisans of the port city of Callao, where the riots had occurred, announced the forming of a "Society of Arts and Trades" on December 18, 1858. In the announcement, artisans demanded the creation of schools that would teach them new skills needed to compete with foreign goods. They complained of the lack of protection for the arts and the absence of a school that would enable national artisans to compete "with the elegance of foreign artisans."[18] An article written about the inauguration of another school for artisans set up by the Municipality of Lima (the Municipal Industrial School) in 1873 made explicit the continuity between new artisan schools and the guilds. As the guilds had ceased to perform their assigned functions, the state would create a new institutional environment:

> Thus far, the education in the mechanical arts that has depended on private efforts has been irregular and vice-ridden, for it lacked method and master artisans lacked titles and were not subject to supervision. This situation could only have brought discredit and decadence to industry. The municipality's initiative represents a stimulus for the old master artisans and a hope for the entire country whose peace and progress can only be based on the universal love of work that prepares for the exercise of all republican virtues.[19]

Thus, schools were regarded not only as a means of replacing the old system of apprenticeships and providing young artisans with the necessary training, but also as important vehicles for the transmission of republican values.

The School of Arts and Trades (Escuela de Artes y Oficios)

The School of Arts and Trades was inaugurated in December 1864 with great fanfare. The ceremony at which Sarmiento gave the previously cited speech was presided over by President Castilla and was attended by members of the diplomatic corps, congressmen, senators, members of the judiciary, and members of the American Congress, which met in Lima that year. Although the school would serve to train national artisans, in this age of comparison, Peruvian artisans were measured by the yardstick of things foreign. Europe stood as the model to emulate, and the influence of things European permeated the school. The direction of the school, for example, was assigned to the Frenchman Julio Jarrier, who had previously been in charge of a similar establishment in Chile. The stated aim of such schools was to put artisans in a position to compete with foreign products. The assumption was that Peruvian artisans lacked the skills necessary for their products to compete with foreign ones and thus the artisans needed to be trained, preferably by foreign artisans. Even the uniforms for the school students were imported from France.[20]

The school's mission was to address the problem of foreign competition without reverting to older protectionist policies. In his inaugural speech, President Castilla discarded protectionism as a viable solution to the problem of foreign competition. Instead, the state would support Peruvian artisans by providing technical training. Castilla's diagnosis of the state of the Peruvian mechanical arts was grim, echoing the view of the 1859 congressional report. In his inaugural speech he proclaimed:

> The mechanical arts, which never emerged from their infancy amongst us, have had a languid life, and barely gave signs of life, and those who dedicated themselves to them were forced to abandon them due to the perfection of foreign industry that contrasts with the growing decadence of indigenous industry, making competition impossible.[21]

The diagnosis of the problems facing Peruvian artisans placed the blame for the current situation on the inability of artisans to compete with their foreign counterparts.

The inaugural speech made by the French director Jarrier conveyed a demeaning attitude toward national artisans. The School of Arts and Trades, Jarrier claimed, would provide a solution to the sorry state of Peruvian artisans unable to reach a sufficient level of perfection in their work. He lamented the fact that foreign artisans arriving in Peru were not providing the necessary training for Peruvians. Foreign artisans, with "skill and knowledge naturally superior to those of the of sons the country... do not, due to indifference or some worse feeling, contribute to initiate them in their perfected work procedures."[22]

In the speech that followed, the prominent Argentine liberal Domingo Sarmiento further elaborated on the importance of work as the basis for progress. In the case of Peru, Sarmiento claimed, the School of Arts and Trades would contribute to reverse Peru's historic reliance on easy metallic wealth. By learning "mathematics applied to the arts," the students at the school would help to transform the products of nature into lasting wealth. While Peru could now boast the existence of railroads, telegraphs, piers, museums, steamboats, and gas lighting, the true engine of progress lay in technical education. Sarmiento ended his speech comparing the task of the school to the independence of America from Spain: "The School of Arts and Trades is the corollary to the battle of Ayacucho to which our forefathers came from every part of America."[23]

The budget allotted to the school by the state reflected the serious nature of the commitment to artisan education. In May 1862, Jarrier had been given a working budget of approximately 500,000 pesos to set up the infrastructure for the school.[24] The school was housed in what had been the old Royal College, a large building built around spacious courtyards. With the government budget, Jarrier equipped the school with seven workshops, chemistry and physics laboratories, a museum, a refectory, and an infirmary and purchased the necessary objects for religious worship. Despite its secular leanings, the Peruvian state at this point remained firmly tied to Catholicism. The workshops included a fashion-design shop, a foundry, a blacksmith shop, a carpentry shop, a boilermaker shop, a coach builder's shop, and a tanning shop. Many of the workshops operated on steam-run machines imported from Europe.

Aiming to "modernize" and complement the traditional apprenticeship system, the School of Arts and Trades admitted and funded students between the ages of fifteen and eighteen, with preference given to "the sons of honest artisans."[25] In theory, the scholarships were to be distributed at a national level among students from the nation's various departments.[26] The education offered lasted four to five years and combined trade-related and general education. In addition to offering artisans technical training in its various workshops, the curriculum included courses in arithmetic, algebra, geometry and trigonometry, and chemistry as well as two years of French language and two years of English. Students boarded at the school and had very little contact with their parents. Vacation lasted twenty-five days per year, fifteen of which were to be spent on-site at the school.

Once students graduated from the school, they were expected to set up their own workshops as master artisans. The artisan workshop would thus be put at the service of the liberal project of spreading both technical knowledge and the appropriate norms of civilized behavior taught at the school. In theory, the state would either offer graduating students employment or provide the necessary economic assistance for them to set up their own workshop. The transmission of the skills and values learned at the Escuela de Artes y Oficios would hopefully occur on a national level, as graduating artisans were expected to return to their department of origin to set up workshops and pass on their skills to other artisans.

Although it is unlikely that any such scheme was ever implemented, particularly given the mounting financial difficulties faced by the Peruvian state, the commitment to give the school a national dimension was sufficient to generate public debate. When two foreigners were admitted into the school's first class, the newspaper *El Comercio* raised the issue of compliance with the rule of setting up a workshop in one's department of origin. The newspaper suggested that the problem be solved by assigning the foreign students a department in which to set up workshops.[27]

The aim of offering Peruvian artisans technical training went hand in hand with the liberal project of inculcating moral behavior among the masses. The state sought not only to train artisans but also to instill the virtues considered necessary for these artisans to become good citizens of the republic. The moral dimension of the enterprise was clearly spelled out in the inaugural speeches by director Julio Jarrier:

> Work is today the general law of the march of humanity, and not
> only from the point of view of material interests that constitute one
> of the primary needs of modern times; it is also the most powerful
> cause of our moral perfectibility. . . . Work, in whatever form it
> may take, always contributes to the development of intelligence,
> the most beautiful faculty in man; it elevates his ideas, it gives him
> a consciousness of his own dignity and worth as an individual, and
> thus also puts him in a better position to resist the evil passions
> and to triumph over them.[28]

These words expressed the liberal view on the moral significance of work for society. Work thus constituted a central feature of the liberal recipe for nation building.

The rules of the school reflect the way liberals sought to achieve their goals through a strict disciplinary regime for the students. The school regulations indicate that students would be under constant surveillance with the aim of teaching them behavior considered appropriate. Gootenberg has commented on the military discipline imposed on the students and characterized the school "as a controlling welfare response to the social problem."[29] Indeed, after the resignation of Jarrier, the school was put in the hands of a military director, General Manuel Mendiburu. Another military officer in the school, after 1872, was sergeant major José Mora, named as inspector.[30]

There is certainly a Foucaultian aspect to the rules of the school, which mandated an elaborate system of vigilance for regimenting every aspect of student life.[31] According to the rules, "The student's main duty is to observe the strictest subordination. . . . He must approach his teachers and masters with trust and as though he were a member of the family."[32] The relationship between student and teacher was thus both hierarchical and paternalistic. A school inspector would be specifically in charge of discipline. Simultaneously, the teachers and even the students themselves were expected to reinforce the disciplinary regime. For this purpose, the student body was divided into sections with students chosen as "corporals" (*cabos*) to help with supervision.[33] The inspector would receive a written report from the teachers indicating "the fault that a student may have committed that day in the workshop."[34] Students were to proceed from one activity to another in an orderly fashion. Even during rest and recess periods, students would be subjected to the disciplinary gaze of the sub-inspector. Punishment for improper behavior ranged from missing recess and performing extra tasks in the workshops to expulsion for more serious misbehavior.

The school would thus train its young students to conform to certain norms of virtuous behavior both in and outside the school. Such behavior included order, silence, and cleanliness. One of the rules stated: "Everybody must abide by the cleanliness rules with regard to themselves, their dress and their beds, and must develop habits of good domestic order in the dining room and during other activities."[35] In the afternoons, the school inspector would ensure that students in the courtyard cleaned themselves and retired in "good order." The inspector would also ensure that students kept silent and observed orderly behavior while in the classrooms and during meals. The inspector "will frequently be present during the meetings in classrooms and in the dining room where the sub-inspector will also be present so that order not be inverted in any way. And he will be sure to remove from the table and set aside anyone not observing the required moderation."[36] The rules demanded that students abide by certain criteria of courtesy. The regulations on cleanliness were so thorough that they even covered the activities of the chaplain, who was ordered to keep his chalices, ornaments, and altarpieces in "the best state of cleanliness."[37] As for students' appearance in public, on their days off, students had to maintain their cleanliness and "decency" and wear the school uniforms. Those who did not wear the uniform in public would be punished.

The Foucault-like aspect of the institution on paper may say more about liberal ideals than about actual practice. As in all realms of life, the divergence between theory and practice in Latin America is often great. It is unlikely that the constant surveillance called for in the rules actually worked as stringently as it was supposed to—when does it ever in any educational institution?[38] In some cases, the strict schedules were even officially changed to accommodate important religious festivities—for example, on March 2, 1867, the newspaper *El Nacional* announced the postponement of the school's exams due to the celebration of *carnaval*.[39]

The public aspect of the school certainly marked a definite transition from the corporate social identity of guilds to a public connection between artisans and the nation. In contrast to the guild examinations that strengthened the identity of artisans within a specific guild, the school linked the work of the artisan to the nation. Every year students passed public examinations, received prizes, and had their workmanship publicly displayed. The examination dates were announced in the city newspapers.[40] The school ceremonies were sometimes attended by the president. Some of the products manufactured at the schools were put on display at the National Exhibitions that began to take place in 1869, discussed later in this chapter.

The products displayed at the National Exhibition included devices such as a distillery and various cast-iron works.[41] Some of the machines built at the school were intended not only for exhibition purposes; some were actually sold for use outside the school. A water pump made at the school was used by the German Fire Brigade.[42] A soap-cutting machine was used at a local soap factory.[43] Other products made at the school included a machine to arch tires, hammers, compasses, iron grilles, pumps, buckets, kettles, and carpentry works such as a dining room table, a screen, a door, and wheels for carriages. In 1873, for the first time, students at the school built an eight- to 10-horsepower steam engine.[44]

While the institution remained restricted to a small percentage of the total artisan population, those artisans trained at the School of Arts and Trades had access to new opportunities and prestige. In 1870 the government named fourteen of the school's students as assistants to engineers.[45] Between 1868 and 1873, seventy-nine artisans graduated from the school and found employment in a diversity of trades ranging from blacksmiths to mechanics to fashion designers.[46] However, the more ambitious initial scheme of offering government assistance for graduates to establish workshops in their place of origin was never implemented.[47]

The dire financial situation of the Peruvian government during the 1870s placed severe limitations on the functioning and impact of the school. Over the course of the 1860s, the Peruvian government had become increasingly indebted, relying on future guano revenues. By the early 1870s the government was bankrupt, and when Manuel Pardo became president in 1872, he severely cut the government budget. In July of that same year, the director of the School of Arts and Trades, General Mendiburu, wrote to the government complaining that for three months he had not received the assigned funds to pay the school's employees.[48] By 1877 Mendiburu claimed to have drawn on his private funds to meet certain school costs.[49] At about this time he submitted a report recommending that the number of classes be limited and that the school be restricted once again only to boarders (it had been open to day students by the government under General Balta, who was president from 1868 to 1872).[50]

The school continued to operate until 1880, when the Chilean army invaded Lima during the War of the Pacific. As part of the war trophies, the Chilean invaders stole the machinery and carried it off to Chile.[51] Peru's defeat proved devastating and put an end to this particular attempt by the Peruvian state to offer artisan education. Many years after the war, in 1905, the school reopened.

The Municipal Industrial School (Escuela Industrial Municipal)

The School of Arts and Trades was not alone in its mission to educate artisans. The state involvement in the education of artisans was paralleled at the municipal level by the founding of the San Pedro Municipal Industrial School in 1873. In 1873, reforms aimed at decentralizing government administration were implemented. These reforms involved the creation of administrative bodies at the level of the department, the province, and the district. The reforms gave municipalities greater financial independence. Inspired by an 1871 French model of decentralization, these reforms were seen as a step toward greater democracy according to Basadre: "The authors and defenders of the new organization put in place spoke lucidly about what municipal freedom means for a democratic nation, in other words, the self-management of interests at the local level."[52] As a result of these reforms, over the course of the 1870s, the municipal government once again became a prominent institution in the life of the city. The municipal presence had a direct impact on artisans not only as a result of the newly established school but also because the patente tax (also imposed on artisan establishments) now fell under municipal jurisdiction. The decentralized municipal structure continued to operate until 1880.[53]

Like the School of Arts and Trades, the Municipal School offered artisans both technical training and education as citizens. In his speech at the inaugural ceremony in 1873, the mayor of Lima, Federico Marriott, pointed out that the school would offer both a primary and a technical education. Both types of education, he claimed, were important for the making of citizens. Without a primary education "one would be unable to give society useful members or the Republic dignified citizens."[54] Offering a primary education, he said, was the state's only obligation. Such an education was seen as having both a moral and a political dimension and included courses in grammar, calligraphy, arithmetic, geometry, drawing, and civics (*catecismo político*).[55]

In addition to receiving an education, children attending the school would be trained as artisans. In his speech, the mayor of Lima repeatedly stressed the importance of work and savings:

> Preparatory education is not enough to enter in a dignified and
> fruitful way into the life of society. The individual must find
> something further, in himself, to consolidate his independent
> life and be truly useful to his fellow citizens. Only love of work
> and the knowledge of an industry can guarantee welfare for
> the individual.[56]

In addition to being trained in the school workshops, students would be given an allowance. A part of the allowance was for their daily expenses and a part was to be put in a savings bank (*caja de ahorros*) to set up funds that would then be used to establish an independent workshop after graduation.

The inaugural ceremonies themselves exemplified what were considered the correct norms of polite society. One of the rooms of the school had been decorated with flags and shields, and a wooden stage had been put in place for the guests of honor: the president, accompanied by members of his cabinet and of the municipality. A special commission from the municipality ushered guests to their seats "with great civility," according to a newspaper account.[57] The ceremony began with a band playing the national anthem and students singing along.

The mayor's speech was followed by a speech by President Pardo in which he further elaborated on the distinction between a regular and a practical or technical education. Pardo presented work as a cornerstone of the educational task. In his speech, he claimed that in their efforts to offer a professional education, countries often forgot to train their manual workers. It was not enough to train a few skilled artisans; it was necessary to "train all men in work and for work."[58] The emphasis was thus not on the technical skills to be acquired by Peruvian workers but rather on the moral value of work. Although studying could develop qualities such as intelligence, imagination, and memory, work played a crucial role in shaping an individual's personality: "applied to the education of the child, work constitutes the most powerful means of cultivating character, that bedrock of the human personality which is subsequently merely modified by education."[59] Work contributed to develop qualities such as will, patience, perseverance, firmness, energy, and independence as well as modesty, resignation, industriousness, and thrift. These qualities, "combined with the cultivation of intelligence, yield as their fruit that divine faculty that allows man to concentrate in his own spirit the means of overcoming the obstacles put in place by society or nature, and that all together, form the essence of the human personality, and hold the secret of the true and permanent grandeur of nations."[60]

What was the role of the artisan within Pardo's general views of training working people? It seems contradictory that at the inauguration of a school for training artisans, Pardo should downplay the training of skilled artisans in favor of a broader moral training of workers. Yet his words are consistent with Pardo's overall views of national development. Among Pardo's main concerns was the issue of devising a plan for national development without relying on guano resources. In Pardo's conception of national development, skilled workers could be brought from Europe while Peruvians needed to be trained to work in mining and agriculture.[61] Neither aspect of this development project envisioned a role for the skilled urban artisan, whose products could be cheaply replaced by imports.

Like the School of Arts and Trades, the Municipal School relied heavily on foreign skills for the training of national artisans. The predominance of non-Spanish names among the masters in charge of the workshops is striking. The ironworks workshop was run by Leon Perdriel & Company, the printing press by Carlos Prince, the bookbinding workshop by Teodoro Fischer, the gilding workshop by M. Quesnell and Company, and the carpentry workshop by Alberto Hoechlin.

The school's first director was Julio Jarrier, who had previously presided over the School of Arts and Trades. Jarrier resigned the post of director at the Municipal School shortly after beginning the assignment, citing "family and health reasons." He was temporarily replaced by Petrus Blanc, who worked for the Medical School and had contributed to running the municipal school's chemistry lab.[62] Many of the materials for the school were imported from France, including tools for the workshops and some of the textbooks, including arithmetic and geometry.[63]

The school would admit students between the ages of fourteen and twenty, who were required to have mastered the basics of reading, writing, arithmetic, and religion to gain admission. Students would be accepted into one of the school's seven workshops: printing, ironwork, locksmith, carpentry, cabinetmaking, sculpture, and bookbinding workshops. The original plan for the school also included a music teacher, although it is not clear whether the school ever had one.[64]

As a day school, the Municipal School was less able to implement as stringent a program of student education as the School of Arts and Trades. The Municipal School's rules made brief reference to the need for students to follow basic norms of discipline and cleanliness. In contrast to the highly regimented School of Arts and Trades, the municipal artisan school seems to have focused more on the technical education of artisans than on attempting to encourage "civilized" norms of behavior. While the School of Arts and Trades stated the lofty goal of "giving the nation honest and educated artisans," the municipal school stated its goal more modestly as offering "the children of the capital an upper level primary education, supplementing their classic studies with the practice of a manual profession or trade."[65]

The following wages were paid at the school in 1876: the director had a salary of 120 soles a month; the professor-secretary, eighty soles; the acting priest, forty; the doorman, twenty-five, and the servant, twenty.[66] Student apprentices also received a small wage of twenty cents a day for first-year students, thirty cents a day for second-year students, and forty cents a day for third-year students.[67] The number of students is unclear from available documentation but probably did not exceed the number at the School of Arts and Trades.

Only a year after the school began to function, problems were already being reported resulting from the country's general impoverishment. The *Municipal Bulletin* for 1874 reports two kinds of difficulties. The first was the fact that apprentices were not staying for the entire three years but were leaving the workshops after only a year. The second had to do with the general economic situation and demand for the products made in the school's workshops. Like the School of Arts and Trades, the Municipal School relied to some degree on outside contracts. The *Bulletin* reports that the lack of demand for the products made at the school had led to the closing of four of the school's workshops. The *Bulletin* also complained about the quality of the education offered at the school. Although the documentation on the school is sketchy, there are already certain indications of financial problems early on, and it is fair to speculate that the school would have faced numerous problems related to the general economic downturn of the 1870s and the weakness of the municipal government.[68]

Liberal Elites and the Education of the Masses: The Sociedad Amantes del Saber

Parallels to the state and municipal projects for artisan education can be found in the efforts of a number of private associations. As early as 1856, the Sociedad Filotécnica showed concern for the education of artisans. The Sociedad, which opened on July 27, 1856, had as its objective "to spread among artisans and industrialists the fundamental knowledge of their profession. It has been formed through the spontaneous meeting of various philanthropic individuals interested in enlightenment and social progress."[69] In 1864, another society, named Los Hijos del Pueblo (The Sons of the People), sought to offer artisans a general education. This society included artisans among its members. A notice appearing in the newspaper *El Hijo del Pueblo*, published by the society, stated that the purpose of this association of "youth and honest artisans" was to work "for the education of the people and for its triple progress: intellectual, moral and material."[70] The society was founded on February 2, 1864, with a membership of 27, which had grown to 193 three months later. The society established an evening school and Sunday school for artisans as well as a library.[71] Yet classes and activities at the Sociedad Los Hijos del Pueblo were interrupted when the president, Colonel Mariano Bolognesi, was called away for military service at the outset of the conflict with Spain that led to the war with Spain.[72]

A more lasting effort took place in the 1870s, headed by a group of intellectuals who founded a society under the name Amantes del Saber (Lovers of Knowledge). Among the members was prominent intellectual Joaquín Capelo, who would later publish a four-volume sociological work on Lima (1895–1902). Another member was Manuel Osma, from an elite Lima family.

The members of the Sociedad Amantes del Saber had embarked on a highly humanistic and idealistic project. As part of their society, they founded the Artisans' School (Escuela de Artesanos). Without workshops, the school could offer only general education. The program at the school was divided into three sections. The first, practical education for workers, lasted twelve months (spread out over the course of two school years). The second, "education for the citizen," lasted four years. This type of education was referred to specifically as "political education." The last subdivision encompassed education in certain specialties that "albeit not indispensable, constitute a necessary adornment for all men, and will last indefinitely."[73] In addition to the education considered "practical," the school also offered classes in political economy, Spanish grammar, geography, experimental physics, English, and French.[74] The curriculum differed substantially from the more technically oriented education of the state and municipal schools of arts and trades.

Given the lack of technical training, why did the school use the name Artisans' School? The fact that it was oriented toward artisans demonstrates the degree to which the very name *artisan* had come to be associated with working people considered socially acceptable by liberals. More than a mere occupational category, the term *artisan* now had broader connotations. At this point in the midst of the liberal period, artisans had succeeded in stepping into the role of an emerging middle sector and of distinguishing themselves from the plebe. Thus the term itself indicated a degree of social mobility and a willingness to embrace many of the ideals set forth by liberal reformers.

Although the Artisans' School had its own set of teachers, members of the society were also obliged to offer thirty hours of services a year to the school. According to the statistics presented in the society's own periodical, the number of enrolled students climbed from 113 in 1874, to 177 and 172 respectively during the two semesters of 1875, and finally to 437 students in 1876.[75] In addition to the artisan school, the Sociedad ran an engineering school, the Escuela de Ciencias é Ingenieros, which had begun as an algebra class taught at the Sociedad by Joaquín Capelo and Francisco Choucherie.

The education offered to artisans at the Artisans' School had a strongly scientific component. Classes included practical arithmetic, practical trigonometry, practical mechanics, and drawing.[76] Classes were offered at night: arithmetic classes on Mondays, Wednesdays, and Fridays from 8 to 9 P.M.[77] There was even a proposal to open an astronomy class.[78] The Sociedad published a mathematics textbook covering the subjects of arithmetic, algebra, and geometry as well as textbooks on practical mechanics and English. Publication of the texts began in 1872. An edition of 1,000 arithmetic books sold out, leading to a second edition. The Sociedad's monthly periodical,

El Siglo, ran a column with mathematical problems and printed the solution to the problems in the following issue. The column demanded a knowledge of calculus from the reader: for example, the September 1, 1875, edition asked the reader to find the derivative of log sin arctan $g\,x$—lge/$2x$.[79] The periodical often published on mathematical subjects. One issue included a detailed proof of the theorem of Budan (written in Paris in 1811) and another, in a column titled "Famous Mathematicians," the biography of the French mathematician Adrien Marie Legendre (1752–1833), known for his theory of numbers.[80]

The teaching of such specialized subjects formed part of a broader project of educating artisans to become citizens. The Sociedad Amantes del Saber's monthly newspaper made explicit this need: "Convinced that it is a need of every people, and more so of peoples like our own governed by democratic institutions, that each person know his duties and rights as a citizen, persuaded of that need, we intend to teach our disciples the most indispensable notions of Natural and Constitutional Law."[81] Despite the stated purpose of instructing artisans on basic legal notions, the list of courses does not include courses in law. Nothing resembling a civics course appeared in the curriculum.

In the face of possible attacks from conservatives, the Sociedad Amantes del Saber considered it necessary to defend its project of educating workers. Such a defense did not respond to any specific attacks but rather anticipated likely conservative objections. The two main objections addressed were that educated workers would be susceptible to "delusive theories" (probably referring to socialist ideas) and that studying would take valuable time away from work. Members of the Church continued to offer opposition to secular education, and some even sermonized against a popular educational periodical of the period that covered a variety of subjects, including moral tales and home management.[82] As Frederick Pike writes: "In addition to not wishing to see their monopoly over instruction jeopardized, many Peruvian ecclesiastics questioned the usefulness of mass education, regarding it in the liberal nineteenth century as more likely to corrupt than to uplift the soul of the child."[83]

Despite ideological differences with conservatives, the liberals behind *El Siglo* still bore the mark of the strongly Catholic culture of Peruvian society. While the article on the mathematician Legendre indicated that he followed in the path of the "immortal Newton," a brief section titled "History for the People" gave a series of definitions of history including the following: "An era is a group of years. The main ones are that of Creation and that of Jesus Christ."[84]

Nonetheless, the liberal defense of artisan education hinged mainly on a classic Enlightenment view of history as a march toward democracy and the triumph of reason. During past epochs "the people" were kept in ignorance, according to *El Siglo:* "Fortunately, the times are over in which science was the sole patrimony of the priests of Egypt and Greece, and of the Brahmins of India."[85] The ignorance of "the people" was a central cause for the perpetuation of despotism and demagoguery; education is thus presented as a bulwark against these evils. It would be very difficult for a Louis XIV or Napoleon I to take power in an "enlightened nation" such as the United States. As a locus for the formation of enlightened citizens, the school would help to protect Peru from the evils of despotism, demagoguery, and violence.

The other set of objections—that studying would keep artisans away from their work—was also dismissed by supporters pointing to the link between education and work and to the moralizing value of education. The school would keep artisans away from the everyday evils of drinking and other vices associated with taverns. This defense of artisan education ended with an idealized portrait of the artisan attending school: "What a beautiful spectacle is offered by those artisans who, after finishing a day's work, rather than go rest eagerly come to hear our lessons, and pay us with their gratitude for the education that we offer in fulfillment of our duty!"[86] In addition, the Sociedad claimed that it was teaching artisans subjects useful for their work, such as drawing, arithmetic, algebra, and geometry.

A lecture given by one of the students at the school reveals its theoretical and somewhat naive spirit. Artisan Miguel Melgar, who had attended the Artisans' School, gave a physics lecture defending a thesis on the theory of heat waves. The lecture received much attention in the Sociedad's periodical, and Melgar was highly praised for all aspects of his performance. Even his language was noted for being "simple and clear . . . , without unnecessary ornaments or figures."[87] The report in the society's periodical indicates that the lecture was attended primarily by artisans and makes the claim that artisans would be the ones to find such a lecture most useful.

The scene presents a Pygmalion-like quality. One can almost imagine the room, the artisan Miguel Melgar stiff and awkward in his role as lecturer on theoretical physics. His first words were almost apologetic, thankful to those who had given him this opportunity to be the first artisan to talk about such subjects. It is worth quoting them at length since they are one of the few records of an artisan's words. These words reveal much about the persistent hierarchies in the relationship between artisans and elite and the need to adopt the liberal discursive framework:

> To fulfill the obligation imposed by my professor, I come to present to you this small work, the fruit of my scarce knowledge. I would not have dared to do so were I not encouraged by the hope that you will listen to me with indulgence, both because of the complexity of the issue at hand and because this is the first time that an artisan will have his voice heard in an act of this nature. Allow me, gentlemen, before beginning to address the issue that I will talk about, to express on my own behalf and on behalf of my fellow students the enormous gratitude we feel as a result of the benefits we receive from the society Amantes del Saber. This institution, having understood the state of ignorance of the working class, as well as the vices that beset it because of the lack of an appropriate institution, decided to found the Escuela de Artesanos.[88]

The characterization of a working class menaced by vices because of the "lack of an appropriate institution" constituted a rather direct challenge to the moral authority of the Catholic Church. Melgar continued for a few more sentences with his words of gratitude and ended with a baroque flourish of emotion that somehow clashed with the ideal of simplicity of language sought by liberal reformers: "Having satisfied the need that I arduously felt to express my gratitude, I will now address the topic."[89]

Melgar continued with a lecture that proved that the theory of waves was superior to the theory of emissions in explaining the nature of heat. According to the first theory, bodies lose heat because they get colder; according to the second, bodies lose heat because they begin to move more slowly. Melgar offered the example of making fire from rubbing sticks together as proof for the theory and cited various experiments: those of Davy, Baumont, and Mayer and Tindall. The theory of emissions, he claimed, "must be discarded and removed from our sight, for to some degree it presents insurmountable obstacles to the development of science."[90] He then explained a series of phenomena having to do with heat: dilation, fusion, ebullition, solidification, radiation. His speech was interspersed with remarks in praise of science. The event concluded with a speech in which the society's president underlined the unique character of that day's talk and presented it as an illustration of the fact that the working class took an interest in learning.

As part of its educational program, the Sociedad Amantes del Saber had plans—which remained unfulfilled—to encourage the virtue of thrift by promoting special savings banks, cajas de ahorro, for artisans. The idea was not a new one in Peruvian society. Such institutions had originally been linked to the world of theater and been intended as a means of supporting artists unable to perform. The most prominent caja de ahorros was founded by the Beneficencia de Lima on December 17, 1868.[91] This savings bank for the city's popular sectors accepted primarily small deposits and paid an interest rate of 6 percent. The savings were to be invested by the institution to purchase various types of government bonds.[92] The first account was opened by José Pardo y Barreda, the son of Manuel Pardo, at that time director of the Beneficencia.[93] By participating in that institution, Pardo was setting an example for "the people" in the classic liberal manner.

Liberals attributed a moral value to such savings institutions. The very discipline of saving would keep artisans from wasting their money on vices. The Sociedad's newspaper offered a vivid description of the dangers facing artisans on this front: "On a Sunday or a holiday, the artisan who has no work that day reaches into his pocket and finds the week's savings, and does not hesitate to lose himself in the orgy where the fruit of his labors will be consumed."[94] The savings banks would act in conjunction with the school to channel artisans' resources in a productive direction. Yet as stated earlier, the Sociedad never founded any such institution.

All three schools for artisans discussed thus far—the Artisans' School, the School of Arts and Trades, and the Municipal School—each in its own way embarked on the task of training artisans both as workers and as citizens of the republic. The school programs reflect the multifaceted nature of the liberal project that sought to train skilled laborers while inculcating a series of moral values in them. The methods for transmitting these values, particularly in the case of the state-run school, involved attempting to impose a highly disciplinary regime. Those few artisans who were successful within the liberal schooling system had the opportunity to receive some national recognition through the participation of artisan schools in the first national expositions to be held in Lima.

Incentives for National Artisans:
The Expositions of 1869 and 1872

Toward the end of the period of guano-led prosperity, an entirely new kind of festival took place in the city of Lima: the Industrial Exposition of 1869, held at the School of Arts and Trades. This exhibition, as well as a second one held in 1872, reinforced the importance of labor as a central value in the liberal nation. At a time of growing criticism of the country's reliance on guano, the exposition can be seen as a sign of the need for Peru to base its economic development on the unleashing of the nation's productive forces. Although liberal thinkers increasingly envisioned national prosperity as based on the export of raw materials, the notion of developing national industry remained an important theme among some elite thinkers. In a speech during the closing ceremony of the 1869 exposition, Luís Benjamín Cisneros, a promoter of protectionist policies, claimed that with the exposition, justice had finally been done to national industry. In an 1866 study of economic issues, Cisneros had warned against the dangers of the state's reliance on guano and proposed greater state participation in national development, including the fostering of protection for national industry.[95]

The 1869 exhibition was held at the School of Arts and Trades and included displays of a wide array of national products. The workshop of carpenter Vicente Zavalaga presented furniture, both carved and gilded, for a salon. Other displays included furniture from the warehouse of Kunh, Karauslach, and Company, an importing firm. Various smaller objects, such as a silver coffeepot, a silver card holder, a silver miter, and jewelry, were displayed. The theme of the Incas also appeared in the exhibit: on display were eight pieces of Inca gold and silver figurines of an Indian, two llamas, two sheep, and two pheasants.[96] Thus to a small degree the Inca past was included as part of the national heritage.

A number of items on display had been produced at national establishments ranging from the School of Arts and Trades to Lima's new penitentiary.[97] Both the students of the School of Arts and Trades and the penitentiary inmates presented furniture exhibitions. The state arms foundry displayed boxes for ammunition and homespun cloth. The School of Arts and Trades received a gold medal as a prize for the work produced. The Medical School (Escuela de Medicina) presented various objects, including a set of artificial dentures. The agricultural section included products such as molasses, olive oil, and flour as well as various Peruvian wines, some of which had been sent to expositions in Paris and in Santiago, Chile.

The exposition celebrated utility and productivity as criteria for the products displayed. The zoological collection, for example, was deemed to be quite poor, as it lacked any animals specially bred to be of use to man. The assessment of the collection in one of the city's main newspapers exhorted Peruvian hacienda owners to make their livestock more productive: "It would be desirable for our hacienda owners[98] to begin experimenting in order to produce, for example, fatter and more muscular cows for slaughter, horses better suited for racing, stronger donkeys for work . . . etc. . . . experiments that would demonstrate the advance of the country and be profitable and useful for the public in general."[99]

The exhibition of live animals underscores the gap between the realities of a poor nation and the hopes of industrial and agricultural progress. One of the courtyards of the School of Arts and Trades held a seemingly haphazard collection of animals: a bull and cow "of not very good race," two English pigs, a small bear, an anteater, two "very talkative" parrots, three small deer, some goldfish, a beautiful greyhound, four species of duck, and a rooster with four legs. The strange creature had allegedly been born from an egg with two yolks that had undergone an unusual development process. The group of animals belongs more readily in a García Márquez story on the shortcomings of progress than in the liberal libretto for national prosperity.

Despite its emphasis on agricultural themes, the exposition placed artisans and national industry in a central position. The event itself was housed at the School of Arts and Trades and was officially called the Industrial Exposition. A number of independent artisans were awarded prizes for their work: shoemaker Fermín Quintana, hatter Miguel Rios, and silversmith Lorenzo Zavala all received silver medals. Zavala had made a teakettle, as well as a silver shovel intended for the upcoming January 1, 1870, inauguration of work on a section of the railroad to the central Andes.[100] A handful of incipient industries had appeared in Peru during the previous decades, and the exposition recognized these efforts by Peruvian industrialists. Francisco Garmendia, owner of the Cusco woolen textile factory, established in 1859, and Carlos López Aldana, who had just that year begun a cotton textile mill near Lima, both received medals of honor.

Despite the prominence of national products, the exposition reflected the growing attraction of foreign products in Lima. A detailed newspaper description of the exposition praised the work done by the director of the botanical gardens, Carlos Klugg, in adapting foreign species to Peruvian soil. These included twelve types of eucalyptus and seventy-eight types of conifers.

The article dwelt on the "elegant eucalyptus, for upon seeing them, the hope has arisen amongst us of having them someday adorn our public avenues."[101] Eucalyptus were considered superior to other trees because of their height and because their wood would be useful for shipbuilding. By contrast, the collection of Peruvian medicinal plants received scarce attention.

The presence of a commission sent by the Sociedad de Artesanos to thank the municipality attests to the favorable opinion of the event in the highest artisan circles.[102] The speech by one of the members of the Sociedad dwelt on the usual liberal theme of the need to stimulate work as a way of encouraging morality and civic virtues.[103] A number of institutions that educated and employed national artisans were awarded prizes. The School of Arts and Trades received a medal of honor "for the industrial advancement of its students." The Bellavista Naval Foundry received a silver medal for a "maritime machine" and a bronze cannon, as did the Arms Foundry (Maestranza de Artilleria) for firearms and a gun carriage for a cannon. Two School of Arts and Trades students, Jacinto Marticorena and Juan Olaechea, received copper medals for a threading machine and anvil respectively. The penitentiary received a prize for a dresser-desk and a sewing table. A number of foreign artisans also received prizes.

The appearance of women both in the official discourse and among those receiving prizes illustrates attitudes toward women and work during the period. In his concluding speech, Pardo, then mayor of Lima, made a passing reference to the "interesting issue of work among women" when discussing the potential for the development of a silk industry. Pardo portrayed women as "weak" workers who could conduct the relatively easy task of taking care of silkworms. A number of prizes were awarded to women, primarily for sewing, embroidering, and making artificial flowers. Josefa Rodriguez received a medal for a chair cover, as did Isolina Rossell for an embroidered bedcovering and Elvira Derteano for a silk cushion and a wool rug.[104]

This official view of women contrasts with the actual role of women as laborers in the city. Women sometimes worked alongside their husbands in workshops. Sometimes widows continued to operate a workshop after their husband's death. For example, in 1878, Melchora Flores was continuing to make shoes after her husband's death, although she had scaled down the work in her small workshop.[105] In addition, a number of women worked as seamstresses throughout the city.

The aim of encouraging national industry went hand in hand with the classic liberal concern with moralizing the masses. The speech by Manuel

Pardo at the closing ceremonies for the event made reference to both issues. On the one hand, he highlighted the efforts made to develop national industries, both manufacturing and agricultural, that would serve to make Peru a prosperous nation. On the other, he emphasized the need to educate Peru's working classes and encourage them to develop good habits, such as saving. A poem written to honor the plumbers Kemish and Melson reveals the close links between work and national prosperity:

The works exhibited today
By Lima's most famous plumbers,
Honor our exposition
And they achieve special esteem. . . .

Eternal renown for the happy worker
Who fulfills his mission upon earth.
Expending on true work
all the energies of his heart.
Work will be the great poison
That will eliminate the frightening chaos
That has enslaved Peru's people and made them
Subject of the ambitions of the fiercest.

Kemish and Melson, among the first
Who love and venerate work,
Sincere friends of Peru
Wish the country a happy future;
Pleasant days of the fatherland.[106]

The products on display included pumps and bathroom fixtures such as lavatories and bidets, probably not to be found in artisan homes.

The National Exposition of 1872 replicated the events of 1869 but on a much grander scale. By 1872, an entire pavilion had been built in Italian Renaissance style to house the new exposition. Named the Palace of the Exposition (Palacio de la Exposición), the building lay outside the boundaries of the old colonial city.[107] The national exposition had no precedent in colonial festivities. Basadre has described this event as indicative of "the enthusiasm for visible prosperity and the spirit of imitation of major world events."[108] The event thus offers a valuable window into ideas of nationhood and the role of artisans in the modern nation.

FIG. 8. *Present-day view of the Palacio de la Exposición, which housed the 1872 National Exposition, where many artisans exhibited their crafts (author's photo).*

Inaugurated on July 1, 1872, the Exposition of 1872 had two stated objectives: first, to bring together Peru's natural and industrial products, and second, to present foreign machinery, plants, and animals applicable to Peruvian agricultural or manufacturing industry.[109] The products to be placed on display would include the country's animals, vegetables, minerals, and works of art. The foreign "models" at the exposition referred primarily to new trees and plants as well as domestic animals "belonging to perfected breeds."[110] The exposition remained open for three months.

In the minds of writers and politicians of the period, the exposition helped to place Peru among the civilized nations of the world. An article written by Carolina Freyre de Jaimes, a writer from the Southern department of Tacna and wife of Bolivian journalist Julio Jaimes, traced the history of such expositions back to those organized by France and subsequently by other European nations.[111] While she recognized the limitations faced by American nations with respect to their Old World counterparts, Freyre de Jaimes nonetheless saw the exposition as a sign of progress and claimed that "today Peru stands up with the scepter of progress in hand and with the symbols of peace and universal confraternity under its flag."[112] At the closing ceremony, the new president, Manuel Pardo, repeated the usual praise for work as the basis for national prosperity: "The work of each man is the basis for the greatness of a people, and not so much a source of material wealth as of a condition for its virtues."[113] His speech touched on a classic Enlightenment theme when he considered these "festivals of work" as part of the moral and material progress of humanity, regardless of national boundaries and languages.

The exposition's organizers had seen to it that the new setting for this "festival of work" had all the trappings of a civilized nation. An orchard on the outskirts of Lima with an area of 192,000 square meters was converted into the grounds for the buildings of the "Palacio," complete with sprawling gardens. In addition to the main two-story Renaissance-style building, there was a concert hall, a greenhouse for tropical plants, and a Turkish-style gazebo. A fountain was crowned with a large statue of Hercules fighting the Hydra. An Arch of Triumph was adorned with the national shield and with symbols representing the arts. Crowning the arch was a statue of liberty. Inside the main building were paintings, including the reproduction of a French landscape. Peruvian themes were not entirely absent from the exhibit: various portraits of prominent Peruvians included two paintings by renowned Peruvian painters of the period: Francisco Laso's *Santa Rosa de Lima* and Luís Montero's *Funerales de Atahualpa*. Fixtures such as doors and iron columns and ornaments such as statues and vases as well as furniture had been imported from France.[114] Italian architect Antonio Leonardi was responsible for the design. Even the master builder had come from abroad: José Bisini traveled from Chile to supervise the construction.

The main building housed numerous products divided into industrial and agricultural sections. The agricultural products included potatoes, maize, and fruits. There was also a display of minerals exhibited by Antonio Raimondi. The industrial section presented wines, shoes, sewing machines, perfumes from various parts of the world, musical instruments, clothing, silverware and jewelry, a display of coins and bills, weapons, surgical instruments, porcelain, and many other products. A display of machinery included a cotton gin made in the United States, various machines to crush metal made in England, and a portable steam engine and a device for distilling liquids, both made by the students of Lima's School of Arts and Trades. The displays included products from Chile, Ecuador, Bolivia, El Salvador, England, Italy, France, Belgium, Germany, Holland, Switzerland, Scotland, the United States (including California), Japan, and Persia.[115]

One of the most remarkable objects at the exposition was a monumental clock built by a Peruvian inventor, Pedro Ruiz Gallo. A military officer, Ruiz Gallo had worked on the clock for nearly six years and, thanks to the interest shown by a congressman, received some financial support from the Peruvian state. The Sociedad de Artesanos had also been instrumental in seeking support for this public work. The clock marked the hours, days, seasons, years, and centuries as well as the paths of the sun and moon. At five o'clock in the morning, one of the faces of the clock displayed the raising of the national flag while two miniature soldiers saluted, all to the tune of the national anthem. The scene was repeated with the lowering of the flag at dusk. Every hour the clock displayed one of twelve scenes from Peruvian history, beginning with the mythical foundation of the Inca Empire and ending with the battles for independence and finally a depiction of the current president, President Balta, pointing to a map of Peru and decreeing the implementation of various public works.[116]

At the closing ceremonies of the exposition, Ruiz received a diploma for the prize of honor from the president followed by a gold medal from the Sociedad de Artesanos. In his speech, he identified with the workers who were giving him the prize: "A worker and son of the people, like the poor workers who honor me with a medal, I feel happy today hearing their voice of encouragement." He concluded by referring to artisans as "humble instruments of progress."[117]

A man of immense talent, Ruiz had built a work of technology and art and sought public support for his endeavor. His monumental public work stood as a tribute to the transition toward a secular society, one in which time, that most valued of commodities in the modern world, no longer remained attached to religious spaces. The clock with its flags and anthems and pictures represented secular patriotic values and celebrated Peruvian history. Yet it seemed that the nation could scarcely afford the luxury of a public clock constructed by one of its own artisans. Ruiz had expended enormous private efforts for the building of a public work and received little institutional support. Some support came from the Sociedad de Artesanos[118] and some from the state, although never enough to cover the costs of his work. The following year, *El Comercio* complained that the clock had failed to receive adequate maintenance. "Poor Ruiz!" read the article. "When we think that with his genius, in another part of the world, with greater protection and studies, he could occupy a place among the great mechanics of the world. In fact, his name barely reaches the boundaries of the Peruvian territory, and he is forced to despair and sometimes even suffer true deprivations. We feel a great sadness with respect to all things related to the progress of our arts.... As that work has cost its author so many pains and now demonstrates to foreigners the advancement of the mechanical arts in Peru, no effort must be omitted to ensure its conservation."[119]

The exposition reflected a strong optimism about the possibility that Peru would someday reach similar standards of civilization as Europe. An article in the newspaper *La Patria* reflected this optimism. The article spoke approvingly of the good "taste" of the works of the School of Arts and Trades and predicted a bright future for national industry:

> The works presented by the School of Arts and Trades constitute models of good taste and great mechanical combinations and appear full of hope in a better future that will bring an era of wealth and well-being to our national industry. In the present century, mechanical force, locomotion and steam decide the fortunes of a people and the destinies of humanity.[120]

Other articles that appeared at the time of the exposition reflected a similar optimism.

This great optimism seems sadly ironic and distorted at a time when the state had actually become dependent on huge loans based on future guano exports and faced imminent bankruptcy. Contrary to liberal rhetoric, Peru relied not on the industriousness of its citizens but on the sale of guano to Europe. During the course of the three months during which the exposition lasted, a change in the presidency brought Manuel Pardo to power, the country's first civilian president. Under Pardo's predecessor, José Balta, the government had incurred disproportionate indebtedness to finance the building of railroads. Pardo brought a more sober tone to the presidency and recognized the dangerous state of the country's finances. Yet for all his good intentions to diversify the economy, Pardo presided over a worsening economic situation. By the end of the decade, war with the southern neighbor, Chile, brought Peru to bankruptcy. Following the Chilean invasion of Lima, Ruiz's clock would be taken by the Chileans as a war trophy, another great humiliation.

Conclusion

The war with Chile thus brought to an end a chapter in Peruvian history during which liberals sought to implement their vision of a nation of prosperous citizens. Peru's defeat and the Chilean occupation of Lima from 1881 to 1883 would stand as a stark reminder of Peru's failed efforts to become a unified and prosperous nation—in the years after the war, a new chapter began during which efforts to revive Peru's economy involved increasing reliance on foreign capital investment. The model of Peru as an exporting nation emerged much more clearly after the war with the development of agricultural and mining interests.

In many ways, the efforts of liberals before the war point to a vision of national prosperity that involved preparing the national population to face the economic and political challenges of modern nationhood. Within this vision, for liberals, education constituted a prime instrument for reform. The schools for artisans and the national expositions during the 1860s and 1870s sought to put into practice the liberal vision of a working population. The schools were intended to provide artisans with technical training but also to turn them into citizens in the liberal mold. The stated purpose of the School of Arts and Trades was to "give the nation honest and educated artisans."[121]

Certainly the concern of elites revealed a less than enthusiastic view of the popular sectors of their society. The strongly disciplinary regime of the School of Arts and Trades with attention to the issues of cleanliness, noise, and order attests to this view of the need to reform every aspect of working people's behavior. Still, in relationship to conservatives uneasy with notions of popular sovereignty, liberals took significant steps to begin to open up the political arena to participation, albeit limited, by the popular sectors.

Artisans responded actively to take advantage of liberal overtures to the popular sectors. The liberal emphasis on work as a cornerstone of national prosperity put artisans in a favorable position to seek legitimacy within the nation. Although the discourse of work and the establishment of institutions intended to train workers and instill work discipline had one set of connotations for the elite, for artisans the emphasis on work provided a basis for legitimating their social position. The centrality of work in elite discourse allowed artisans to present themselves as working people, distinguished from what was viewed as the lazy plebe. Liberal ideology and institutions gave artisans the opportunity to dignify their work and to leave behind colonial racial categories by presenting themselves as model and useful citizens. The next chapter explores the ways artisans, through their mutual aid societies, increasingly claimed to be legitimate liberal citizens while continuing to pursue their own agendas as artisans.

CHAPTER FOUR

Mutual Aid Societies and Artisan Respectability, 1860–1879

On the working men, at least in the more advanced countries of Europe, it may be pronounced certain that the patriarchal or paternal system of government is one to which they will not again be subject. That question was decided when they were taught to read, and allowed access to newspapers and political tracts . . . when railways enabled them to shift from place to place, and change their patrons and employers as easily as their coats, when they were encouraged to seek a share in government, by means of the electoral franchise.

—John Stewart Mill, *Principles of Political Economy*

Simultaneously with the introduction of elite programs of social reform, the middle sectors of Latin American societies determined to distinguish themselves from the masses, especially by identifying behavior characteristic of civilized people.

—William Beezley and Colin MacLachlan,
Latin America: The Peoples and Their History

OVER THE COURSE OF THE 1860S AND 1870S, a reader of Lima's newspapers might come across numerous public announcements like the following:

Sociedad de Artesanos de Auxilios Mutuos, National Library:
By order of the member and President [of the society], a General
Meeting is called for Sunday the 2nd, at noon, to proceed with the
election of new posts, in accordance with article 90 of our rules.
The punctual assistance of members is called for.[1]

Following the liberal reforms of the 1850s, artisans established a visible
public presence through such mutual aid societies, which were favorably
regarded by liberals. For example, in 1862 playwright Trinidad Manuel Pérez
dedicated his play *La industria y el poder* (*Industry and Power*) to the
Sociedad de Artesanos (Artisan Society) and commended artisans for
"forming an association to encourage national industry, and to help one
another to guarantee work and defend themselves against the idleness that
breeds misery."[2] While liberals looked favorably upon them, artisan mutual
aid societies represented more than a gesture of conformity to liberal ideals.
In forming these new associations, artisans distanced themselves from the
politics of the guilds and guaranteed a political presence for themselves
within the polity of the 1860s and 1870s.

This chapter discusses the appearance and significance of artisan mutual
aid societies during the 1860s and 1870s in the context of the social and political transformations of the guano period and of the broader liberal nation-
building project. I argue that during this period, mutual aid societies gave
artisans both social respectability and an independent political voice. By
heeding the liberal call for voluntary associations, artisans directly contributed to building a civil society or, to use Habermas's term, a public sphere
independent of the state in nineteenth-century Peru. Although mutual aid
societies downplayed their political role—in fact, their rules outright forbade
the discussion of politics—they nonetheless contributed to reaffirm the role
of artisans as active citizens within the emerging liberal polity. Yet artisans
sought to define this public sphere on their own terms: they did not view
themselves as the abstract individual citizens envisioned by liberals, but
rather as a distinct social sector with a set of common interests.

In a society where colonial racial hierarchies survived and continued to
influence social status, mutual aid societies offered artisans a means of leaving behind racial identities. By insisting on their identity as "honest artisans"—a term used in the rules of mutual aid societies—the members of
these societies clearly distinguished themselves from the many day laborers,
domestic servants, or unemployed individuals who made up Lima's plebe

and would still have been identified primarily in racial terms as "indios" or "negros." Given the racial makeup of the city's artisans, it became all the more important to deemphasize race. The 1866 census for the city of Lima, which surprisingly continued to employ racial categories, demonstrates that the artisan population was made up primarily of individuals considered to be mestizo, zambo, negro, and indio.

As members of voluntary associations, artisans could claim a place for themselves as "civilized" members of society, or "gente decente." While they did not specifically use the term *middle class,* artisans can be considered as part of an emerging middle sector. In his study of German liberalism during the nineteenth century, historian James Sheehan offers a definition of the middle strata (*Mittelstand*) that is applicable to Lima's artisans: "The liberal concept of the *Mittelstand* was both a social and a moral category. It depended less on objective criteria than on the existence of shared moral virtues. These virtues meant that the *Mittelstand* coincided with what liberals often called 'the real *Volk,*' those enlightened and progressive men whose political and social virtues would eventually triumph, producing that liberal world to which the movement was committed."[3] While artisans could obviously make no claim to belong to the elite, they could claim to share the social and moral vision of liberal elites.

Artisans heeded the liberal call to form voluntary associations, but their interests in forming such associations differed from those of doctrinaire liberals. Artisans drew on certain aspects of liberalism while rejecting others. In particular, the liberal emphasis on the individual as the basis of citizenship found little echo among artisans, who continued to identify as a sector. While liberals envisioned voluntary associations as a vehicle for educating the "masses" and creating new habits of sociability among individual citizens, artisans saw such societies as independent instruments to further their economic, social, and political well-being as a distinct sector within Peruvian society. Even after protectionist policies had been defeated, artisans continued to pursue their interests as a social sector and to call for the government to take measures to protect the trades. Through their mutual aid societies, artisans conformed to the expectations of liberal ideologues but in a very pragmatic manner that enabled them to further their own social and political position. I argue that artisans saw themselves as artisans first and citizens second.

Not all artisans belonged to these societies, and it is important to emphasize the heterogeneity within this sector. While mutual aid societies tended to be officially conciliatory and noncombative, many artisans continued to participate in more radical forms of politics. Artisans played an important role in the violent uprising of 1872, which led to the assassination of the Gutierrez brothers, who had perpetrated a military coup against democratically elected Manuel Pardo. It is noteworthy that carpenters, with their long tradition of political activism, stood out among those killed in the violence.[4] Furthermore, more recent trades began to emerge and present a less than conciliatory stance: the typesetters stand out for their role in putting forth ideas of class that clashed with the classless language of mutual aid societies, a subject to be explored in the next chapter. To some degree, this fluid identity of artisans between respectable middle sector and plebe gave them a degree of power—the threat of potential violence meant that liberal elites needed to take artisans into account.

The Limits of Political Organization in Mid-Nineteenth-Century Peru

Politically, mutual aid societies allowed artisans to turn over a new leaf during the 1860s and 1870s, a period characterized by historian Paul Gootenberg as a "renascence of artisan politics."[5] It was probably no coincidence that the first of such artisan associations followed closely on the heels of the 1858 protest against free trade. The protest marked the exhaustion of the old trade politics—artisans had little chance of reversing the wave of economic liberalism that swept most of Latin America. It also demonstrated the limits of political violence as the state responded with repression—President Castilla had himself led the troops that quelled the protests. In the aftermath of this repressive response, artisans sought to pursue their political goals through means acceptable to the liberal establishment by forming new associations. Mutual aid societies helped to reclaim artisan legitimacy by distinguishing the honest and hardworking artisan from the potentially dangerous plebe, which had frequently participated in acts of violence.

Artisans had to proceed with caution in the potentially volatile political environment of mid-nineteenth-century Peru. During the heyday of classical liberalism and at a time of frequent political conspiracies, Peruvian nineteenth-century governments did not welcome political interest groups of any kind. The risks involved in forming associations among workers had become clear when a dockworker in the port of Callao attempted to form an association, the Sociedad Democrática Filantrópica del Callao (Democratic Philanthropic Society of Callao). Salazar y Zapata had attempted to found the society since the late 1840s and encountered opposition from the conservative regime of President José Rufino Echenique (1851–54), who suspected that the society was a front for his political enemies. President Echenique even ordered that Salazar Zapata be deported, although the order was subsequently reduced to house arrest.[6] It was only after Salazar y Zapata fought on the side of President Castilla with the liberals in 1855 that President Castilla allowed him to form the society in the port of Callao in 1858.

In the eyes of the government, the potential political dangers of such societies was further underlined by the presence of radicals in Lima society. The liberal reforms of 1855 were accompanied by a small but visible radical movement that included newspapers and an association, the Sociedad Republicana (Republican Society). A central figure in this movement was Chilean radical Francisco Bilbao, who in 1855 published a pamphlet titled *Gobierno de la libertad,* calling for an 1848-style revolution.[7] Bilbao was no newcomer to radical politics. In 1851 he had been one of the leaders of the Sociedad de la Igualdad, a political organization that mobilized artisans in Santiago, Chile. The organization participated in violent protests and was banned by the Chilean government.[8] Wary of Bilbao's role as political leader, the Peruvian government made him promise not to get involved in politics.

The government's concerns over Bilbao reflect the more general concern over popular political participation in the context of the 1848 revolutions. As Natalia Sobrevilla has shown, these revolutions had an impact among elites and artisans in Lima.[9] Events in the broader Atlantic world contributed to the cautionary stance within the Peruvian political establishment.

Given the charged political climate of the 1850s, it is not surprising that artisan mutual aid societies presented themselves as apolitical organizations. The statutes of these societies invariably forbade the discussion of political matters. For example, the rules of one such society, the Sociedad Fraternal de Artesanos (Fraternal Society of Artisans), stated: "It is forbidden to address political matters in the meeting hall and in any other place where the Society may convene."[10] The consistent disclaimer against political activity in artisan mutual aid society rules was most likely intended to reassure politicians and to protect artisan leaders from the kind of repression faced by Salazar y Zapata.[11]

Yet despite their injunction against political activity, mutual aid societies helped to establish artisan legitimacy within a changing political environment. The liberal reforms of the 1850s had both a democratic and a repressive component: the political arena was opened to a greater number of voters; at the same time the protests of 1858 had illustrated the violent side of political crowds and elicited a repressive government response. Within this political setting artisans walked a fine line. While the protests of 1858 suggested that artisan demands could not be ignored, political violence had nonetheless failed to achieve artisan aims. Following the protests, artisans had attempted to emphasize their role as honest citizens and to distance themselves from the violence. Mutual aid societies contributed to further separate artisans from the volatile plebe feared by Lima's elites and to distinguish artisans as respectable citizens. The achievement of social respectability on the part of artisans who belonged to these societies has been pointed out by Thomas Kruggeler in his study of Cusco artisans during the same period.[12]

Constructing a Liberal Polity

While they had attacked the guilds, liberals nonetheless recognized the importance of the artisan political base. In seeking artisan support, liberals also sought to reform old political habits and thus encouraged artisans to adopt new forms of association. The liberal call for the formation of voluntary associations formed part of a broader set of both political and cultural reforms during the 1850s. The liberal generation behind these reforms has been characterized by Pike as "highly romantic, wanting freedom of competition and unfettered political and economic individualism."[13] In keeping with these ideals, voluntary associations would help to create the ideal citizens envisioned by liberals.

One of the first steps in the process of reform was the 1850 electoral law, which extended suffrage to all taxpayers. Further reforms followed after General Castilla led a liberal-backed revolt against conservative president Echenique in 1854. Liberal reform momentarily reached a crux with the National Assembly of 1855, many of whose delegates advocated radical liberalism. Direct elections were held for the first time in Peru to elect the delegates to the National Assembly of 1855. The brief interlude of direct elections contrasted with the established system of electoral colleges and indirect elections that kept decisions in the hands of propertied notables and thus held in check the possibility of offering excessive political power to voters. Among the reforms stemming from the National Assembly was a final attack on corporations with the elimination of military and ecclesiastical fueros (legal privileges). Although the 1860 constitution reinstated the system of indirect vote, it maintained the earlier broad criteria for suffrage since the voting requirements hinged on literacy.[14] Given the high literacy rates among them, artisans qualified as voters.[15]

In opening up the political system, liberals sought an urban power base to counterbalance the power of rural landowners, who could control the vote of peasants. During the presidency of General Ramón Castilla (1845–51 and 1855–62), according to Peloso, liberals sought "to win broad-based popular support for the liberal economic program and at the same time to channel social change by forging a silent pact with key elements of the populace."[16] This outset of political opening coincided with the guano boom, during which significant numbers among the popular sectors were drawn into the economy. The attempt to draw support from popular sectors follows a pattern set during the early years of the republic. As Charles Walker has noted, despite liberals' relative lack of enthusiasm toward the popular sectors, the attempt to draw support among the poorest sectors of the urban population differentiated liberals from conservatives.[17]

The liberal efforts to broaden the electoral base coincided with the economic expansion brought about by the guano boom. Large numbers of artisans, shopkeepers, and other members of the popular sectors were being drawn into the expanding economy during this period. Although he acknowledges that bribery certainly contributed to increasing the number of votes cast, Peloso hypothesizes that a growing civic consciousness also played a role and that the popular sectors "willingly took part in a process that provided them with an opportunity for legal political expression."[18] According to Peloso, "Despite limited and sometimes misleading guidance, voters learned political lessons that far surpassed the intentions of liberal reformers."[19]

While inviting segments of the popular sectors into politics, liberals also feared the power of the enfranchised people and discouraged any form of class- or group-based political activity. Thus, while liberal reforms brought a greater number of voters into politics, liberals never attempted to establish an interest-group politics that drew on the support of a given class or sector. Liberals still sought votes on an individual basis. Their reforms affected the popular sectors, leading to greater voter registration. Yet as Peloso points out, liberals were averse to interest-group politics: "The liberal electoral system did not encourage the expression of sectoral or class interests. Voters had little opportunity to express their political interests in the pre–National Assembly period, and at the apex of liberal reforms (1855–57) liberal leaders failed to mobilize their followers in a systematic effort to implant a liberal state in Peru."[20] In keeping with their ideas, liberals saw individuals as the basic civic unit.

Liberal fears of the potential for political violence from below were borne out over the course of the 1850s as elections became real loci for political competition. Basadre considers the 1850–51 elections that brought conservative General José Rufino Echenique to power the first real elections to be held in Peru.[21] All the candidates in this election understood the importance of artisans and made efforts to seek their support.[22] The greater importance of elections as arenas for disputing political power brought increasing levels of violence and fraud. The stakes became higher with the increased state revenue from the guano trade: "Between 1845 and 1872, especially once the Castilla-era reforms got under way, disputed elections became a sign of social change and conflict in Peru as the electorate grew and became more contentious."[23]

Liberals criticized the electoral practices characterized by fraudulent tactics. The liberal lawyer and extraordinarily prolific writer and journalist Manuel Atanasio Fuentes described the 1855 elections as follows: "Who didn't realize that the voting booths were turned into marketplaces? Who didn't know that the candidates sent their agents to the electoral stand in the capital and that they stood on either side of the voting tables and bought the votes of the freed slaves and of the abject men who arrived at the ballot box looking lost?"[24] A common method of winning elections involved taking over the voting tables in order to modify the votes in favor of a given candidate. The custom of fraudulence in these elections was such that in his 1855 *Diccionario para el pueblo* (*Dictionary for the People*), liberal Juan Espinosa began his definition of the term *elections* as follows: "All elections are held under the influence of the dominant power in a society, or of a political party supported by force; all elections intended to support an individual rather than a set of well-defined and known political principles will be considered legally void as well as unjust and oppressive."[25] Espinosa wrote the *Diccionario para el pueblo* with the intention of educating the "people" in republican values.

At the heart of political patronage networks was the political club, an institution that emerged only at the times of elections and was used by candidates to mobilize voters. The mobilization tactics included offering gifts in exchange for the vote. It was not unusual for politicians to provide their followers with weapons and to attack the voting booths in order to affect the winning candidate. Hilda Sábato offers the following general definition of clubs: "The clubs were not . . . closed circles, as the accusations of rival groups might suggest, nor were they democratic spheres for popular expression, an image that the groups themselves liked to portray. These clubs constituted political networks that linked various leadership groups and their supporters."[26] According to Carmen McEvoy, political clubs became vehicles for co-optation and targeted a wide social cross section, including members of the military, artisans, printers, blacks, and rural inhabitants.[27] Both presidents General Ramón Castilla and General Rufino Echenique made use of political patronage networks and brought their followers to elections through such clubs.

Liberals had political clubs of their own. As early as the 1840s, liberals made much more direct overtures to bring the popular sectors into politics. The Club Progresista (Progressive Club), founded in 1849 to support the candidacy of civilian Domingo Elías, stood for a number of liberal causes, including direct elections, shortening of the presidential term, reduction in the size of the army, and establishment of a national guard. The club sought artisan support by advocating the need for artisan schools.[28] Yet according to Safford, the political platform of Elías also revealed some of the contradictions of liberalism in calling for European immigration: "The Peruvian society also called for the encouragement of immigration, something which could hardly have appealed to its working-class constituency."[29]

Liberals criticized the patronage politics of caudillismo and contrasted them with the behavior to be expected from the citizens of a civilized nation. Manuel Atanasio Fuentes played an important role as a critic of President Castilla and started a political newspaper that was later closed down by Castilla. In practice, liberals also attempted to distance themselves from traditional political practices. When the liberal-leaning Civilistas came to power in 1872 with Manuel Pardo, Peru's first civilian president, their political campaign attempted to redefine political culture along liberal lines.

As part of the effort at political socialization, the Civilistas' electoral society, the Sociedad Independencia Electoral, attempted to differentiate itself from the maligned political clubs. Safford wrote, "As a result of the aforementioned process, the political clubs were reorganized and acquired an air of respectability, to the degree that the new sought-after social groups responded and began to actively participate in them."[30] As McEvoy phrases it, the Civilistas were "in search of citizens." The most striking sign of this attempt to restructure political customs was a march through the streets of Lima.[31] Thousands of Civilista supporters marched in silence: "The evident intention was to make a public display of the control of a unified and well-disciplined political body."[32] This march contrasted with the traditional violence associated with political campaigns. McEvoy suggests that such an attempt to establish a distance from traditional political practices may have been welcomed by artisans and others tired of the usual manipulative tactics.[33]

Although Pardo and the Civilistas sought to distance themselves from the old form of politics, new systems of patronage developed that revealed links between artisan leaders of the mutual aid societies and the Partido Civil, the civilian political party. Manuel Pardo saw the need to establish a broad social base for his government.[34] Almost a third of the 600 supporters present at the founding of the Sociedad Independencia Electoral that launched the Pardo candidacy in 1871 were artisans and workers.[35] The campaign that preceded the election of Manuel Pardo reflected these goals of institutional change. Pardo and the Civilistas came to power at a point when the model of development based on guano had reached a crisis. The Civilistas offered alternatives to the guano model. According to Kristal, "The civilistas called for a restructuring of Peru's institutions."[36] In their campaign they relied on the symbolism of artisans as hardworking citizens.[37]

At the heart of such efforts at political socialization lay the notion of a polity based on individual citizens whose reasonable choices would add up to the common good. To convert the potentially unruly political crowds into disciplined liberal citizens, liberals encouraged the formation of voluntary associations. The most direct call for the formation of such associations was penned by one of nineteenth-century Peru's most ardent defenders of liberal values, Francisco de Paula González Vigil.

A priest and a doctrinaire liberal whose political career stretched back to the early years of the republic, Vigil battled consistently in the name of liberal ideals. He did battle both to uphold constitutional principles in the face of caudillo political power and to establish a secular society based on a clear separation of church and state. His battle for constitutional values reached a crux when, as a congressman in 1832, he accused President Agustín Gamarra of not abiding by the constitution and ended his speech in Congress with the words: "It is my duty to accuse, and I accuse." Vigil became disillusioned with caudillo politics and dedicated his energies to religious issues. Defending the separation of church and state, Vigil published a lengthy work, *Defensa de los gobiernos contra las pretenciones de la curia romana* (*A Defense of Governments*

Against the Pretensions of the Roman Curia) (1848, 1849), that led both to denunciations from Peruvian conservatives and subsequently to his excommunication by Pope Pius XI in 1851.[38]

Vigil's ideas were disseminated in the press. His 1858 pamphlet titled *Importancia y utilidad de las asociaciones* (*The Importance of Utility of Associations*) was published at least twice in the press. The first time, it appeared in the liberal newspaper *El Constitucional*, which ran from April to August of 1858 and opposed Castilla.[39] It was subsequently reprinted in the newspaper *El Hijo del Pueblo* (1864), published by the liberal Sociedad Los Hijos del Pueblo, which included artisans among its members. Vigil also played a direct role in advising mutual aid societies on the principles of association.[40]

The pamphlet *Importancia y utilidad de las asociaciones* reveals the blend of liberalism and Christianity in Vigil's thinking. As Gonzalo Portocarrero points out: "He considered solidarity a fundamental value expressed through emotional ties to the family, the nation and all of humanity. His liberalism is ethical and romantic reflecting Vigil's belief in progress, reason and science, but also in religion, providence and charity."[41] Carlos Forment uses the term "civic Catholicism."[42] Vigil no longer espoused the traditional Catholic view of a society based on religious foundations; rather, he saw association between men as a function of utilitarian principles. At the outset of his pamphlet he pointed to association as the characteristic that distinguished men from animals and claimed: "Only man is able to join with other men, because he is convinced of the utility that will result to all from such a union."[43] Yet while he espoused utilitarian principles, Vigil warned that individualism brought the danger of egoism: "When an individual acquires more and thinks more of himself, he runs the risk of focusing only on himself, considering only his own interests, and will be so committed to them that if he does not forget the public interests, he postpones them and his main pursuit becomes his egoism."[44]

For all his adherence to liberal ideas, Vigil's thought remained grounded in a corporatist tradition.[45] He pointed to the limitations of the individual, unable to act alone and therefore needing to cooperate with other human beings: "Private societies demonstrate, by their very name, that people convinced that their isolated faculties would not be enough to carry out their stated purpose in the midst of civil society have agreed to join forces to achieve this aim."[46] He departed from a secular view of associations by attributing a moral dimension to associations and claiming that only those with good, as opposed to evil, objectives were to be tolerated.

Vigil advocated that associations ought to act publicly. He cautioned against secret associations although he did not dismiss them altogether, arguing that at certain times in their history, Christians had been obliged to form such secret associations for fear of persecution. Vigil emphasized the importance of strengthening such associations in order to achieve social goals rather than counting on the government to resolve all problems. Here his thought reflected the classical liberal rejection of excessive reliance on government: "It is a disgrace for societies that governments should have to do everything and that everything be expected and feared of them."[47]

While Vigil approved of the political nature of associations, his view of politics remained clearly within the liberal mold: politics was to be based on the action of individual citizens rather than social sectors. He argued that "it is an absurdity to wish that citizens refrain from politics in a democratic Government."[48] His primary concern in advocating a political dimension for associations was the defense of republicanism against absolutism. Republican governments ought not to fear associations; only absolutist governments would oppose the formation of political associations. In this sense his opinions coincide with those of Simeón Tejeda, who claimed that the people would not normally participate in politics unless their dignity was threatened.[49] Vigil's remained an idealized view of politics in which the individual citizens, strengthened by their associations, would act in defense of the republican system.

Voluntary Associations as the "Civilized" Form of Sociability

Voluntary associations of the most diverse kind began to appear in Lima during the 1850s, offering a new model of the kind of organization deemed culturally acceptable for the citizens of a "civilized" nation. The first mutual aid societies had been formed to help theater actors who were out of work. It is noteworthy that actors, who had traditionally been considered a disreputable profession, should have attempted to gain security and a measure of respectability through such associations. In 1854, a group of Lima doctors formed a professional society, the Sociedad de Medicina (Medical Society). Musicians followed suit with the Sociedad Filarmónica Santa Cecilia (Saint Cecilia Philharmonic Society), first founded in 1856 and then reestablished in 1860 as the Sociedad Filármonica (Philharmonic Society). The members of Lima's various foreign communities also established mutual aid societies of their own, such as the Sociedad de Beneficencia Italiana (Italian Beneficent

Society) and the Société Française de Secours Mutuels (French Mutual Aid Society). Given the importance of European immigrants for the liberal nation-building project, the popularity of such organizations among the members of Lima's communities of British, French, and Italians certainly contributed to their prestige.

These associations rejected any formal adherence to a hierarchical social order and were premised on contractual relations among equal individuals. In their formal organization, mutual aid societies thus reflected a new democratic form of sociability that had become more prominent over the course of the national period.[50] Historian Carlos Illades in his study of artisans in Mexico City offers the following general definition of the mutual aid society:

> A voluntary association of free and equal individuals with a
> democratic structure that enables members to vote and to be
> elected. It is formally independent of the government and of
> religious and civil corporations, pertains to the private sector,
> does not use coercion as a means of control, does not demand
> the total allegiance of its members . . . in the sense that it is limited to
> private objectives, previously defined by contract, and it is secular.[51]

Mutual aid societies can be considered as a subset of a wave of associations formed in Lima during this period with multiple aims ranging from the associations formed by liberals for educational purposes (Hijos del Pueblo, Amantes del Saber) to social clubs such as the Callao Club, founded by the British in 1867.[52]

The notion that voluntary associations constituted the most appropriate form of organization for the citizens of a nation seeking to conform to European notions of progress became widespread. It is significant that even the Catholic Church began to fight its political battles on terms set by liberals and adhered to the new organizational paradigm. Given the trend of greater secularization, the Church was forced to influence policy by attempting to mobilize popular sectors. In 1867, a group of "notables" formed the Sociedad Católico-Peruana (Peruvian Catholic Society) to defend religion in the face of liberal attacks.[53]

When in 1855 Lima's printing workers formed one of the city's first mutual aid societies, the Sociedad Tipográfica de Auxilios Mutuos (Typographical Mutual Aid Society), the newspaper *El Heraldo* commended them and stated the hope that the spirit of association would take root in Peru: "Hopefully their example will not be wasted and the spirit of association will now rise from its tomb!"[54] In 1859 the popular newspaper *La Zamacueca Política* lamented the scarcity of these associations and echoed the liberal view of voluntary associations as a sign of progress and civilization: "The system of associations is quite widespread in Europe and has brought enormous advantages. There are societies of writers, of artists, of workers; political societies . . . while amongst us [the spirit of association] hasn't yet awoken. For this reason, the isolated efforts have remained unfruitful of those amongst us who have sought to achieve a greater objective through literary, political or welfare associations"[55] *La Zamacueca Política* criticized Castilla as an enemy of republican ideals and expressed popular sentiment by upholding the artisan cause for tariffs. The newspaper was eventually closed by the Castilla regime in 1859.[56]

Artisan Mutual Aid Societies and Social Respectability

In 1860, five years after the typesetters had formed their association, a tailor, Juan Antonio Zubiaga, founded a mutual aid society for artisans, the Sociedad de Artesanos de Auxilios Mutuos (Artisan Mutual Aid Society). At least two other exclusively artisan mutual aid societies appeared in the city of Lima: Artesanos Firmes por la Union (Artisans Firmly United) and the Sociedad Fraternal de Artesanos (Fraternal Artisan Society). The Sociedad Fraternal de Artesanos, also founded in 1860, emerged as a result of divisions among the founding members of the Sociedad de Artesanos de Auxilios Mutuos.[57] Over the course of the next two decades, such associations would become widespread, both in Lima and in other large Peruvian cities. In 1870 Cusco artisans founded their own Sociedad de Artesanos, and an artisan society also appeared in the city of Arequipa.

The social welfare offered by mutual aid societies guaranteed artisans a certain level of income during hard times and thus prevented them from slipping into a state of complete destitution. At a time of growing unemployment in Lima and of shrinking opportunities for national artisans as a result of imports, such security could mean the difference between holding on to a "middle-class" status and becoming part of the destitute popular sectors. Shane Hunt has speculated on the threat to the social status of artisans posed by the unemployment brought about by the guano age: "The factors released by the contracting artisan industries could not possibly be absorbed in an expanding guano industry. Any absorption in agriculture or the sectors producing non-traded goods has passed unnoticed. It is likely to have been limited by downward wage rigidity, since the employment alternatives available to artisans would have signified reduced income and social status. The result of such partial adjustment was chronic unemployment."[58] Competition came not only from foreign products, but also from foreign artisans, who began to establish successful enterprises in Lima. As Crossick has noted for London artisans during this period: "Disaster was always a real possibility for even the most secure of artisans."[59]

During times of illness, a member of the Sociedad Fraternal de Artesanos would receive one sol per day. The society had its own doctor to supervise those who fell ill. In the case of illnesses lasting more than two months, members would be assigned a lower stipend of twelve soles a month. A similar sum would be paid to any member who became disabled.[60] In order to receive these benefits, the members of the society paid an initial fee of three soles, twenty centavos, and a monthly fee of fifty centavos (in addition, members had to pay one sol every time a member died and needed funeral expenses covered). Shane Hunt calculates the average yearly wage for poor artisans exempt from taxation at this time (1876) at 832 soles, well above the average daily wage for the city of Lima—0.29 sol.[61]

The records of meetings of the Sociedad Fraternal indicate the discussion of the cases of members requiring such funds. At one of the regular Thursday meetings, for example, a member named José María Bustamante asked for thirty soles in order to go outside of Lima for health reasons and presented a certificate from a doctor. He was finally allotted ten soles.[62] His ailment may have been a respiratory one since Lima is excessively humid.

In addition to providing economic assistance during times of hardship, mutual aid societies contributed to place their members within the confines of respectable society. By their very nature as democratic associations based on principles of equality, mutual aid societies conformed to the prevailing ethos of progress and stood apart from earlier corporate organizations.[63] Mutual aid societies ignored both the corporate identification by trade and the traditional hierarchies within the trades between masters, journeymen, and apprentices. The liberal notion of the hardworking citizen thus replaced social hierarchies and opened up the field for artisans to establish a common social identity. In the definition of their membership, mutual aid societies emphasized the respectability of those who belonged. In its rules, the Sociedad Fraternal de Artesanos stated: "The members are all honest artisans who reside in the Capital and in Callao, and who perform a known art or trade, regardless of nationality."[64]

Membership in such societies, with their meetings taking place at churches and announced in the newspapers, gave artisans a foothold in respectable society at a time when long-standing prejudices against artisans persisted in Peruvian society. Prominent nineteenth-century liberal jurist Francisco García Calderón noted the persistence of such prejudices against the mechanical arts despite liberal reforms, "and we who have proclaimed freedom of work and equality of citizens still feel the consequences of the concerns regarding industrialists. European immigration has made us realize that the worker deserves consideration; but some professions are still regarded as less dignified."[65]

The prejudices against artisans were compounded by racial prejudices—a high proportion of artisans were of Indian and African heritage (see Fig. 3).[66] The following satirical poem, written during the late colonial period about Lima's customs, reflects the double prejudice against artisans and people of mixed race. The poem refers to artisans with a variety of racial epithets with derogatory connotations such as *zambo, mulato,* and *churupaco* and portrays artisans as thieves:

> *The next day you will see*
> *Many black artisans*
> *Chinese, zambos and mulatos*
> *Churupacos and other "skin colors."*
>
> *If one hires them,*
> *They ask for a loan,*
> *And before finishing the piece*
> *They've already received the money.*
>
> *They then sell the piece to another,*
> *while the owner is left with nothing,*
> *And if you lodge a complaint*
> *The artisan pays you one peso a month.*[67]

These attitudes about artisans so permeated Lima society that they even appeared in the newspapers intended to defend artisan interests. A satirical piece in the newspaper *El Artesano* narrated an incident in which an artisan charged his friend excessively for a pair of shoes.[68]

Membership in a mutual aid society clearly differentiated artisans from the growing plebe. The need to establish social distance from the urban poor became more pressing during this period. The guano boom had brought both social and political change: the abolition of slavery, the arrival of Indians in the city as a result of army recruitment, and the introduction of Chinese coolies were altering the face of Lima's popular sectors. The abolition of slavery in 1854 increased the number of free blacks in the city. In addition, liberal reforms of the 1850s contributed to bring the lowest social classes into the political system. A contemporary observer describes Lima in the following terms at the end of the 1870s: "Lima contained a dangerous class, like London or Paris, not so numerous, but, in some respects, more formidable. There was a mass of 30,000 idle negroes and half castes ready for any mischief, numbers of bad characters of all sorts and a Chinese colony."[69]

While membership in a mutual aid society clearly placed the artisan above the members of the plebe, the benefits afforded at the time of death further emphasized this distinction. The possibility of having a dignified funeral was considered a source of respectability. A fictional piece with strongly moralistic tones titled "The Rich and the Poor," which appeared in a Lima workers newspaper, dated 1875, illustrates this point. In the story, a carpenter at the verge of death tells his son that all that he can leave him is his work. After the father dies, the son is able to collect money for the funeral from other workers and can thus bury his father in luxury: "The hearse that would take the corpse was first class and extremely luxurious." Meanwhile the "ignorant crowd" stands by, watching the funeral, and members of the crowd wonder at the fact that a worker can be buried in luxury. A passerby enlightens the masses, explaining that workers will always receive a decent burial because they support one another in times of need.[70] While a luxurious funeral was an indication of respectability, the article also cautioned that luxury should never lead to indebtedness and preached the values of thrift.

Various aspects of institutional life within a mutual aid society contributed to reinforce the social status of artisans as respectable national citizens. The first was the fact that as secular and democratic associations, mutual aid societies marked a clear break from the earlier religious and corporate organizations considered "backward" by liberals. Second, the mutual aid society established social and political links between artisans and elites while separating artisans from the plebe, whom liberal elites considered lazy and in need of reform. The figure of the "honest artisan" stood apart from the plebe, made up of servants, vagrants, and criminals. In establishing an identity as a middle sector, artisans also relied on liberal views. In the eyes of liberals, artisans constituted part of the middle class needed to establish a prosperous modern nation. In his *Diccionario del pueblo*, Juan Espinoza, a journalist and defender of liberal ideas, offered a number of definitions of key terms intended to educate the popular sectors in the ways of republicanism. His definition of *artisan* begins with an identification with the middle classes: "ARTISANS constitute the middle class of society, between the proletarian and the wealthy."[71]

By belonging to mutual aid societies, artisans publicly established a distance between themselves and the colonial religious brotherhood, an institution associated with notions of hierarchy and racial segregation, as well as with baroque festivities considered distasteful by liberals. Dating back to the colonial period, brotherhoods attended to the cult of a particular saint, provided health benefits for their members, and covered funeral costs. During the nineteenth century, the brotherhood was not subject to the same kind of direct attacks as the guild. Yet the process of secularization brought about by liberal reforms eroded the power and prominence of brotherhoods. Newspapers reported on the financial problems faced by brotherhoods. In 1865, a government edict placed brotherhoods under the centralized government administration, the Beneficencia Pública.

Throughout the colonial period and into the national period, brotherhoods continued to reinforce social hierarchies through their racial identification. Despite the fact that such racial divisions had theoretically been abolished with nationhood, the racial affiliation of some of these institutions persisted into the national period. An internal brotherhood document dated 1835, fourteen years after the declaration of an independent republic, accused an individual named Miguel Macalaya of being unfit to hold a position within the brotherhood as he was neither an Indian or a mestizo, but a *chino,* one of the many complex colonial racial categories for someone with African and Indian ancestry.[72] While artisans continued to participate in brotherhoods during the first half of the century, and they surely must have continued to belong to them well into the nineteenth century, these, like the guilds, ceased to be the most visible artisan institution within a changing economic and political setting.[73]

The hierarchies within the brotherhood contrasted with the nominal equality of mutual aid society members. The rules of a nineteenth-century

FIG. 9. *Present-day members of the Sociedad Fraternal de Artesanos (2001)*
founded in 1860, which continues to operate today. Standing, left
to right: Angélica León, Manuel Bohorquez, Felicita Rodriguez de
Corcuera. Sitting, left to right: Miguel Tristán (now deceased), Felipe
Valentini, Cesar Valentini, Ricardo Corcuera (author's photograph).

brotherhood illustrate the persistence of these intense hierarchies with
regard to funeral rites. Such features as music and number of candles had
traditionally signaled a clear distinction in social status. The rules of the
Cofradía del Niño Jesús (1848) gave explicit instructions on the number of
candles to be used at the funerals of members with different ranks. At the
funeral of a child of the highest-ranking officials, the *prioste,* or mayordo-
mos, fourteen candles were to be used; for the child of one of the *hermanos
veinte y cuatros* (presiding brothers), six candles; and for the children of
other members of the "guild," four candles.[74] It is noteworthy that the rules
of the brotherhood continued to use the old concept of "guild" to refer to
the organization. Death and its commemoration were central aspects of the
brotherhood, and members were also obligated to participate in certain
funeral rites: the day designated for commemorating the deaths of members, the entire brotherhood was expected to be present. In case of the death
of the treasurer (*prioste bolsero*), they were obliged to attend the funeral.

Following in the tradition of Bourbon enlightened reformers, nineteenth-century liberals criticized the baroque nature of festivities at the time of funerals and of saint fiestas sponsored by brotherhoods. An example of the liberal distaste for such rituals appears in an article in the Lima newspaper *El Obrero* (1875), which criticized the pomp and circumstance that accompanied funerals.[75] The article expressed disapproval not only of what it considered to be a pompous funeral but of the fact that the family would have incurred debt to pay for the ceremony. Such religious customs were associated with the "centuries of obscurantism," a reference to the colonial period. They were seen as customs unbefitting an enlightened period such as the nineteenth century. The author recommended that the funeral be conducted in a more sober style: "Let us take the corpse of our beloved one to the general cemetery without pomp or ostentation, and let us use those soles that we would have been spent on songs and lights to satisfy our most pressing needs."[76]

While mutual aid societies reproduced many of the religious functions of the brotherhood, as secular organizations mutual aid societies assigned a more discreet role to religious festivities. The difference between brotherhood and mutual aid society in this respect is clearly reflected in the rules. The brotherhood was organized around the public cult of the saint, and its rules dealt in detail with the cult. In the case of the Cofradía del Niño Jesús, the very first ordinance specified that the members of the brotherhood must partake of the celebration of the Feast of the Circumcision.[77] The sixth ordinance mandated that the brotherhood's officials attend a meeting one month prior to the fiesta in order to "address the issue of how best to conduct the celebration with the greatest devotion and solemnity."[78] The cult of the saint contributed to funding the brotherhood through the collection of alms during the fiesta.

While their main purpose was no longer the celebration of saints' fiestas, mutual aid societies retained their ties to the religious establishment, and most held their meetings at churches and convents. The patron saint remained an important feature of the mutual aid society, but the society itself was not dedicated to the celebration of the saint's festivity as was the brotherhood.[79] Rather a special commission was named for this purpose. The rules primarily addressed the issue of meetings and the functions of the various elected officials. The patron saint of the Sociedad Fraternal de Artesanos was San Francisco Solano. The duties of the society's members included attending funerals and the main religious festivity. The section of the rules outlining the responsibilities of the members states the obligations of members "to attend the General Meetings of the Society, the swearing in of members, their funeral and the celebration of our Patron Saint."[80] Funeral benefits remained an important service offered by the mutual aid society. The rules also enjoined members to visit those members who were ill.

The most detailed instructions in the rules of mutual aid societies referred not to the cult of the patron saint, but rather to the functioning of the society itself, including the meetings of its members. Meetings were publicly announced in the city's newspapers. In the case of the Sociedad Fraternal de Artesanos, for example, these meetings were to take place on Thursdays and were open to the public. The rules of the society specified that at these meetings, members were allowed to participate three times, while the person who was forwarding a given motion would be allowed to talk four times. The rules outlined a rather complex administrative structure with a number of elected positions. The mutual aid society was to be led by a presiding committee composed of a number of members: a dean, a president, two vice presidents, two secretaries and two extras, a treasurer, a supervisor, an adjunct, and a supervisory secretary, as well as the welfare committee. Officials were elected for four-year terms. The regulations spelled out extremely detailed rules on the frequency with which the director's board was to meet and its functions as well as those of each of its members and included procedural rules for the weekly board meetings.

Public and Political Connections:
The Sociedad de Artesanos de Auxilios Mutuos

In addition to providing for its members, artisan societies helped to establish connections with Lima's elites. In some cases the connections proved to be very direct through the membership of elites, such as painter and politician Francisco Laso. Although the membership of such individuals was most likely of an honorary nature, it had great social significance: other members of the Sociedad of more modest means could thus claim to belong to an association in which they were considered equals with these men. Such was the case of industrialist Francisco Hurtado, who owned a carpentry business, the National Factory, that employed twenty-seven artisans, including blacksmiths, carpenters, and gilders. Hurtado identified himself as an "artisan" in his dealings with the government and belonged to two artisan societies, the Sociedad de Artesanos and the Sociedad Fraternal de Artesanos.[81] The

FIG. 10. *Certificate of membership of Francisco Hurtado, Sociedad de Artesanos de Auxilios Mutuos, 1868, emphasizing the honesty of members (Archivo Histórico Municipal de Lima).*

Sociedad de Artesanos could also count Emilio Dancuart, a member of the elite, among its members.[82]

A prominent member of Lima's elite, artist, writer, and politician Francisco Laso joined the Sociedad de Artesanos. In addition to his successful career as an artist (he is now considered one of Peru's major nineteenth-century painters), Laso was politically active and participated in congressional politics.[83] Having a figure of such stature as a member of the society guaranteed a degree of respectability for artisans, who could count Laso as one of their own. In 1873, the newspaper *El Artesano* commemorated the fourth anniversary of Laso's death with an article singing his praises. It began by stating that Laso had been a member of the Sociedad de Artesanos de Auxilios Mutuos. Other worker mutual societies also attracted prominent individuals. In 1863, President San Roman reportedly sought to become a member of the mutual aid society Sociedad Filantrópica Democrática (Philanthropic Democratic Society).[84]

In addition to such ties to individual members of the elites through honorary membership, artisan societies established connections to members of

Lima's political and ecclesiastical authorities through public ceremonies. Despite the injunctions against politics in the rules of mutual aid societies, these societies enabled artisans to establish important political connections that were qualitatively different from the old patron-client relationships with caudillos. In addition, some individual members pursued political activity and developed direct links to the political establishment. For example, the founder of the Sociedad de Artesanos, tailor Juan Antonio Zubiaga, was a candidate for Congress in 1866, although he did not win a seat.

Unlike caudillos, with their protectionist policies, the politicians of the liberal age could no longer offer any concrete material benefits in exchange for artisan political support. Mutual aid societies stood as independent institutions, some of whose leaders were recruited to help promote support for the Partido Civil, the country's first modern political party. The interest of political authorities in supporting mutual aid societies attests to their political importance. Members of the elite and of the political establishment considered it worthwhile to pursue the relationship with this politically active sector of the population.

Furthermore, societies created links with one another and thus constituted an organized segment of the electorate at a time when elections were important loci for political battles. The broader political significance of mutual aid societies has been noted by Hilda Sábato for Buenos Aires. Sábato has remarked on the dual nature of the mutual aid association as an institution that provided services to its members and also linked them to public life:

> They functioned in the context of the spaces created by the institutions themselves, and dialogued amongst themselves, thus creating intense exchanges among associations. Banquets, homages, commemorations, various festivities, protests or social meetings gave a concrete shape to these relations and led to the formation of specific circuits of action and communication. Associations also served as mediators with the State.[85]

Such links existed among Lima's mutual aid societies. For example, societies would invite each other to fund-raisers and inform one another of the results of internal elections. In May 1872, the Sociedad Fraternal de Artesanos received an invitation to a bullfight organized by another mutual aid society, the Sociedad de los Andes de Auxilios Mutuos, to raise funds.[86] On another occasion, the Sociedad Tipográfica informed the Sociedad Fraternal de Artesanos about who had been elected to preside over the society that year.[87]

The public nature of the associations set mutual aid societies apart from the cofradía. While the religious aspect remained a part of the mutual aid society, the public life of the mutual aid society was more linked to emerging secular society. The Sociedad de Artesanos established a public presence in a number of ways. Meetings were announced in various city newspapers. These meetings took place at various locations during the first two decades of the society's existence. In 1864 the Sociedad was holding its meetings in the convent of San Francisco, in the hall known as the General.[88] In subsequent years, the Sociedad met at the National Library and at the church of San Agustín until eventually, in 1872, the Sociedad de Artesanos received its own building from the government for meetings and a Sunday school.[89] The new location was at the site of the old Espíritu Santo church.

Soon after its foundation, the Sociedad de Artesanos de Auxilios Mutuos caught the attention of the playwright Trinidad Manuel Pérez, who dedicated his 1862 play *La industria y el poder* to it. Pérez formed part of a midcentury generation of romantic intellectuals. The play had an honest and hardworking artisan as its protagonist. In the dedication, Pérez praised the members of the Sociedad for having formed an association to further their interests, to seek protection for national industry, and to assist one another in times of need. The play was performed on various occasions after its opening in 1862, and the script was published three separate times.[90]

In its public functions, the Sociedad established connections to the political establishment. An 1867 religious celebration for the society's patron saint, San Francisco Solano, was attended by various political figures, including "various ministers, the general inspector of the army, a large number of congressmen and other distinguished people.... At the conclusion of the ceremony, the attendants received small gifts. It is apparent that the invitation of the Sociedad de Artesanos has been satisfactorily attended by the notables in our society."[91] The sober tone of this ceremony held in the presence of members of the government differed greatly from the more popular nature of brotherhood celebrations, which took the saint in procession out onto the streets and could thus be witnessed by the general populace. In another example of an artisan society establishing social ties with government officials, the Sociedad Fraternal de Artesanos in 1873 invited the president, Manuel Pardo, to celebrate the thirteenth anniversary of its foundation. Although the president was unable to attend, he sent a representative.[92] In both cases, politicians considered it worthwhile to attend events organized by each of these artisan societies.

The Sociedad maintained good relations not only with civil but also with ecclesiastical authorities. In June 1873, for example, the Sociedad sent a delegation to congratulate the new archbishop. Archbishop Orueta received the delegation, and in thanking the Sociedad de Artesanos, he praised the work that the Sociedad was doing in favor of the working class: "I am happy to see the working class united in a moral and welfare association. This conduct is very praiseworthy and they do well, as man has been born not to live and pass away like other creatures, but rather to do as much good for his fellow men as possible."[93] The archbishop's words reflect the identification of artisans as part of a working class by the 1870s, a subject to be addressed in the following chapter.

In addition to establishing relationships with civil and religious authorities, the Sociedad de Artesanos participated in patriotic civic festivals. The Independence Day celebration of 1866 reveals the prominent social standing achieved by the Sociedad de Artesanos and its strong association with national symbols. On July 27, the day prior to Independence Day, the Sociedad de Artesanos assembled at the Portada del Callao, one of the portals of the old colonial city walls, together with various patriotic associations. The participants included the Society of Founders of Independence, the Veteran Corps from both the independence wars and from the War with Spain (concluded only months earlier), and the national fire brigades. Together they sang the national anthem while standing at the foot of a Tree of Liberty, a symbol dating to the American and French Revolution.[94] They subsequently marched into the city for two days of celebrations that included fireworks displays and an intricate reenactment, in Lima's central plaza, of the recent naval combat with Spain. Such festivals reveal continuities with colonial festivities in which the place of a corporate group in the celebrations indicated the social importance of such a group in society.[95]

In the course of the ceremonies, two artisans were presented with prizes, one for the most outstanding piece of craftsmanship (in the 1866 celebration the prize was won by Vicente Pedraza for making an organ) and the other for the artisan who had shown the most bravery during the recent military encounter with Spain. The prizes were each 200 soles.[96] In the course of the celebrations, the chief of the Artisan Fire Brigade gave a patriotic speech, and following the speech a young girl offered the president of the republic a laurel wreath in the name of the artisans.[97]

The existence of an artisan fire brigade during the battle reflects the respectable position of artisans in society. During the 2nd of May Battle in 1866, in which the Spanish fleet bombarded Lima's port Callao, the population organized to defend the port. All of Lima and Callao's fire brigades stood by during the battle with Spain to help put out the fires caused by Spanish bombs. Lima's foreign communities each ran fire brigades: the French, the British, and the Germans. The Bomba de Artesanos, the artisan brigade, was organized by the well-known painter Francisco Laso.[98] By participating as firemen, artisans were following a historical precedent: an 1839 edict required that artisans keep equipment in their workshops for putting out fires.[99] Yet the actual formation of a fire brigade reflected the greater degree of institutional organization attained by artisans during this period. In the course of everyday life, firemen played an important role in a community where construction materials were highly flammable (*quincha*, a combination of reeds and mud, was a common building material in the city). In civic celebrations, the city's foreign fire brigades often made elaborate displays with their ladders.

Beyond the ceremonial role in civic festivals that reinforced their connection to the nation, artisans became directly involved in politics during this period. Carmen McEvoy points to the Partido Civil's reliance on artisans and in particular on the connections between the party and the Sociedad de Artesanos de Auxilios Mutuos: "Thus it was not out of context for the Sociedad Independencia Electoral, an association that sought to find the citizen vanguards among working men, to have established a close link to the 'Sociedad de Auxilios Mutuos,' the most important artisan society of the period."[100] The Sociedad Independencia Electoral co-opted a number of artisan leaders from this society, including Ignacio Albán, José Zavalaga, José Ríos, Juan Pajuelo, Manuel Polo, Luque, Gregorio Basurto, José Bustamante, and Enrique del Campo. The first artisan elected to Congress was a member of the Cusco Sociedad de Artesanos, Francisco González, congressman from 1876 to 1879.

Conclusion

Why did artisans create mutual aid societies that for the most part seemed to reproduce the social functions of the brotherhood? Although there is no evidence to show that mutual aid societies engaged directly in political activity, these associations were a crucial underpinning of artisan politics during the mid–nineteenth century. At a time when liberal electoral reforms had enfranchised large sections of the plebe, artisans strove for a degree of respectability to separate themselves from the plebe and offer legitimacy in the eyes of the elite. A member of the Sociedad de Artesanos de Auxilios Mutuos enjoyed the support of other artisans and belonged to an association that included members of the elite and played a central role in civic celebrations in which the artisan stood proudly as a valuable citizen.

Adherence to the nation and to liberal institutions allowed artisans to gain a more solid footing in the emerging polity. Ties to the past were maintained: artisan mutual aid societies continued to play an important role in the saint-day celebrations, an inheritance of the brotherhoods. Yet they also played a new role within national civic festivals in which artisans could claim to represent the nation, thanks both to their craftsmanship and to their patriotism. Mutual aid societies gave artisans a social and political platform and allowed them to continue pursuing sectoral interests after their guilds ceased to be viable political organizations.

These societies reflect the interdependence between liberal politicians and artisans. On the one hand, liberal politicians needed artisans as an important urban base of support, and liberal ideology portrayed artisans as model citizens. On the other, artisans sought proximity to liberal politicians in order to further their own sectoral demands. As long as they were associated with popular protests, artisans were perceived as dangerous by liberals. The specter of violence was not so distant: artisans had participated in the protests of 1858 and in the political violence of 1872, in which a mob executed the Gutierrez brothers, three military officers who had staged a coup. Violence had also erupted in 1865 when a crowd attacked and destroyed merchandise in English, North American, German, French, and Italian stores.[101]

While mutual aid societies contributed to reinforce a sectoral identity among artisans, they did not yet constitute class-based organizations. Theirs was the rhetoric of patriotism and conciliation with the government. These societies grouped upwardly mobile artisans—probably only a few hundred per society—while the majority of the city's artisans remained outside these organizations. To some degree, the mutual aid society also cut across classes by incorporating members of the city's elite.

Nonetheless, references to artisans as part of a working class became common during this period. Lima's printers became instrumental in furthering the notion of a working class through various artisan and worker newspapers that appeared during this period. With the worsening economic conditions during the 1870s, the notion of artisans as part of a broader working class that included unskilled labor gained prominence.

CHAPTER FIVE

"Artisan Liberalism" and the Beginnings of a Working Class, 1860–1879

For no one will doubt that journalism is an easy and inex-
pensive and quite obvious school for the advancement of a
people. The enlightenment brought by the press regenerates
humanity: the speed at which it travels has had an impact on
the progress of civilization; many have been enlightened and
others immortalized as great men. In conclusion, the enlight-
enment spread by the press makes of all men a single family
in the realm of reciprocal communication.

—El Artesano, March 15, 1873

We need to explore how new social identities among both men
and women were formed . . . how they represented their work-
ing identities, and how workers defined their roles and articu-
lated their thoughts in response to the wider political culture
and the moralizing discourse to which they were subjected.

Susan Deans Smith, "Working Poor and the Colonial State," in
Rituals of Rule, Rituals of Resistance

ON NOVEMBER 26, 1872, A COMMISSION
of artisans presented newly elected President Manuel Pardo with a petition
demanding that the national congress take some action to control the
impact of the escalating cost of living on artisans and in general on the.

"impoverished people." The petition reflected the country's worsening economic situation. Over the course of the 1860s, deficit spending based on loans obtained on the basis of projected guano revenues had finally brought the government to the verge of bankruptcy. In the coming years, Pardo, who had campaigned as a critic of the easy guano wealth and sought to put the country on a more solid economic footing, faced the worst economic depression thus far in the nation's history. A slump in the price of guano during a period of world economic depression worsened the government's already dire financial situation.

In some ways, the artisan petition echoed the political rhetoric of Pardo and the Civilistas in criticizing the easy wealth of guano. Artisans considered Pardo's political victory as their own and referred to "our sacrifices and patriotism, thanks to which, with God's protection, we won the most splendid victory over those who trampled upon our laws and committed fraud with the national income."[1] Yet the petition also showed a new political assertiveness in which artisans sought to strengthen their demands by making common cause with other workers. In the petition artisans claimed not only to be citizens but to be a privileged set of citizens, in this case the majority:

1. That artisans have the right to petition by virtue of the fact that they form the majority of the citizenry that constitutes the political association of the nation.
2. That industrialists and workers form part of the same body [corps] as artisans because they knead the bread for their families with the sweat of their brow.[2]

Thus, a half century into the national period, artisans were not only casting their demands in the language of republicanism but also claiming to be a majority of the citizenry. They bolstered their political legitimacy through reference to their role as laborers in common cause with other workers. This kind of claim was only possible as a result of artisan identification with a broader working class.

In this chapter, I examine the political discourse of the 1870s that identified the demands of artisans with those of other workers. During this period artisans began to use the language of class.[3] While the notion of artisans as part of a working class was not entirely new, the artisan press of the 1870s made this link explicit and gave it an overtly political dimension.[4] The press actively sought to politicize its readership and make artisans and workers aware of their common interests. A new group of "artisans"—Lima's printers—were at the forefront of the newspapers that constituted a prime example of this discourse and an early manifestation of class consciousness.

The assertiveness of artisans contrasted with the ambivalence of liberals toward popular political participation. While liberals defined citizenship in terms of education, artisans now claimed rights as citizens based on their role as laborers. The discourse of the workers' press borrowed some elements and rejected other elements of liberal discourse. The figure of the honest and hardworking artisan remained a cornerstone in the defense of workers' political rights, while the moralizing tone of liberal discourse receded somewhat into the background. By formulating their demands in class terms, artisans departed from the liberal blueprint of a society of individual citizens and thus from the liberal model of the polity. The notion of a working class also contributed to leave behind the racial categories of colonial society.

This chapter draws primarily on the two available newspapers linked to mutual aid societies during this period, *El Artesano* (1873) and *El Obrero* (1875–77). The presence of such newspapers is a remarkable phenomenon that must be understood within the context of a process of political modernization.[5] The appearance of these newspapers, intended to reinforce an identity among artisans of all trades and workers, represented a qualitative step away from the earlier use of the press by artisans to voice their concerns. While artisans had frequently used the press to express their demands both to the government and to a broader public, the workers' press was aimed specifically at artisans and workers. The newspaper itself became a political instrument for broadening the numbers of those who defined themselves as artisans and workers. It sought to extend the links between workers and educate them about their political rights and their common interests as a class. These newspapers put forth the notion of a working class with political rights.[6]

Of the new republican institutions, the press was the most accessible to those with limited means. In her study of Brazilian artisans, historian Halpern Pereira notes that for those with meager resources, the press was the most available means of expressing their interests:

> A relatively accessible means of expression for individuals and
> social groups with scarce economic resources, the press during
> this period, both here and in other countries, constituted an
> important vehicle for socio-political participation for the most
> diverse groups with the most varied goals. To some degree, one

can say that it became more important than the simple petition, usually presented to those in power, and gave such a petition a new potential through the use of public opinion on a scale that had been previously impossible.[7]

In his recent study of Cusco during the early national period, Charles Walker has pointed to the importance of the press in the political battles of the period.[8]

While in numerous ways the artisan press was cut in the liberal mold, the formulation of artisan and worker interests in terms of a working class represented a pragmatic interpretation of liberal views to suit the purposes of artisans.[9] This artisan liberalism sometimes clashed with mainstream liberal values. For example, the portrayal of a society divided into social classes challenged the classic liberal view.

The notion of a society divided into social classes remained outside the liberal repertoire. In his 1855 *Diccionario para el pueblo,* intended to educate "the people" in the ways of republicanism, Juan Espinosa reflected the liberal aversion to the notion of social classes. His definition of "social classes" is worth quoting at length for the richness of texture that combines references to republicanism, religion, and a critique of social hierarchies and reference to artisans as potentially more socially useful than aristocrats:

> In a republic the only social class should be that of the citizen; no first, second or last. However, those knowledgeable on such matters claim that even in heaven there are hierarchies. We are not familiar with such regions, but we have noted that here there is a universal habit of dividing the inhabitants of every town into classes, the most noteworthy of which are the wealthy and the poor. . . . Let us do away with classes: if it someday becomes necessary to classify individuals in society, rather than refer to them as being of first, second or third class, let us classify them as honest or base, skillful or clumsy, useful or pernicious to the community: the useful ones will be hard workers and healthy of heart while the harmful ones will be the lazy and base, in which case a shoemaker can be of the first class and a marquise of the last. Man of the people! Keep in mind that you are the son of God, and that as such nobody can be nobler than you! Was our father Adam a count or a marquise?[10]

During the 1870s, Manuel Pardo and the Civilistas continued to envision a republic of citizens rather than one divided into social classes.[11]

The artisan press took the earlier symbolic association between artisans and hardworking citizens a step further by clearly spelling out notions of political rights. It combined the new language of political rights with religious arguments on the centrality of work to society and formulated an "artisan liberalism," a conception of the working class that drew primarily from liberalism but also from a variety of sources, including Christianity and socialism as well as the experience of Lima's artisans.[12] The artisan as hardworking citizen remained at the heart of this ideological formulation.

The discourse on work and citizenship can be placed in the context of broader trends within the Atlantic world. The link between work and citizenship formed part of the repertoire of nineteenth-century political ideas. In his study of labor in late–eighteenth- and nineteenth-century France, William Sewell writes: "The argument that labor was the source of all wealth and that laborers were therefore 'the people'. . . became commonplace[s] of workers' discourse in the 1830s."[13] Given the increased flow of ideas through newspapers and travelers during the nineteenth century, it is fair to assume that Peruvian artisans would have been influenced by these general trends.

Within the Peruvian setting, the notion of the artisan as a legitimate citizen based on his work resonated with the prevailing concern of the period: a concern with the depletion of guano resources and the need to find new sources of wealth on which to base national prosperity. As part of his political campaign, Civilista Manuel Pardo emphasized the need to base national prosperity on the work of individual citizens. He played on a long-standing liberal theme of criticizing the excessive reliance on government bureaucratic positions (a phenomenon commonly described as *empleomanía*).[14] During the 1870s, Manuel Pardo and the Civilistas attempted to diversify the economy to steer the nation away from its dangerous reliance on guano. Excessive indebtedness was quickly eroding government revenues: by 1875 the service of the foreign debt nearly equaled the government's guano revenues of 2.6 million pounds sterling.[15] The precarious situation of national finances was worsened by a worldwide economic depression. The war with Chile in 1879 plunged the country further into turmoil and poverty, a situation from which it would not begin to recover until the end of the century. Such circumstances may have helped to formulate artisan interests in terms of a broader political bloc in an effort to seek increasing leverage during rather desperate times.

The Changing Nature of the Artisanry and Work

The changes in artisan discourse over the course of the first half century of the republican period in Peru were accompanied by changes in the relative importance of certain trades. While silversmiths had dominated the social and political scene during the colonial period, new trades emerged at the forefront of artisan politics during the national period—the loss of power of silversmiths correlates with the weakening of the Church and the fall of the colonial aristocracy, the main consumers of silver products. During the period of caudillismo, shifts occurred in favor of some of the trades who benefited from government patronage—in particular those trades producing goods for the military, such as tailors, ironmongers, and tanners. During the battles over commercial policy, and in particular during the 1858 protest, carpenters emerged as one of the most politicized trades among the artisanry.

As the number of newspapers in the city of Lima grew, typesetters became increasingly prominent. Typesetters played an important role in the shift from an artisan to a worker identity. The nature of their work with the pressure of producing newspapers to meet firm deadlines meant that the rhythms of work were probably more demanding than those of a more traditional artisan workshop. In fact, the newspaper *El Obrero* refers to this difference in a somewhat exaggerated way in a vignette that presents the life of the artisan as one of leisure, with time to read, while the typesetter works from morning until night.

An increasing number of mechanized factories began to appear in Lima over the course of the 1860s and 1870s. Many of these factories used steam-operated machinery. These included three beer factories, a biscuit factory of Arturo Field, and a chocolate factory.[16] Some industries attained a fairly large size, such as the cigar factory of Antonio Pouchan and Co., which during the 1870s employed over 400 workers (both men and women).[17] In addition, a textile factory operated on the outskirts of the city (in Vitarte). Various artisan workshops employed numerous artisans. For example, the National Factory built furniture and employed twenty-seven artisans, including carpenters, blacksmiths, gilders, and an upholsterer.[18]

Nonetheless, mechanization was not widespread, and the majority of artisan establishments continued to operate on a small scale. Studies of nineteenth-century Britain have shown the degree to which artisan workshops survived alongside new industries during this period of intense industrialization. The argument can certainly be extended to conclude that artisan workshops in Lima did not suffer a process of displacement as a result of the modest growth of industry during this period.[19]

In some cases, smaller workshops incorporated new machinery into the production process. The shoe factory of a Mr. Pease employed ten people and used machinery.[20] The novelty of such a method earned this establishment newspaper coverage, and the reporter commented on the machinery and claimed that the workshop could produce up to 200 pairs of shoes in a day:

> Having been invited to visit the shoemaker's shop owned by
> Mr. Pease on Baquijano Street, we have done so today and have
> been surprised to see the various machines for making shoes.
> We will not describe them because only by seeing them can one
> grasp their curious and complicated mechanisms; let it simply
> be said that all the work is done with these machines, from the
> easiest to the most difficult. Mr. Pease, with ten workers and his
> mechanical devices, can make up to 200 pairs of shoes a day.[21]

The words reflect the novelty of machinery that was beginning to be used for manufacturing in Lima. They also reflect the shifts in the relative prestige of trades, as a newspaper featured a shoemaker—normally on the low end of the status scale. The foreign origin of the shoemaker certainly must have contributed to this greater prestige.

While artisans' discourse was primarily a male discourse, women nonetheless constituted an important presence among the artisanry. Outside the workshop environment, many women worked as seamstresses, probably often in their own homes. The 1866 census for the city of Lima includes a large number of these seamstresses. At the time, sewing machines also began to appear on the market in Lima. The increased availability of sewing machines during this period may have impacted the work among seamstresses.[22]

Despite the fact that artisans decried the woes of economic liberalism, some of the city's artisans seem to have adjusted in various ways to the new environment. As a new elite associated with guano wealth emerged in Lima, artisans learned to cater to their tastes. Some workshops took out ads in the newspaper offering goods made in Peru. One such advertisement announced that a shirt workshop (with no specific name) had just received a shipment of thread and cotton and could make a series of items of clothing for customers, including "very fine flannel shirts, collars and stocking . . . for ladies who love good taste."[23]

The beginning of the guano period in the 1840s had forced artisans to adjust to the new economic realities of free trade, but the end of the guano period in the 1870s brought a period of severe depression. This downturn contributed to weakening the economic position of artisans. Jorge Dulanto Pinillos notes that at the tail end of the guano boom, when people could no longer afford luxuries, Lima's commercial establishments suffered severely.[24] Dulanto Pinillos also cites the newspaper *La Opinión Nacional,* which gives the figure of 20,000 unemployed in Lima in 1875.[25] This economic environment offered scarce opportunities for artisans to prosper and created a pressure of downward mobility. It was within this general setting that printers in particular began to put forth more assertively the notion of a working class with a common set of political interests.

Public Opinion in Nineteenth-Century Peru

The establishment of a common identity among artisans and other workers relied on the mechanisms of public opinion. The significance of the artisan press cannot be understood without discussing the role of the press and of public opinion in nineteenth-century Peru. As early as the Independence period, the press and public opinion became a primary form of political engagement, a radical departure from the past. The appearance of newspapers signaled a turn away from the secrecy of politics under the monarchy toward a more open discussion. Around the time of independence, in a society with low levels of literacy, a number of newspapers appeared. Pablo Macera points to the way journalism both depends on and constitutes public opinion and represented an entirely new form of politics within Iberian societies:

> Journalism presumes the existence of and simultaneously constitutes "public opinion," a concept that did not exist under the political systems—such as the Spanish Empire—where authority proceeds from the elevated will of Providence.
>
> A Spanish viceroy was only responsible to the monarch and to God for his acts. Under the colonial regime, both Hapsburg and Bourbon, government decisions could only be based on consultation among a small group of advisers who surrounded the supreme vice governor. These advisers were called upon to

implement a set of rulings whose ultimate rationality they were (legally and psychologically) forbidden from questioning.[26]

The notion of public opinion in the nineteenth century represented a qualitative shift. Social groups were now able to voice their views on specific matters of policy affecting their interests. Artisans became one of the first groups to do so. The "public sphere," to use Habermas's term, thus included non-elite actors.

The 1870s were a particularly prolific time for the press. Amid the flurry of often short-lived political newspapers that appeared in 1873 with titles such as *La Bala Roja* (*The Red Bullet*), claiming "to make audible the voice of popular indignation, to bring to justice all those who commit abuses, and point out to peoples the road that duty prescribes,"[27] *El Artesano* stood out for claiming to speak in the name of artisans. Together with worker newspapers, women's newspapers appeared during this period. These newspapers appeared at a time when the printed word was increasingly contributing to disseminate the idea of Peru as a nation.[28]

The artisan press reflected an awareness of the importance of public opinion during this period. *El Obrero* pointed out that in the United States, even women with marketplace stands and women butchers (*placeras y carniceras*) read the newspapers that defended their interests. The article defined public opinion in the following terms:

> Public opinion is the prestige enjoyed by a government. You know this as well as we do. Who is it that elevated the present ruler to the first position in the nation? Public opinion. Who is it that has formed national guards throughout the country to quell the antiliberal revolution headed by doctor don Nicolás de Piérola? Public opinion. Who is responsible for the current crisis that we suffer with such resignation without rising in revolution against the existing order of things? Public opinion, i.e., the opinion of the great majority of the nation, which is liberal.[29]

The conservative caudillo Piérola, Pardo's political rival, had strong ties to the Catholic Church and at the time had begun to plot against the Pardo regime. Evidently *El Obrero* saw a role for itself in the process of forming public opinion and claimed that public opinion supported liberal views.

Readership of the artisan press extended beyond Lima. In May 1873,

Francisco González, president of the Cusco Sociedad de Artesanos, ordered thirty issues of the newspaper to be sent to Cusco.[30] Published letters to the editor came from provincial cities such as Cusco and Arequipa. The newspaper even received and published a letter from someone in Paris who, identified as an artisan, praised the newspaper, discussed worker events in Europe, including a socialist meeting in Germany, and signed the letter "your friend and colleague."[31]

While it is difficult to determine the exact readership of the artisan press, recent historiography suggests a wider readership among non-elites than was previously assumed. In his recent study of Cusco for the early republican period, Charles Walker argues that large numbers among the urban poor would have had access to newspapers: "Through the various links between written and oral culture, the newspapers informed far more people, including illiterates, than could read them."[32] Walker points to the fact that newspapers were sometimes displayed publicly and that news would have been discussed in various public spaces such as taverns and *chicherías* (taverns that served *chicha,* a fermented corn beer).

The findings of some European historians reinforce the notion that the written word had a significant impact among the popular sectors. In an essay on early modern France, Natalie Zemon Davis comments on the impact of the printed word on popular culture as early as the sixteenth century.[33] In his study of late-nineteenth-century Russia, Jeffrey Brooks notes the importance of literacy among the popular sectors of Russia: "The belief that the printed word is a means to attain power over oneself and one's environment was at the heart of the demand for literacy in Russia. Growing numbers of ordinary people took the trouble to learn to read before the October Revolution because they became aware of the practical and cultural uses of literacy in their daily lives."[34]

Brooks's observation on the possible religious connotations of written texts is particularly suggestive: "For both workers and peasants . . . the printed word retained something of its original religious significance, which enhanced the power of the printed word, and the idea of spiritual self-perfection was translated into a quest for personal self-improvement in the secular texts."[35] It is safe to assume a strongly religious cast of mind among the urban popular sectors during this period. A letter written to *El Artesano* by a reader in the Andean city of Huánuco explicitly draws a parallel between the pages of the Bible and those of the newspaper by claiming that *El Artesano* "will be the worker's holy book containing the divine religion of work."[36] Such a statement suggests that Brooks's observations for Russia may be relevant to Peru. Whatever the religious resonance of these newspapers, many of their articles had an explicitly political component.

A Voice for Artisans

The newspapers *El Artesano* and *El Obrero* marked a new stage in artisan politics, a direct attempt to voice the concerns of artisans and to present their demands in terms of a broader working class. These newspapers differed from liberal newspapers such as *El Hijo del Pueblo* or *El Siglo,* which sought to educate the masses. Rather, the workers' press spoke more directly to the issues affecting artisans following the defeat of protectionism. *El Artesano,* edited by Ignacio Manco y Ayllón, was published biweekly between March 15 and December 1, 1873. *El Obrero,* edited by José Enrique del Campo, was published weekly beginning on March 20, 1875, and ending in 1877.[37] *El Artesano* claimed to speak directly in the name of artisans, while *El Obrero* presented itself as the voice of the working class. The claims were more than rhetorical. In its opening editorial, *El Artesano* announced that its pages would be open, free of charge, to artisan societies and to any individual seeking to voice concerns.[38] Both newspapers had ties to the Sociedad de Artesanos and the printers' mutual aid society, the Sociedad Tipográfica de Auxilios Mutuos (Typographical Mutual Aid Society). The editor of *El Artesano,* Manco y Ayllón, belonged to both societies and was elected president of the Sociedad Tipográfica in 1873. He also worked as a printer at the newspaper *El Comercio.*

Their work as printers placed both Enrique del Campo and Manco y Ayllón socially in proximity to the popular sectors. Enrique del Campo could be considered a classic case of an individual facing the pressures of maintaining a precarious social status. His father had been a public prosecutor, whereas his mother belonged to a family that included a poet and a doctor. Enrique del Campo himself began to study medicine, but his family's financial situation forced him to discontinue his studies. He became a typographical worker and succeeded in becoming administrator at various of the city's printing presses. He eventually was elected permanent president of the Sociedad de Artesanos and also held a municipal post as "inspector de Instrucción" at various municipal schools. Jorge Basadre comments on del Campo's position between middle- and working-class status: "Enrique del Campo stood between . . . a middle-class origin and a gradual movement into the working class, and then a return to the middle class."[39] As a member of the national guard, he lost his life fighting against the Chilean invasion.[40]

As for Manco y Ayllón, he claimed ancestry from Inca nobility, a rather striking fact in a city increasingly drawn to European and particularly French culture as a paradigm of civilization. Manco y Ayllón claimed to have documents that proved he was a direct descendent of the royal family of the Incas. In a petition to Congress in 1868 he demanded an investigation of a corpse found in the Lima hospital of San Andrés that he alleged might be the remains of the Inca emperor Huayna Capac. Were they the remains of the Inca, they should be given a dignified funeral and a monument should be erected. The document is worth quoting from because of the blend of modern concepts of citizenship and patriotism with ancient notions of nobility. Manco y Ayllón himself claimed that his concern stemmed both from his identity as a Peruvian and as a descendant of the royal family. The document outlined the conquests of Huayna Capac, claiming them as important for the Peruvian nation: "Your Excellency, here is the indefatigable monarch whose many noteworthy merits require that our patriotism take his cadaver into account, and that the Peruvian Nation dedicate to him a monument worthy of his high status and notable civic virtues. Huayna Capac, Sir, has no fewer merits than Christopher Columbus and Bolívar."[41] Manco y Ayllón thus reinterpreted Inca history in the light of republicanism and sought to integrate the most famous Inca ruler into a national pantheon.

In his writing, Manco y Ayllón also indirectly addressed the more immediate issue of social and racial prejudices in Lima society. In a fictional piece published in serial form in *El Obrero* titled "Two Neighbors," a man falls in love with a woman of a higher social class than himself. The protagonist, Omairo, of Indian descent, falls in love with Victoria, the woman living next door. At first she expresses disdain because of his Indian blood, and when he declares his love, she responds by calling him *"cholo,"* a derogatory word referring to a person of Indian ancestry who has moved to the city and attempts to assimilate to urban life. But gradually she falls in love with him. Although Omairo descends from Inca nobility (the author dedicates an entire section of the story to tracing Omairo's lineage), in Lima he is still considered an Indian, and when he approaches Victoria's mother to declare that he loves her daughter, the mother brushes him aside and refers to him with the derogatory term "Indian." She later advises her daughter "not to ever take interest in an *hijo del pueblo* (son of the people), a worker and much less an

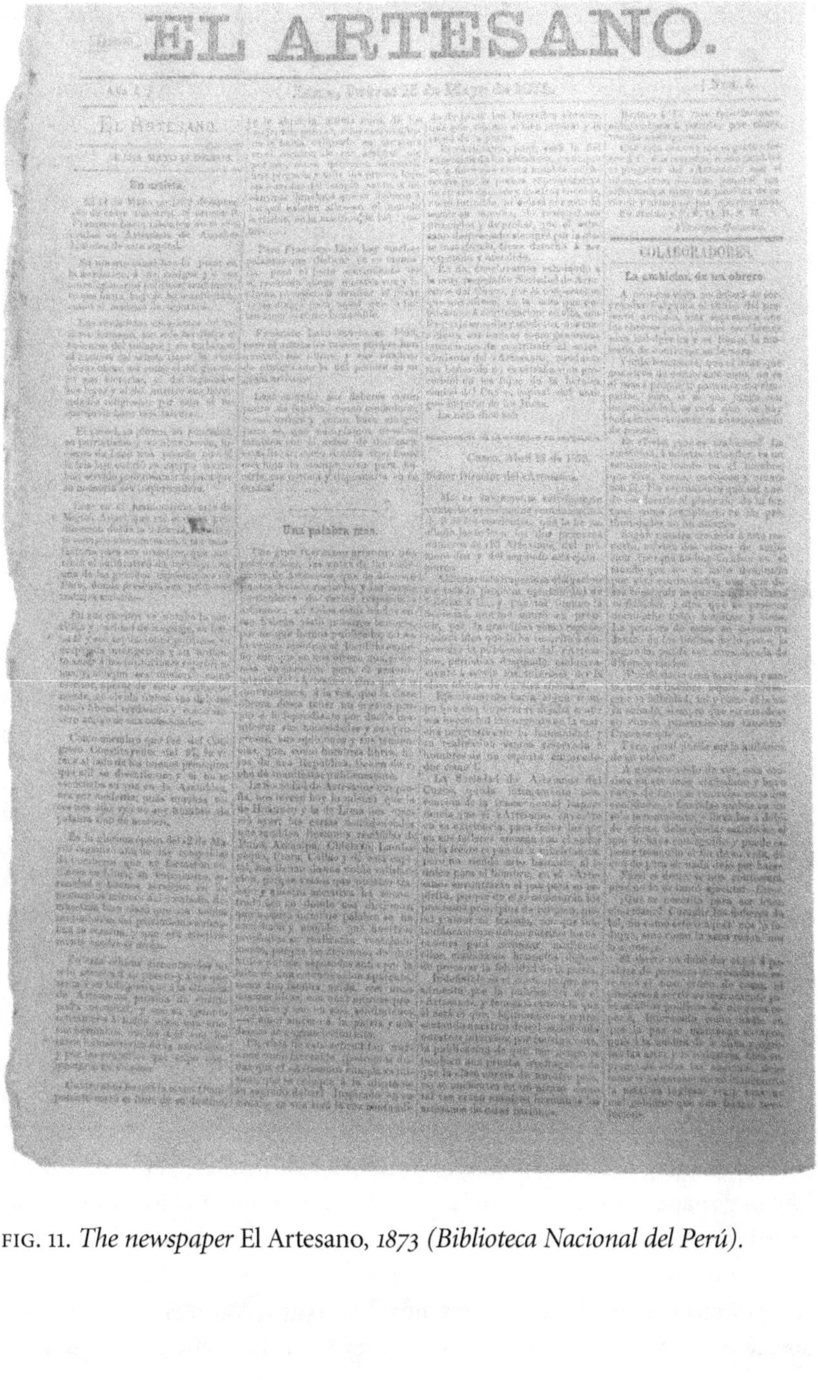
EL ARTESANO.

Un artista.

Una palabra mas.

COLABORADORES

La ambicion de un obrero

FIG. 11. *The newspaper* El Artesano, *1873 (Biblioteca Nacional del Perú).*

Indian."[42] Omairo then joins the army in order to attain a higher social position that would make him worthy of Victoria. The story ends with Omairo and a companion in the army singing a *yaraví* (a traditional Andean musical form) declaring his love for Victoria and bidding her farewell.

The story illustrates a number of themes on race and class in Peruvian society. Foremost, of course, is the prevalence of social prejudices against Indians in Lima and the barriers to social mobility based on race. The story may reflect some of Manco y Ayllón's own frustrations. In the story, even descent from Inca nobility doesn't create social legitimacy: the protagonist must seek other channels, such as the military. Even so, he remains condemned as an outsider for his connections to Andean culture.

This story, together with a number of articles in both the newspapers edited by Manco y Ayllón and Enrique del Campo respectively, reveal a social awareness of the disadvantages affecting artisans and workers. *El Artesano,* for example, denounced the fact that patrons often failed to pay artisans adequately for their services. It portrayed the situation as one in which artisans remained powerless in the face of influential individuals: "The one who abuses is a gentleman with numerous connections, either in the Government, the militia, in the financial sector, in the magistracy or in the courts, and what can be done against such an individual?"[43] Even with recourse to a fair judge, the artisan lacked the resources to pursue the legal path. The author of the article claimed to know many artisans who had faced such abuses.[44] This specific complaint about artisans is followed, in the same article, by a complaint about the ways politicians manipulate artisans for electoral purposes. The article equates artisans with the working class: "It is well known to all that anyone with a set of [political] aspirations makes constant promises, and that none of the classes into which our society is divided has been more showered at all times with promises than the working class."[45]

The defense of artisans sometimes clashed directly with liberal ideals. At one level this clash stemmed from the evident distance of liberals from the everyday concerns of the artisans they sought to turn into citizens. The issue of Sunday schools is a case in point. In contrast to *El Hijo del Pueblo* (the newspaper of the elite-run society Los Hijos del Pueblo), which suggested that people attend Sunday school even on Easter Sunday, *El Artesano* took a more realistic view on the issue.[46] While it supported Sunday schools and praised the Sociedad de Artesanos de Auxilios Mutuos for organizing one, it also commented on the difficulty for workers to attend such schools on their only day of rest: "We will not deny the importance of such an institution, but we believe that it will not produce the expected results for the simple reason that, as Sunday is the artisan's only day of rest, since he dedicates the other six days of the week to work in order to support himself and his family, he must necessarily dedicate this day to rest."[47] The problem was compounded by the duties imposed by the National Guard, whose participants needed to be available two Sundays a month.

The newspaper pointed to the hardships facing artisans required to participate in the National Guard, one of Manuel Pardo and the Civilistas' main projects. Pardo reorganized the National Guard during the 1870s and saw it as a quintessentially republican institution that would increase the power of civilians over the military. *El Artesano* addressed the issue of the economic hardships presented by artisan participation in the National Guard. One article criticized a move by the heads of regiments to give up their salaries to benefit the institution, as this would create pressure for officers under them to do likewise:

> The opposite occurs with these officers. Formed primarily of artisans who have no other capital or income than that produced by their personal labor, and since most of them are heads of a household, how could they fulfill their obligations, if, as we previously stated, they chose to emulate their superiors and also renounce their salaries? They will then be forced to miss their obligations to their family in order to demonstrate to their leaders that they are not indifferent to the patriotic sentiment that moves them.[48]

In another article on the issue, the newspaper mentioned the hardship imposed on an artisan who would normally bring in two soles a day but had to participate in the National Guard, where he would be paid only sixty centavos a day.[49] The newspaper also addressed the issue of forced recruitment of artisans and denounced a specific incident in which members of the 6th Battalion of the National Guard broke into the shop of an artisan given the pseudonym Radials, who lived on the street Descalzas, with the pretext of looking for men evading service.[50]

In its pages, *El Artesano* dealt with immediate issues affecting artisans, such as the rising prices of food and rents in the city of Lima: "The immoderate rise in the price of properties that has now been prevalent for a long time and that grows worse every day is now followed by a rise in the price of meat. And to further alarm the people with the awful prospect of pauperism that awaits them, they are now faced with the new eviction law that gives property owners greater security and guarantees."[51] It also informed on specific incidents, such as the smaller-scale denunciation of the theft of a jeweler's shop, and assumed a civic role by criticizing politicians in Congress for their numerous absences due to "illness."

El Artesano also echoed long-standing sectoral concerns on the issue of protectionism. It called for the government to give work to national artisans: "They have ordered from Europe or from the United States what is needed for equipping the offices of the State, for the army uniforms and for the constructions made by the supreme Government, by the Municipality, etc., even though we could have manufactured them."[52] The shift toward foreign suppliers had come with the process of liberal reforms. By the 1860s, a reader of Lima's newspapers could find advertisements such as that of the London firm Lawrence Philipps and Sons, listing goods such as "uniforms and clothing for the navy, army and diplomatic corps...swords and sheaths for the navy and army."[53] Yet the issue of protectionism, so prominent during earlier decades, now formed only part of a broader call by the newspapers for artisans to exercise their rights as citizens.

Artisan Citizenship

The artisan press of the 1870s reflected none of the ambiguity expressed by liberals about the political role of artisans. Liberal publications had been intended primarily to educate the masses rather than to mobilize them as a conscious political sector. For example, the newspaper *El Hijo del Pueblo* (1864 and 1868), published by liberal intellectuals, saw itself specifically as expressing the views of the mutual aid society Los Hijos del Pueblo, whose aim was to "further the moral progress and enlightenment of the masses."[54] While *El Hijo del Pueblo* emphasized education, *El Artesano* presented itself from the outset as a vehicle for expressing the demands of artisans. In its opening editorial, *El Artesano* stated that artisans had rights and duties and needed to participate in public affairs, particularly when their interests were at stake:

> His position remains the same, and suffering disappointments on
> a daily basis, the artisan has had to silence his voice and even his
> feelings due to the lack of a medium of his own to make himself

heard, and at the same time he has not forgotten his rightful
duties nor his sacred obligations. Such a lamentable situation
cannot continue; it is necessary for artisans, reinforcing their
word, to take part in public affairs, and particularly when their
own interests are being discussed, when others seek to dominate
them or when their best intentions are maliciously distorted or
undeserved charges are launched against them, of which we have
some sad examples.[55]

El Obrero echoed this position and stated that "the people and only the people
must direct its destinies and be the legislator of its democratic institutions."[56]

What was meant by citizenship? The artisan press reveals the development
of an artisan conception of citizenship, a blend of liberalism and earlier corporate political traditions. On the one hand, the conception of
citizenship presented in these newspapers followed classic liberal paradigms
of the need for individual citizens to make their political choices based on
reason. On the other, the definition of citizenship was strongly skewed to
favor artisans and workers—there are thus echoes of the old notion of corporate privileges as these groups claim a special status as citizens.

In an article titled "A Worker's Ambitions," *El Artesano* outlined the elements of good citizenship. The newspaper strongly emphasized independence
and reason. The good citizen would fulfill his duties "not according to what
this or the other person told him, but rather as advised by healthy reason."[57]
He would "guide himself mainly on the basis of his good judgement."[58]
Citizens would take interest in the affairs of the nation by participating in
elections, avoiding revolutionary activity, and abiding by the laws. They would
also be patriotic and therefore ready to defend the fatherland in case of attack.

While echoing liberal conceptions of citizenship, the newspapers also
moved beyond the ideal public sphere imagined by liberals to take into
account the realities of politics. After two decades of electoral politics, artisans had become wary of the attention lavished on them during elections.
Both *El Artesano* and *El Obrero* expressed concern that politicians would
manipulate artisans in their favor. The newspapers strongly insisted on artisan nonpartisanship and cautioned against political manipulation of artisans for electoral purposes. For example, the article "A Worker's Ambition"
cautioned workers not to become the pawns of politicians, warning that they
"should not allow themselves to be dazzled by the sonorous phrases of demagogues or of political [merchandisers]."[59] The newspaper also criticized

political clubs for their role in manipulating artisans.[60] In *El Obrero,* an article titled "The Issue of Elections and the Working Class" criticized the manipulation that occurred during elections. While workers should be involved in politics, they should also remain above the passions associated with political parties: "The worker must not be indifferent to political issues, nor should he be a mute witness of discussions; neither should he be a blind instrument of the passions, nor of the parties fighting for control in the electoral field."[61]

El Artesano presented itself primarily as a newspaper for artisans and as a means for artisans to participate in public affairs by influencing public opinion. Artisans, it claimed, constituted the majority of the citizenry: "A portion of citizens who perhaps constitute the majority of the Republic seeks for the first time to present themselves to public opinion, to fulfill the important role that nature itself assigns them and that their social position demands of them."[62] The editors of *El Artesano* referred to themselves as artisans and invited other artisans to participate in the newspaper: "In the name of our own interests, of our own public education, of our social advantage, of our advancement, of the advancement of the arts, of political tranquility and of national prosperity, we invite our brother artisans of Peru to work and to help the editors of `El Artesano.'"[63] The newspaper struck chords beyond the confines of Lima, as indicated by the receipt of letters from members of artisan societies in the Andean towns of Cusco and Huánuco. These letters and the fact that various artisan societies were advertising their meetings in the newspaper suggest a national readership among artisans.

While the artisan press opened its pages to artisans and workers, it also insisted on the need for education. Education, it claimed, constituted a primary tool for workers to assert their political rights. In this sense, the artisan press conformed to liberal ideas but also went much further than liberals by advocating that workers defend their own political rights: an educated working class would have knowledge of its rights. One article in *El Artesano* made this connection clear: "Can someone ignorant of his rights and duties be a good citizen? Impossible. And how can a person learn these rights? By receiving education and by not being exposed to the bad faith of this or that individual willing to take advantage of other people's ignorance and to turn others into instruments of his own designs."[64] The article warned that lack of education could lead artisans to be swayed by demagogues, including revolutionaries.

While advocating political empowerment, the artisan press firmly rejected both socialism and any kind of revolutionary activity. One article spelled this out in no uncertain terms by citing "the English maxim: 'better a bad government than a good revolution.'"[65] As early as the 1858 protests, artisan announcements in the city newspapers took distance from violent protest.[66] By the 1870s, the power of popular violence had once again been felt in the city of Lima when in 1872 an uprising by the people of Lima against the military coup of the Gutierrez brothers had ended in bloodshed. The coup, organized by a group of military officers, the Gutiérrez brothers, had intended to prevent Pardo from taking power. The officers were killed by a mob of protesters, and the bodies of brothers were hung from the towers of Lima's cathedral. The city's inhabitants were reminded of the dangers of popular political participation. Artisans quickly took distance from the image of a disorderly populace. In their petition to President Pardo, cited at the outset of the chapter, they denounced revolutionaries "who try to make us appear like an idiotic people who overthrow those whom we applauded yesterday."[67]

By emphasizing the pursuit of political goals at the level of public opinion, *El Artesano* also clearly distanced itself from political protests. *El Artesano* was quite emphatic in rejecting protest as a means of political action. In a number of places, the newspaper warned artisans against revolution. A letter to the readers, signed with the pseudonym Compás, affirmed the need for order and rejected protest: "My party, like that of all artisans, is the party of order and it could not be otherwise, as political revolts bring nothing but irreparable losses."[68] In stressing its adherence to peaceful politics, *El Artesano* contributed to reinforce the image of the artisan as respectable citizen.

Work as the Basis for Political Legitimacy: Liberal and Religious Traditions

Just as artisan discourse combined elements of classical liberalism with older traditions of corporate privilege, it also drew on both liberalism and older Catholic ideas to emphasize the legitimacy of artisans as workers. *El Artesano* argued that artisans were the hardworking citizens envisioned by liberals and had rights of citizenship derived from their role as workers.[69] In 1855 Juan Espinoza, author of the *Diccionario del pueblo,* acknowledged the power of workers but claimed that they lacked political awareness.[70] Two decades later, in his speech accepting the candidacy for the Partido Civil, Manuel Pardo referred to the "laboring men who constitute the nation."[71] The connection between labor and citizenship was reinforced by drawing on religion. An article titled "The Dogma of Work" presented the Catholic view that work was man's way of expiating for Adam's original sin; hence "the divine origin of the artisan," whose role as worker fulfilled a mission from a religious perspective. Furthermore, Christ had not been a monarch who resided in a luxurious castle but a carpenter who sought "the support, the guidance and the advice of an artisan; this strengthens our position, and demonstrates once again the divine nature of work, the sublime quality of that great apostolate of workers."[72]

By affirming that the artisan played a central role from a moral point of view, the newspaper sought to further legitimize artisan demands. Anyone who opposed artisans, the article claimed, also opposed God: "The enemies of this guild [artisans] can therefore be called impious; they contradict the commands of the Eternal One, they rebel against the mandates of the Sovereign Architect, that Worker without an equal, that Artisan *par excellence*; they are criminals."[73]

The artisan discourse made a clear distinction between the moral and the social role of the artisan. Having made a religious argument, the author of this piece goes on to make a secular one. From a social perspective, the artisan also had a role to play: his hard work would serve as an example to other members of society: "He is a living doctrine, a living book, and with his example he helps to moralize and perfect his fellow men."[74] This argument drew not on the religious notion of artisans fulfilling a divine mandate but rather on the secular notion, going back to the Enlightenment, of improvement through education and experience.

From this discourse emerged an idealized conception of the artisan as a paradigm of saintly virtue and family values:

> Review the ranks of the artisanry, and together with robust health, you will find among them a scarcity of illness, a quietude of spirit, and a face glowing with happiness by the side of an honest wife, surrounded by agile and robust children, who constitute his hope; finally you will find him in the company of his friends and companions, which is what most satisfies a working man.[75]

Work was considered the supreme virtue, standing above even liberty and patriotism: "But it is no less true that liberty inspires great actions when combined with love of the fatherland. . . . The love of work is the first of all social virtues."[76] Artisans could act as a bulwark against the forces of atheism, a doctrine considered to have been invented by those averse to working.

The newspaper highlighted the inherent utility of artisans and their work to society through contrasts with other social groups. A letter signed "Ricardo" complained that artisans were not valued as they should be. The letter pointed out that while the murder of two army colonels had received much publicity, the murder of an artisan elicited no such attention. The situation is referred to in verse:

This makes me realize
That in this cruel world
If one is to be assassinated
It is better to be a colonel
The life of an artisan;
Is not even worth an anise seed
While that of a Peruvian officer
Is worth an entire Potosí[77]

It is noteworthy that the author compares artisans to one of the highest ranks in the military.

The letter claimed that the work of artisans was as socially useful as that of soldiers: "Meanwhile, I consider an artisan to be as much a man as any other and that society in particular and the Fatherland in general can be served as well with a needle, a hammer. . . the pencil, paintbrush and so many other tools of the liberal and mechanical arts as it can be by a soldier with a sword, a rifle or a drum."[78] In another case the hardworking artisan is contrasted to the wealthy young men who spend their time drinking and gambling. In a fictional vignette, artisans encounter some wealthy young men in a bar. While honest artisans work from six in the morning to six in the evening, these wealthy youth lived on their inheritance.[79]

The figure of the hardworking artisan was accompanied by direct references to issues of social injustice through the image of the suffering artisan, described in the following terms: "Here are a group of misunderstood and poorly treated beings."[80] The suffering artisan is presented as a patriotic individual willing to selflessly sacrifice for his nation, "each of his own accord, helping to make the fatherland great, to which he has sacrificed so many times with the greatest abnegation and without the least bit of self-interest."[81] The following passage from the first issue of the newspaper sets the tone for an image of suffering that recurs at other points in the newspaper and reiterates the notion that the artisan has not previously had a voice: "The artisan, who has always kept silent even after the most bitter disappointments, dedicated exclusively to his austere work, has had his tranquility exploited one thousand times, and at other times his dearest hopes have been shattered and mocked."[82]

The reaffirmation of the artisan as outstanding citizen contributed to challenge long-standing social prejudices against artisans and manual labor. *El Artesano* made reference to the phenomenon of empleomanía (reliance on government employment) and contrasted the independence of artisans with the servile nature of public servants who relied on the government:

> those who disdain the thought of taking a tool in their hands and yet have no remorse at staining their hands in other ways. Those who think they would lower their dignity by dedicating themselves to an art and yet don't find it indecorous to kneel down, and risk breaking their backbone, before a magnate asking for a position that would give them a salary that drains the Budget.[83]

In the face of such prejudice, *El Artesano* reaffirmed a sense of artisan pride: "For if now I am a writer as I am writing, I am also an artisan, and this does not weigh upon me but rather causes me pride."[84] The author of this article explains that the source of his pride is his self-sufficiency and ability to satisfy his own needs.[85]

In addition to stressing artisan independence, the political discourse of the period may have also drawn on an older sense of artisan pride that predated liberalism. Historians of other regions have noted the phenomenon of artisan pride. Ronald Schultz discusses this pride in his study of Philadelphia artisans in the transition from colony to nation:

> Perhaps the oldest notion in the artisan's lexicon was the sense of pride that craftsmen derived from the social utility of their labor. We have lost much of this feeling today, but for an artisan, work was never merely physical labor performed for a requisite number of hours each day. Whether laying the keel of an oceangoing merchantman or fashioning something as simple and prosaic as a shoe, craftsmen looked upon useful labor as a moral and social, as well as an economic act. This was not self-serving rhetoric....

Before the rise of widespread markets and advanced manufacturing processes, the everyday functioning of all communities rested on the artisan's vital contribution to the local economy.[86]

Despite the prejudices against manual labor in the Hispanic world, artisans had held a similarly important position within the preindustrial urban economies.

A specific reference to pride in the work of national artisans appears in an article discussing the construction of a church in the city's port Callao. The Matriz church in the port was being built by Peruvian artisans: "Don Pedro Ortega, who worked on the monitor *Victoria,* [a battleship] today holds the position of director of the construction of the *matriz* (church). He is an honest and intelligent artisan, a true patriot and founder of the 'Society of Artisans' of Callao." The author asserted the dignity of the artisan by referring to the Bellavista Naval Foundry: "Its diverse machines, its capacity and the order that prevails, attest to the fact the leadership is good and that the workers are not vulgar welders but rather masters in their profession."[87]

Defining a Working Class

While *El Artesano* focused primarily on specific artisan grievances and occasionally equated artisans with the working class, *El Obrero* claimed more consistently to be the voice of the working class. The notion of the working class eventually appeared in the title of *El Obrero*—in 1877 the forty-fourth issue of the newspaper was subtitled *"organo de la clase obrera"* (the voice of the working class).[88] The newspaper presented itself as the voice of the working class: "*El Obrero,* whose sole object is to serve as a medium for the republic's numerous working class, and especially that of Lima and Callao, will publish any article sent to it either by artisans or others, as long as it corresponds to the objective of the newspaper, and avoids dealing with political issues, hurting personal sensibilities or offending public morals."[89] The sober tone of the newspaper echoed the changes in the political culture of the 1870s, accelerated by Manuel Pardo and the Civilistas, that sought to bring a greater civility to the political process.

Who composed this working class, according to *El Obrero*? Artisans clearly held a somewhat privileged place within it. An article titled "The Life of the Lima Typesetter" complained that typesetters had even fewer hours of leisure than artisans. While the article clearly presented a highly idealized conception of the life of the artisan, the distinction in lifestyle that it pointed to suggests that the mechanization of labor in printing presses was creating new pressures on workers:

> The carpenter, the mason, the blacksmith, and even the Chinese, whose condition is seemingly a sad one, have the first hours of the evening at their disposal and use them to go to theater, and to enjoy that productive sociability so necessary for those who aspire to beauty: they read when and what they want, they invent something useful, and in general take advantage of that time for whatever they wish to do. The printer, on the other hand, goes from the workshop to bed and from bed to the workshop.[90]

Another article that admonished workers to become educated and be knowledgeable about society's affairs further suggests a social distinction between artisans and workers, with artisans at the top of the hierarchy. It used the term *artisan* rather than *worker* when urging individuals to become politically educated: "The artisan must study political, social and economic matters so that he will not become the instrument of those who claim to be our tutors. Civilization, in accordance with our interests, advises it. The Gospel itself says, 'Help yourself and I will help you.'"[91]

Together with artisans, *El Obrero* considered typesetters as central to this "working class." The content of many of the articles seemed geared toward typesetters. A column that covered a number of issues titled "Memories of a Typesetter" chronicled the travels of a typesetter. Another column gave the history of Gutenberg and the printing press. Beyond these two groups, *El Obrero* remains somewhat vague about other occupations.

The working class as defined by *El Obrero* had strongly religious values. The first issue of the newspaper emphasized the religious convictions of the working class. Referring to the newspaper, this first issue stated: "For...it will be the instrument of the working class, and its voice, although lacking eloquence, will be the sincere word stemming from true feeling, living desires and the firm conviction of those who live in strict fulfillment of the Divine mandates."[92] In an article that continued over a number of issues titled "The Working Class and the Future," political rights were traced back to Christ, who was considered a forerunner of various eighteenth- and nineteenth-century thinkers both in the liberal and socialist traditions:

FIG. 12. *The newspaper* El Obrero, *1875 (Biblioteca Nacional del Perú).*

Nineteen centuries ago a martyr sacrificed himself on the summits
of the Golgotha and proclaimed a holy doctrine. Let us study it
in depth and we will know our rights. Later other apostles of
humanity have preached and proclaimed the rights of man:
Rousseau, Volney, Diderot, Lammenais, Luis Blanc, Bérander,
Adam Schmit [sic], Proudhon and others. Let us read their
works and our reason will be the true judge.[93]

Such a mixture of ideological traditions, a blend of Catholic and Enlightenment traditions, is not unusual in *El Obrero.*

The article "Modern Societies" also displayed this ideological eclecti-
cism by discussing the concept of citizen rights in the United States in
terms of French social theorist and anarchist Pierre Joseph Proudhon
(1809–65). The United States is presented as an example of a country that
upholds the rights of its citizens: "There, on the banks of the Mississippi
and the Hudson, liberty and the rights of the citizen are such palpable
truths that they can be felt by every citizen, from the first to the last."[94]
The author claimed that while Proudhon's ideas could be considered sub-
versive in Europe, this was not the case in the United States. Europe maintained an unjust land tenure system, with the wealthy holding vast
amounts of land that never benefited proletarians. The United States, on
the other hand, had a fairer distribution of property than any other country in the world.

El Obrero portrayed the working class as part of society's march
toward progress in the terms expounded by the nation's liberal leaders.
Thus, manual workers were advised to cultivate their spirit: "The worker,
because his work is purely physical, must not think himself removed from
this law common to all men: the need to cultivate his spirit."[95] The article
titled "A Step Forward" praised artisan Miguel Melgar, schooled at the
Sociedad Amantes del Saber, who gave a talk on physics.[96] In its adherence to liberal values, *El Obrero* resembled its predecessor *El Artesano,*
which had defended a number of liberal causes, including the call for voluntary associations. *El Artesano* strongly praised the Sociedad de
Artesanos of Cuzco (which had just organized an "exposition") and
invoked artisans to form similar associations.[97] *El Obrero* ran moralizing
articles such as the piece "The Science of Man," published over a number
of issues and intended to instill moral virtues in the reader. Both newspapers openly declared their adherence to liberal principles:

Regarding politics, [the newspaper] will uphold public peace, the constitutional regime and liberal principles: it will disregard party colors, will do justice to all: it will forcefully demand the reforms needed for the advancement of the arts: and, although naturally its word will lack eloquence, it will be full of truth and good faith, sincere love of the fatherland.[98]

The sober tone (in contrast to that of other newspapers, which put themselves in the fray of politics with political satires and open criticisms of politicians) indicated the affinity of both newspapers to liberal sensibilities. *El Artesano* even ran an obituary of liberal polemicist Simeón Tejeda, who had openly criticized the guilds.[99]

The adherence to liberal ideas translated into support for the Civilistas. Despite its avowed apolitical stance, *El Obrero* took sides within the Peruvian political spectrum with Pardo and the liberal Civilistas. The newspaper openly criticized conservative Nicolás de Piérola, who had been minister of the treasury in 1869 under the presidency of Balta and had pursued a policy of deficit spending relying on guano resources in order to finance railroad building.[100] Pardo's government initiated legal proceedings against Pierola and other members of the Balta government, accusing them of the country's disastrous economic situation. Piérola in turn launched a failed coup against Pardo and spent much of the decade in exile, plotting to return to politics.

The praise of the working class went hand in hand with a classic liberal critique of various aspects of popular culture. The pages of *El Obrero* echoed the liberal rhetoric on the need to reshape working-class culture to conform to new "civilized" standards. Funerals were a frequent subject of criticism. The pomp and the fact that families incurred debt to pay for such funerals were deemed inappropriate for a civilized country. Associated with "the centuries of obscurantism," these religious customs were unbefitting to the nineteenth century, an enlightened century. In specific reference to the ensuing impoverishment for an artisan family, one article commented: "Is this not an embarrassment in a civilized country?"[101] The author recommended that funerals be conducted with less pomp: "Let us carry the body of our deceased one to the general cemetery without pomp or ostentation, and let us use those soles that we would have spent on songs and lights to meet our most pressing needs."[102]

In the article "Burials with the Corpse in State" we find a similar criticism.

The article supported a government ruling that would reduce outward displays of religiosity and complained of the fact that workers had to spend excessively on funerals. The critique of popular culture echoed classic liberal views dating to the period of Bourbon reforms in the late eighteenth century. A common target of such reforms was the perceived excessive lavishness of popular religious rituals. During the eighteenth century, a number of edicts had attempted to regulate religious rituals, including prohibitions of nighttime celebrations in churches and limits on displays of fireworks.[103]

The reformist impulse extended beyond religious mores to general habits, including everyday behavior in the streets and popular entertainment such as cockfights. An article titled "The Police" suggested that the police play a role in reforming popular customs and thus bringing progress to the nation. The United States, as in various other articles, appeared as an exemplary nation. The police in the United States played an important role in keeping people away from lives of vice and turning them into citizens—although no explicit example is offered. In Peru some improvements had occurred between 1864 and 1875, but still the Peruvian police fell short of their task. Policemen in the city simply stood at city corners, disregarding the uncivilized behavior around them. The following passage is worth quoting at length because it also offers an image of daily life during the period:

> He does not see that a carrier comes down the sidewalk rolling
> a barrel and has the insolence to obstruct pedestrians, he does
> not see that a cook with her pots puts such a large stain on our
> clothing that it cannot be removed except by buying another set
> of clothes, that a glassmaker transporting glass under his arm
> will either lift up your garments or will leave one of your children
> blind in one eye, that a vehicle rounding a corner goes up on
> the sidewalk and destroys it, that from such and such a balcony
> someone throws onto whomever is passing by waters that are
> not perfumed.[104]

The police were presented as potential agents of enlightened reform. In a fanciful vignette of what life ought to be like, the police were criticized for mistreating street drunkards rather than reasoning with them and convincing them to relinquish their bad habits.

The critique of popular customs extended to Peru's Indian population. In the pages of *El Obrero*, the Indians, who made up the majority of Peru's population, were considered uncivilized in their customs. A small series of articles about the Andean region reveals the view of indigenous populations as still "barbaric" and engaged in "uncivilized" religious rituals.

Radical Ideas of Class

Together with more mainstream liberal conceptions, *El Obrero* occasionally presented a bolder class analysis in its pages. In some instances *El Obrero* pointed to the potentially conflictive relationship between social classes, and some articles in the newspaper reveal the influence of socialist ideas. In his study of liberalism, Gavarito Amézaga notes the existence of a radical tradition in nineteenth-century Peru, albeit a minoritarian one, that included the famous Chilean radical Francisco Bilbao, who was exiled to Lima during the 1850s.[105] The surfacing of socialist ideas at certain points indicates the heterogeneity of artisan thought and the persistence of more radical groups among the artisanry. While mutual aid societies and newspapers primarily subscribed to republican values, clearly certain groups offered a more radical analysis. In May 1875, a few months after the paper first appeared, *El Obrero* fired a group of writers for presenting ideas considered too radical.

These ideas appeared in an article titled "The Worker and His Moral Conditions." The article stressed the need for education as a means of improving the lives of artisans but also pointed to deeper inequalities inherent in society. It claimed that the miserable condition of artisans was due to their ignorance and their indifference. In contrast to the usual liberal recipe of education for the masses, this article pointed to deeper social maladies: "Undoubtedly, with respect to the distribution of wealth and social welfare, labor has had the worst part. The enormous injustice of our century is the obvious exploitation of labor by capital."[106] Another article praised advances in industry but noted the latent class conflict in society: "Despite the opposition that exists in Peru between the wealthy and the working class, it is undeniable that some advances have been made in industry as evidenced by the 1872 Exposition, but still the situation remains deficient."[107] The article expressed the hope that workers would save and become property owners but pointed out that in order to save, workers needed to be paid better wages.

One of the most poignant portrayals of the relationship between classes dwelt on the fact that workers could not enjoy the benefits of the very products they themselves make: "The weaver whose hands have produced such beautiful cloths shivers with cold under the thin cloth of his dress, the printer does not nourish his spirit with the book that he has put together, the mason lives in the filthiest house, and all of them thus have access only to the last and worst of the things they have produced, as they are the only ones they can afford with their salaries."[108] In no subtle terms, the article thus touched on the socialist theme of worker alienation.

An article titled "The Working Class and the Future," written by M. F. Horta, a expressed radical ideas beyond the tolerance of the newspaper's editorial board. The article historicized class conflict and engaged in a criticism of religion that led the author to be dismissed from the newspaper. The history of humanity, the article argued, could be seen as the history of oppressors and oppressed. In a reflection of a classic Enlightenment theme, the author portrayed priests as instruments of oppression in an unjust world. The oppressors "abused certain beliefs and natural practices, inventing vengeful gods that protected tyranny, offering eternal life after life on this earth, in an ethereal region for those who suffered with patience the whip of their oppressors, and who like docile lambs followed the route pointed to by their pastors of divine right."[109] Eventually, the French Revolution brought liberation and workers finally broke their chains and overthrew the villains who had been oppressing them. The article proclaimed the values of "Liberty, Equality and Fraternity," praised the French Revolution, and excused the bloodshed by pointing to the achievements of the revolution: "Until last century, a people joined efforts and proclaimed to the world the rights of man, broke the chains that enslaved it, and asked its executioners to account for their crimes and atrocities, and the sharp blade of the guillotine was tainted with the blood of thousands of wolves."[110]

Such radical ideas with echoes of atheism were too extreme for *El Obrero,* which openly declared itself a liberal newspaper. While *El Obrero* upheld the separation of church and state, it was careful to take distance from any atheistic position. After three installments of the article praising the French Revolution by Horta, *El Obrero* ran an editorial distancing the newspaper from the views of this author: "We cannot accept the negations, guised as philosophical ideas of the eighteenth century, made by one of our contributors in his third article titled 'The Working Class and the Future.'"[111] A brief notice following the editorial announced the departure of a group of members of the society that printed the newspaper, including Horta.

Conclusion

The emergence of a language of class in the artisan press of the 1870s marked a new stage in artisan politics, clearly differentiated from the early guild-based politics. Within the new liberal order artisans succeeded in developing a political identity that transcended their separate crafts. While using the language of class to further their political interests, artisans did not stray far from mainstream liberal values and asserted their allegiance to the republican project while taking distance from any form of revolutionary action. Theirs was a pragmatic position: they sought to strengthen their political position without offending liberal elites. The harsh government reaction against the 1858 protests stood as a reminder of the forces of order in Peruvian society.

For artisan leaders, the invocation of a working class offered the opportunity for political involvement on the basis of a pride that broke down traditional guild-based identification and extended beyond master artisans to potentially encompass the entire working population. Such a discourse thus challenged long-standing prejudices against the mechanical trades and lifted the artisan to a central position within the emerging republican political culture. This affirmation of social and political respectability was no small step for artisans, whose dignity had traditionally been called into question both as a result of their occupation, considered menial, and of their racial status as Indians, blacks, and mestizos.

Conclusion

WHILE THIS BOOK TELLS THE STORY OF the persistence of artisans inspired by liberalism's promises of citizenship and equality, it also tells the story of the limitations of the nineteenth-century liberal state and of the disappointments of many thousands of men and women who did not see liberalism's promises fulfilled. Artisans clearly constituted a middle sector, hailed by liberals as hardworking and as potential model citizens, but these artisans never became the prosperous middle class envisioned by liberals as an engine of national progress. The mobility available through education and through the formation of voluntary associations had its limits in a society where racial and social hierarchies continued to matter. By the 1870s, a worldwide depression together with the failings of the guano-based prosperity made dreams of progress seem all the more distant for artisans and others in Peru. Soon thereafter, the War of the Pacific and Chilean invasion further shattered liberal dreams. Its aftermath ushered in a new era of national soul-searching and a greater awareness of the fact that most Peruvians still lacked a voice within the national polity.

Following the war and as the nineteenth-century drew to a close, a working class gained prominence in Peru as it did throughout Latin America. I have argued in this book that Lima's artisans played an important role in the making of a Peruvian working class. Peru's first syndicalist confederation, founded in 1878, bore the name "Confederación de Artesanos 'Unión Universal.'" While this study does not intend to trace the origins of subsequent labor movements, it has attempted to show that many liberal paradigms contributed to the early definition of a working class among artisans in Lima. The story of a modern working class began with artisans' struggles as they came to terms with liberalism.

This study has sought to trace these struggles and has asked: How did artisans respond to liberal reforms and contribute to the process of nation building? The predominant image in the historiography is one of artisans defeated by liberal reform, in particular by the arrival of free-trade regimes that introduced a series of products that competed with national production. Yet evidence suggests that artisans not only survived the transition toward a commercial policy of free trade but actually strengthened their position with the establishment of the liberal state. They did so by creating a number of new institutions ranging from mutual aid societies to artisan newspapers. Lima's artisans thus developed a distinct national political presence and maintained a sense of pride based on their adherence to patriotic values. Within the liberal polity artisans sought to increase their prestige and respectability.

I have argued that the emergence of a polity based on republican principles set the stage for artisans to actively seek integration as citizens in the new nation. From the earliest years following independence from Spain in 1821, artisans in Lima figured as active participants in the political arena. During the first decades of republican life, when the issue of commercial policy occupied a prominent place in political debates, artisans supported protectionist policies that would limit the influx of imported goods competing with artisan production. The city's guilds were sufficiently well organized to join in a common cause and petition the national congress to legislate in favor of protectionist policies. When the tide turned toward economic liberalism, artisans engaged in protests and subsequently demanded that the state offer technical training to help them compete with foreign products.

By the 1870s, artisans had succeeded in presenting themselves as productive citizens and cornerstones of national prosperity. They had published two newspapers of their own and had even managed to have an artisan elected to the national congress in 1876. Over the course of the first half century of the national period, colonial social hierarchies and attitudes toward manual labor had been challenged to such a degree in public discourse that artisans were able to present themselves as central to national well-being. This is not to say that prejudices and social hierarchies did not persist in Lima society. Yet by subscribing to new definitions of citizenship set forth by liberal reformers and by embracing various liberal institutions, artisans sought to distance themselves from their colonial identity based on racial categories.

Artisans have traditionally been portrayed as casualties of the process of liberal reform that gained strength in many parts of Spanish America at midcentury. Historians have noted the uneasy relationship between artisans and liberal elites throughout Latin America, and for the most part liberalism has been seen as damaging to artisan interests.[1] This view is not surprising given the often-vociferous protests of artisans against policies that put them in competition with foreign goods. The Callao protest of 1858 described in this book—a "Peruvian tea party" of sorts—is certainly an important example of artisan hostility to liberal political economy.

Perhaps the visible instances of opposition to economic liberalism have hidden the numerous ways artisans interacted with liberal elites and contributed to the broader liberal nation-building project. This study has shown that artisans were linked to elites in numerous ways. During the 1850s, 1860s, and 1870s the economic stability brought about by the guano boom enabled the state and liberal elites to make substantial efforts to build the institutions of a democratic society. These efforts had their counterparts among artisans with the formation of artisan mutual aid societies and newspapers. The liberal nation-building project thus had echoes among artisans, who had already been politically mobilized in earlier decades during the period of caudillo politics.

Over the course of the period studied, the way artisans viewed and presented themselves changed significantly. Compare the way the cigar maker García referred to artisans in his presentation to Congress in favor of protectionism in 1849, with the rhetoric of a petition protesting the rise in rents in 1872. In 1849, García presented his case, excusing artisans who might not be considered worthy of participating in politics: "It does not perhaps befit an artisan to address these issues of such high interest and whose effects will have such a great impact."[2] By contrast, the 1872 petition asking for lower rents begins by stating the centrality of artisans to the body politic: "By virtue of the fact that artisans constitute the majority of the citizens who form the political association of the nation, they have the right to take the initiative."[3] The printed word allowed artisans to leave behind some of the deference that characterized personal addresses and to take on a much bolder rhetorical stance.

While subscribing to many aspects of liberal ideology, artisans also challenged liberalism by continuing to identify as a distinct social sector and by eventually adopting the language of class. In a society beleaguered by the economic failings of export-led growth and marked by persistent social hierarchies, the hardworking "sons of the country" failed to become the propertied middle class envisioned by liberals. Instead, artisans challenged the liberal model of society by voicing their political demands in the press and becoming increasingly identified as a working class.

The story of Lima's artisans sheds light on the difficulties of liberal nation building in the postcolonial scenario. The language of liberalism allowed artisans to leave behind the colonial guilds and cofradías to seek full membership as citizens in the liberal polity. The language of class gradually emerged as a powerful political tool, and as artisans came to formulate a class identity, they challenged the liberal model of the polity. By the 1870s, the very category "artisans" had ceased to be merely an occupational descriptor and became an integral part of the period's political culture. By speaking out and participating in politics, the shoemakers, tailors, carpenters, cigar makers, and printers of Lima helped to forge the young Peruvian nation.

Notes

Introduction

1. Thanks to lack of rainfall, guano, bird dung, accumulated over millennia on numerous islands off the Peruvian coast.

2. See Paul Gootenberg, *Between Silver and Guano* (Princeton: Princeton University Press, 1989).

3. The most extensive study of nineteenth-century artisans for Peru appears in the works of Paul Gootenberg. Yet Gootenberg's main interest remains elite politics and economic thought. Thus he considers artisan politics primarily from the perspective of elite politics while inviting further study of artisan thought. See Gootenberg, *Silver and Guano*, and *Imagining Development* (Berkeley: University of California Press, 1993).

4. Recent historiography has emphasized the importance of elections in nineteenth-century Latin American politics. See Antonio Annino, ed., *Historia de las elecciones en Iberoamérica, siglo XIX* (Buenos Aires: Fondo de Cultura Economica, 1995).

5. James Sheehan, *German Liberalism in the Nineteenth Century* (Atlantic Highlands, NJ: Humanities Press, 1995), 172.

6. See Frederick Bowser, *The African Slave in Colonial Peru 1524–1650* (Stanford: Stanford University Press, 1974), 125–46.

7. The census is located at the Archivo Histórico Municipal de Lima. It provides racial information on the population of Lima yet at the same time reflects the ambivalence toward the notion of categorizing by race, a hallmark of colonial administration. Race is not included as one of the official categories of information sought by the census: the printed census sheets include no column with the printed category of race. Rather, race has been handwritten in as

an additional category and appears in a final column. While most of the census provides racial information, certain census sheets exclude it.

8. I give the proportions for the entire city from the information provided in the 1876 national census. To my knowledge, the data from the 1866 census for Lima have not yet been processed. I am thus assuming that proportions by race remain unchanged over the ten-year period separating the two censuses.

9. *Plebe,* or *plebeians,* refers to the lower classes. See also note 13.

10. For a discussion pertaining to late-nineteenth-century Mexico of how liberal elites attempted to "moralize the masses" and teach them the values of what liberals considered to be civilized society, see William French, *A Peaceful and Working People* (Albuquerque: University of New Mexico Press, 1996), 63–86.

11. Charles Wagley, *The Latin American Tradition: Essays on the Unity and the Diversity of Latin American Culture* (New York: Columbia University Press, 1968), 166.

12. My argument about artisan respectability parallels that of Thomas Kruggeler in his excellent study of Cusco artisans during the nineteenth century. Kruggeler equates membership in Cusco's artisan mutual aid society with a degree of social respectability by claiming that artisans who belonged to this society were considered *gente decente*—respectable people. The difference between Lima and Cusco artisans lies in their political involvement. While Cusco artisans were removed from national politics during the first half century of the national period, Lima's artisans clearly appeared as actors on the national political arena. See Thomas Kuggeler, "Unreliable Drunkards or Honorable Citizens? Artisans in Search of Their Place in the Cusco Society (1825–1930)" (PhD diss., University of Illinois at Urbana-Champagne, 1993), 166.

13. The term *plebe* was popularized by the work of historian Alberto Flores Galindo, *La ciudad sumergida: aristocracia y plebe en Lima, 1760–1830* (Lima: Editorial Horizonte, 1991), first published in 1984.

14. Fernando Trazegnies, *La idea del derecho, en el Perú republicano del siglo XIX* (Lima: Pontificia Universidad Católica, 1992), 30–35.

15. Torcuato di Tella, "The Dangerous Classes in Early Nineteenth Century Mexico," *Journal of Latin American Studies,* 5, no. 1 (May 1973): 96.

16. John Johnson, *Political Change in Latin America: The Emergence of the Middle Sectors* (Stanford: Stanford University Press, 1958). Johnson's formulation led to intense criticism from the dependency school during the 1960s and 1970s that denied the progressive impetus of the middle sectors and lamented the absence of a European-style "national bourgeoisie" pushing for a capitalist transformation in Latin America. For a detailed discussion of the subsequent scholarly approaches to the issue of the

middle class in twentieth-century Latin America see David Parker, *The Idea of the Middle Class* (University Park: Pennsylvania State University Press), 3–6.

17. Johnson, *Political Change,* 24.

18. Ibid., 5.

19. AHML, Census of Lima 1866.

20. I concur with David Parker's approach and his identification of middle-class identity as a twentieth-century phenomenon: "Peruvians' idea of the middle class was basically an invention of the early twentieth century. At that time, white-collar workers and other similar occupational groups chose to identify themselves explicitly as members of the middle class, in part to gain a sense of identity, but also to lend legitimacy to their fight for social legislation." Parker, *Middle Class,* 6–7. Yet most recent historiography following the decline of Marxist paradigms during the 1980s has turned away from an exploration of the issue of class. As Paulo Drinot points out, the most recent Peruvian historiography shares "an overt or implicit rejection of analyses that prioritize class and Marxism over other analytical categories and theoretical perspectives." Paulo Drinot, "After the Nueva Historia: Recent Trends in Peruvian Historiography," *European Review of Latin American and Caribbean Studies,* no. 68 (April 2000): 70.

21. Ira Katznelson, "Working-Class Formation: Constructing Cases and Comparisons," in *Working-Class Formation,* ed. Ira Katznelson and Aristide Zolberg (Princeton, NJ: Princeton University Press, 1986), 23.

22. E. P. Thompson, *The Making of the English Working Class* (New York: Vintage, 1966), 9.

23. Geoffrey Crossick, *An Artisan Elite in Victorian Society: Kentish London, 1840–1880* (London: Croom Helm, 1978).

24. For the importance of liberalism during the early stages of working-class formation in Mexico, see Maria Elena Diaz, "The Satiric Penny Press for Workers in Mexico, 1900–1910: A Case Study in the Politicisation of Popular Culture," *Journal of Latin American Studies,* 22, no. 3 (October 1990): 497–526.

25. Francois Bourricaud, *Power and Society in Contemporary Peru,* trans. Paul Stevenson (New York: Praeger, 1970), 58.

26. Michael Mann, *The Sources of Social Power.* Vol. II: *The Rise of Classes and Nation-States, 1760–1914* (Cambridge: Cambridge University Press, 1993), 516.

27. For a full account of artisan involvement in these protests, see Francisco Quiroz, *La protesta de los artesanos—Lima-Callao, 1858* (Lima: Universidad Nacional Mayor de San Marcos, 1988). Quiroz includes a number of documents from newspapers and archives relating to the protest.

28. For an account of the participation of Lima's urban populace, including artisans, in these events, see Margarita Giesecke, *Masas urbanas y rebelión en la historia, golpe de estado: Lima 1872* (Lima: Centro de Divulgación de Historia Popular, 1978).

29. This earlier conception had deep roots in traditional liberal historiography and was further reinforced during the 1960s and 1970s by dependency theory. By emphasizing the disadvantages of Latin American economies in the context of a global economy, dependency theory left little room for a study of internal political processes within individual Latin American nations
This problem was partially mitigated in later dependency studies, which gave some degree of agency to national elites rather than portraying them primarily as pawns within an international capitalist system. See Fernando Henrique Cardoso and Enzo Faletto, *Dependency and Development in Latin America* (Berkeley and Los Angeles: University of California Press, 1979).

30. The view can be traced all the way back to the writings of nineteenth-century elites in Latin America. The most poignant expression of this philosophy is to be found in the work of Argentine intellectual and politician Domingo Faustino Sarmiento, whose classic work *Facundo* (1845) portrayed Latin American society as divided between the opposing forces of barbarism and civilization. In the case of countries such as Peru, with a large indigenous population, the pessimism about the possibilities of European style progress has been even more pronounced. The notion that European immigration would contribute to improve the racial stock of Peruvian society became commonplace during the second half of the nineteenth century. The social Darwinism of some Peruvian elites cast the Indian population as a hindrance to modern-style progress and in thinly veiled form continues to mark political discourse today. This dualistic model of society continues to characterize neoliberal thought in the late twentieth century. A good example is the thought of Mario Vargas Llosa, who sees a radical difference between an indigenous Peru and a Westernized Peru and suggests that only further Westernization can bring economic prosperity. See Mario Vargas Llosa, "Questions of Conquest: What Columbus Wrought, and What He Did Not," *Harper's* (December 1990): 43–53.

31. The most sophisticated version of this approach has been presented by Richard Morse, who argues for the continued weight of Iberian political traditions in nineteenth-century Latin America. In Morse's words, "The social, corporatist, and spiritual commitments of the past retained their hold." Richard Morse, *New World Soundings: Culture and Ideology in the Americas* (Baltimore: Johns Hopkins University Press, 1989), 111.

32. Methodologically, Latin American historians have been influenced by the most recent studies of political culture and practices centered primarily

on the French Revolution. See Keith Michael Baker, *Inventing the French Revolution* (Cambridge: Cambridge University Press, 1990).

33. Jürgen Habermas, *The Structural Transformation of the Public Sphere,* trans. Thomas Burger (Cambridge, MA: MIT Press, 1989). François Xavier Guerra argues that the democratic revolutions of the late eighteenth century brought new forms of sociability that clashed with the traditional hierarchies of Latin American society. See François Xavier Guerra, *Modernidad e independencias* (Madrid: Mapfre, 1992), 86–91.

34. For Peru see Cristobal Aljovín, *Caudillos y constituciones Perú 1821–1845* (Lima: Pontificia Universidad Católica y Fundo de Cultura Económica, 2000; for Argentina see Jorge Myers, "Languages of Politics: A Study of Republican Discourse in Argentina from 1820 to 1852" (PhD diss., Stanford University, 1997).

35. Carmen McEvoy, *La utopía republicana: Ideales y realidades en la formación de la cultura política peruana (1871–1919)* (Lima: Pontificia Universidad Católica del Perú, 1997), and Hilda Sábato, *La política en las calles: entre el voto y la movilización, Buenos Aires, 1862–1880* (Buenos Aires: Editorial Sudamericana, 1998). An excellent recent study of nineteenth-century Peruvian political culture supports the idea that the Partido Civil relied on artisans for its 1872 political vitory. See Ulrich Muecke, *Political Culture in Ninteenth-century Peru: The Rise of the Partido Civil.* Translated by Katya Andrusz. (Pittsburgh: University of Pittsburgh Press, 2004).

36. See the articles in Hilda Sábato, ed., *Ciudadanía política y formación de las naciones: perspectivas históricas de América Latina* (Mexico: El Colegio de Mexico y Fondo de Cultura Ecónomica, 1999).

37. See Florencia Mallon, *Peasant and Nation: The Making of Postcolonial Mexico and Peru* (Berkeley: University of California Press, 1995); Mark Thurner, *From Two Republics to One Divided: Contradictions of Post-Colonial Nationmaking in Andean Peru* (Durham: Duke University Press, 1997); Charles Walker, *Smoldering Ashes: Cuzco and the Creation of Republican Peru, 1780–1840* (Durham: Duke University Press, 1999); Sarah Chambers, *From Subjects to Citizens: Humor, Gender, and Politics in Arequipa, Peru 1780–1854* (University Park: Pennsylvania State University Press, 1999); and Richard Andrew Warren, "Elections and Popular Political Participation in Mexico, 1808–1836," in *Liberals, Politics and Power: State Formation in Nineteenth-Century Latin America,* ed. Vincent Peloso and Barbara Tenenbaum (Athens: University of Georgia Press, 1996), 30–58.

38. Walker, *Smoldering Ashes,* 3.

39. Richard Andrew Warren, "Vagrants and Citizens: Politics and the Poor in Mexico City, 1808–1836" (PhD diss., University of Chicago, 1994), 16–17.

40. Mallon, *Peasant and Nation,* 97.

41. Peloso and Tenenbaum, *Liberals,* 4.

42. In Paul Gootenberg's influential study of early national Peru, artisans emerge primarily in this guise. See *Between Silver and Guano,* 46–53. For Colombia see David Sowell, *The Early Colombian Labor Movement* (Philadelphia: Temple University Press, 1992).

43. E. J. Hobsbawm, "Artisans and Labour Aristocrats?" in *Worlds of Labour: Further Studies in the History of Labour* (London: Mendenfeld and Nicolson, 1984), 258.

44. Bruce Laurie, *Artisans into Workers: Labor in Nineteenth-Century America* (New York: Hill and Wang, 1989), 46. A similar moral economy/market economy dichotomy can be found in a number of other works, including Iorwerth Prothero, *Artisans and Politics in Early Nineteenth-Century London: John Gast and His Times* (Kent: Dawson and Son, 1979); David R. Green, *From Artisans to Paupers: Economic Change and Poverty in London, 1790–1870* (Hants, England: Scolar Press, 1995); and William Reddy, *The Rise of Market Culture: The Textile Trade and French Society, 1750–1900* (Cambridge: Cambridge University Press, 1984).

45. Michael Sonenscher, *Work and Wages: Natural Law, Politics and the Eighteenth-Century French Trades* (Cambridge: Cambridge University Press, 1989), 5.

46. William Sewell, *Work and Revolution in France: The Language of Labor from the Old Regime to 1848* (Cambridge: Cambridge University Press, 1980).

47. Sean Wilentz, *Chants Democratic: New York City and the Rise of the American Working Class, 1788–1850* (Oxford and New York: Oxford University Press, 1984).

48. In his study of Cuban urban workers, Joan Casanovas makes a similar observation for Cuban historiography. His excellent study examines the ways Cuban urban laborers formulated an anticolonial identity. Joan Casanovas, *Bread or Bullets! Urban Labor and Spanish Colonialism in Cuba, 1850–1898* (Pittsburgh: University of Pittsburgh Press, 1998). A number of studies of Latin American labor movements present mutual societies primarily as precursors of later developments. Victor Alba, *Politics and the Labor Movement in Latin America* (Stanford: Stanford University Press, 1968); Hobart A. Spalding, Jr., *Organized Labor in Latin America: Historical Case Studies of Workers in Dependent Societies* (New York: New York University Press, 1977); and John Hart, *Anarchism and the Mexican Working Class, 1860–1931* (Austin: University of Texas Press, 1978). For Peru, see Peter Blanchard, *The Origins of the Peruvian Labor Movement, 1883–1919* (Pittsburgh: University of Pittsburgh Press, 1982). Two valuable studies of Peruvian artisans focus primarily on moments of protests: Margarita Giesecke, *Masas urbanas y rebelión en la historia, golpe de estado: Lima 1872* (Lima: Centro de Divulgación de Historia Popular, 1978), and Quiroz,

Protesta de artesanos. For Chile, L. A. Romero, *La Sociedad de la Igualdad: los artesanos de Santiago de Chile y sus primeras experiencias políticas, 1820–1851* (Buenos Aires: Editorial del Instituto Torcuato di Tella, 1978), focuses primarily on protest and presents artisans primarily as pawns of radical liberal elites rather than as actors in their own right.

49. Charles S. Olton, *Artisans for Independence: Philadelphia Mechanics and the American Revolution* (Syracuse: Syracuse University Press, 1975), and Howard Rock, *Artisans of the New Republic: The Tradesmen of New York City in the Age of Jefferson* (New York: New York University Press, 1979).

50. Reinhard Bendix, *Nation-Building and Citizenship: Studies of Our Changing Social Order* (Berkeley: University of California Press, 1964), 78.

Chapter 1

1. This statement must be qualified to take into consideration possible differences throughout recently unified Spanish society. In the Basque provinces and in Asturias, for example, nobles partook of the trades without losing their status. See Mark Burkholder, "Honor and Honors in Colonial Spanish America," in *The Faces of Honor,* ed. Lyman Johnson and Sonya Lipsett-Rivera (Albuquerque: New Mexico University Press, 1998), 20.

2. Ibid., 26.

3. Lyman Johnson, "Artisans," in *Cities and Society in Colonial Latin America,* ed. Louis Schell Hoberman and Susan Migden Socolow (Albuquerque: New Mexico University Press, 1986), 229.

4. Karen Spalding, *Huarochirí: An Andean Society Under Inca and Spanish Rule* (Stanford: Stanford University Press, 1984), 280.

5. Emilio Harth-terré and Alberto Márquez Abanto, *Perspectiva social y económica del artesano virreinal en Lima* (Lima: Imprenta Gil, 1963), 84.

6. Ibid., 87. The association of "don" with nobility during the conquest period was rapidly followed by a more widespread usage. "In the late period the 'don' spread so far that nearly any Hispanic with an established position, for example a master artisan, was accorded it." James Lockhart and Stuart Schwartz, *Early Latin America* (Cambridge: Cambridge University Press, 1983), 318.

7. Spalding, *Huarochirí,* 280.

8. Ibid.

9. See Bowser, *African Slave,* 125–46.

10. Scarlett O'Phelan, *Rebellions and Revolts in Eighteenth-Century Peru and Upper Peru* (Cologne: Bohlau Verlag, 1985), 195.

11. See Spalding, *Huarochiri,* 271, 275, 280.

12. Johnson, "Artisans," 229.

13. Francisco Quiroz, *Gremios, razas y libertad de industria* (Lima: UNMSM, 1995), 33.

14. For a detailed description of relations with the municipality in Lima see ibid., 55–56. For a discussion of municipal control of the guilds in Mexico see Felipe Castro Gutierrez, *La Extinción del la artesanía gremial* (Mexico: UNAM, 1986), 36–46.

15. Quiroz, *Gremios,* 41.

16. *Casta* was the general term used in colonial times to refer to individuals of mixed race.

17. Quiroz, *Gremios,* 6.

18. Ibid., 61.

19. These exclusions and prohibitions appeared in the rules of the brotherhood Nuestra Señora de la Agonía. The sometimes interchangeable role of guild and brotherhood is addressed in the next section. Ricardo Temoche Benites, *Cofradías, gremios, mutuales y sindicatos en el Perú* (Lima: Escuela Nueva, 1987), 21.

20. Quiroz, *Gremios,* 67.

21. Harth-terré and Abanto, *Perspectiva social,* 7.

22. AHML, *Gremios,* Caja 1, Doc. 6 (1809).

23. Bowser, *African Slave,* 142.

24. Johnson, "Artisans," 231.

25. Héctor Samayoa Guevara comments on this phenomenon in relation to the guilds in Guatemala. See Samayoa Guevara, *Los gremios de artesanos en la ciudad de Guatemala* (Guatemala: Editorial Universitaria, 1962), 173.

26. Castro Gutierrez, *La extinción,* 46.

27. Josephe de Mugaburu and Francisco de Mugaburu (son), *Diario de Lima (1640–1694)* (Lima: Imprenta y Libreria Sanmarti y Ca., 1917), 53–54.

28. A discussion of the fiesta as a locus for the display of grandeur is to be found in José Antonio Maravall, *Culture of the Baroque: Analysis of a Historical Structure* (Minneapolis: University of Minnesota Press, 1986), 242.

29. Johnson, "Artisans," 234.

30. Ibid., 232.

31. Corpus Christi celebrates Christ's institution of the Eucharist and dates to 1264, when it was established by St. Thomas Aquinas.

32. Linda A. Curcio-Nagy, "Giants and Gypsies: Corpus Christi in Colonial Mexico City," in *Rituals of Rule, Rituals of Resistance,* ed. William Beezley et al. (Wilmington: Scholarly Resources, 1994), 17.

33. For Mexico see Manuel Carrera Stampa, *Los gremios mexicanos* (Mexico: EDIAPSA, 1954), 223–46; for Guatemala see Samayoa Guevara, *Gremios,* 177–82.

34. Lockhart and Schwartz, *Early Latin America,* 318.

35. Johnson, "Artisans," 231–32.

36. See Flores Galindo, *Ciudad sumergida.*

37. Bowser, *African Slave,* 139.

38. Johnson, "Artisans," 232.

39. Juan Carlos Estenssoro, *Musica y sociedad coloniales: Lima 1680–1830* (Lima: Editorial Colmillo Blanco, 1989), 98.

40. Olinda Celestino and Albert Meyers, *Las cofradías en el Perú: región central* (Frankfurt: Verlag Klaus Dieter Vervuert, 1981), 117–118.

41. Bowser, *African Slave,* 247.

42. Celestino and Meyers, *Cofradías,* 119.

43. Ibid., 122.

44. The shoemakers' cofradía was authorized to fund the cult of its saint through a fiscal mechanism specifically linked to the trade: artisans could charge the *herrete,* or one real, for raw materials associated with their trade entering the city. See ibid.

45. Temoche Benites, *Cofradías,* 20.

46. Celestino and Meyers, *Cofradías,* 122.

47. Quiroz, *Gremios,* 65.

48. Temoche Benitez, *Cofradías,* 20–21.

49. Mark Burkholder and Lyman Johnson, *Colonial Latin America* (Oxford: Oxford University Press, 1998), 203.

50. Lockhart and Schwartz, *Early Latin America,* 15.

51. Clara García Ayluardo, "A World of Images: Cult, Ritual, and Society in Colonial Mexico City," Beezley et al., *Rituals,* 89.

52. Jean Descola, *Daily Life in Colonial Peru,* trans. Michael Heron (New York: Macmillan, 1968), 193.

53. Jean Sarrailh, *L'Espagne éclairée* (Paris: Imprimerie Nationale, 1954), 543.

54. Richard Herr, *The Eighteenth-Century Revolution in Spain* (Princeton: Princeton University Press, 1958), 123.

55. Ibid., 151.

56. Ibid., 126.

57. Sarrailh, *Espagne éclairé,* 518–26.

58. Herr, *Eighteenth-Century Revolution,* 126.

59. Ibid.

60. Although the guilds had been officially abolished during the brief constitutional interregnum that brought the Spanish Cortes of Cadiz into session in 1812 during the Napoleonic invasion of the Iberian Peninsula.

61. Johnson, "Artisans," 246.

62. John Preston Moore, *The Cabildo in Peru under the Bourbons* (Durham, NC: Duke University Press, 1966), 159.

63. For a detailed discussion of the impact of the increase in the sales tax, alcabala, from 4 to 6 percent and its relation to the rebellions in the southern Andes, see O'Phelan, *Rebellions and Revolts.*

64. Ibid., 173.

65. Ibid., 197.

66. Quiroz, *Gremios,* 133–34.

67. Ibid., 131.

68. Ibid., 134.

69. Ibid., 138.

70. Johnson, "Artisans," 245–46.

71. See Francisco Quiroz, "Artesanos y manufactureros en Lima colonial" (master's thesis, Pontificia Universidad Católica del Perú, 1998). The importance of entrepreneurship and artisan production that made use of labor outside the guilds has been noted for the case of France by Michael Sonenscher, who demonstrates that corporate allegiances had significantly weakened among artisans in eighteenth-century France. See Sonenscher, *Work and Wages.*

72. Flores Galindo, *Ciudad sumergida,* 22.

73. For accounts of various dimensions of the Bourbon reforms in Peru, see Scarlett O'Phelan Godoy, ed., *El Perú en el siglo XVIII: La era borbónica* (Lima: Instituto Riva Aguero de la Pontificia Universidad Católica del Perú, 1999).

74. Sarrailh, *Espagne éclairée,* 653–61.

75. García Ayluardo, "World of Images," 90.

76. Estenssoro, *Música,* 92.

77. García Ayluardo, "World of Images," 91.

78. Cited from "Recopilación de las Leyes de Indias," Temoche Benitez, *Cofradías,* 30.

79. More research is needed on the direct impact of such ideas in America during the late colonial period. In his study of Guatemala, Samayoa Guevara discusses the activities of the Sociedad Económica de Guatemala (Guatemala Economic Society) in reorganizing the guilds and educating artisans. See Samayoa Guevara, *Gremios,* 72–74.

80. Quiroz, *Gremios,* 131.

81. Kruggeler, "Unreliable Drunkards," 106.

Chapter 2

1. Jorge Basadre, *Sultanismo, corrupción y dependencia en el Peru republicano* (Lima: Editorial Milla Bartres, 1981), 108.
2. Gootenberg, *Silver and Guano,* 50.
3. Creoles were the descendants of Spaniards, born in America. During the late colonial period Creoles had faced exclusion from the highest ranks of government. Mestizos were people of mixed race with Indian and/or African ancestry.
4. Jorge Basadre, *Perú: Problema y Posibilidad y Otros Ensayos* (Caracas: Biblioteca Ayacucho, 1992), 71.
5. For the most recent appraisal of Gamarra in the context of caudillismo and early state building see Walker, *Smoldering Ashes,* 121–51.
6. See John Lynch, *The Spanish American Revolutions, 1808–1826* (New York: Norton 1973), 344–47.
7. Cristobal Aljovín, "Representative Government in Peru: Fiction and Reality, 1821–1845." (PhD diss., University of Chicago, 1996), 407, 427. The idea of links between the military and republican political projects is not a novel one in Peruvian historiography. Almost a century ago renowned Peruvian intellectual Francisco García Calderón claimed that "militarism . . . was a popular democratic force, and in this sense was an element for building the republic." Francisco García Calderón, *Le Pérou Contemporain* (Paris: Dujarric et Cie. Editeurs, 1907), 81. Jorge Basadre has called this period that of the "Determination of Nationality" and has supported "the thesis that the army had a national content, and in its own way, imperfectly, fostered a sense of democracy." Basadre, *Introducción a las bases documentales para la historia de la República del Perú con algunas refleciones,* vol. 1 (Lima: Ediciones PLV, 1971), 305.
8. Frank Safford, "Politics, Ideology and Society," in *Spanish America After Independence,* ed. Leslie Bethell (Cambridge: Cambridge University Press, 1987), 118.
9. Walker, *Smoldering Ashes,* 6.
10. Ibid., 152–85; Warren, "Vagrants and Citizens," Vincent Peloso, "Liberals, Electoral Reform, and the Popular Vote in Mid-Nineteenth-Century Peru," in *Liberals,* Peloso and Tenenbaum, 186–211.
11. Paul Gootenberg, "The Social Origins of Protectionism and Free Trade," *Journal of Latin American Studies,* 2, no. 14 (1982): 338.
12. Jorge Basadre, "El Perú republicano," in *El Peru en cifras, 1944–1945,* ed. Dario Sainte Maries (Lima: Empresa Gráfica Scheuchs SA, 1945), 638.
13. Gootenberg, "Artisans and Merchants: The Making of an Open Economy in Lima, Peru, 1830 to 1860" (MPhil. thesis, Oxford University, 1981), 134.

14. Ibid., 136.
15. Ibid., 138.
16. AHML, Gremios, Doc. 29, *Oficios del gremio de zapateros—Reglamento Gremial* (1827).
17. Gootenberg, *Silver and Guano*, 76–77.
18. Ibid., 50–51.
19. AHML—Republica—Caja 5—Cupos y Emprestitos—Doc. 9 (1823).
20. The patente was subsequently abolished on October 31, 1827, and then reinstated on December 4, 1828. See Jorge Basadre, "La riqueza territorial y las actividades comerciales e industriales en los primeros años de la República," *Mercurio Peruano*, Año X, vol. XVII (1928):18.
21. Jonathan Levin, *The Export Economies* (Cambridge, MA: Harvard University Press, 1960), 92.
22. Gootenberg, "Artisans and Merchants," 134.
23. Emilio Romero, *Historia económica del Perú* (Buenos Aires: Editorial Sudamericana, 1949), 316.
24. However, this tax was not fraught with the political difficulties attached to Indian tribute, the colonial head tax that survived into the national period. The tax was first abolished by Peru's first independent ruler, San Martín, in 1821. Early leaders of the republic had made much of the abolition of the Indian head tax, *tributo*, associated with a colonial society. Yet tributo was soon restored, as the state relied too heavily on this income to be able to adhere to liberal principles; fully one-quarter of the national budget stemmed from Indian tribute. In its republican form tributo was renamed *la contribución* and was not fully abolished until 1855 under President Castilla.
25. Gootenberg, "Artisans and Merchants," 135.
26. AGN, Protocolos Notariales, Escribano Jose Cubillas, Prot.177, May 11, 1858. Agreda also had some outstanding debts.
27. AGN, OL.297–1286, January 11, 1842. The contract also mentions "helmets, key covers, cloaks and ties" (*morreones, cubre llaves, portacapotes and corbatines*). The latter two objects would most likely have been made of cloth rather than leather. This may indicate that artisans of different trades were working in conjunction with one another.
28. Oviedo (comp.), *Colección*, vol. 4, 87–88, cited by Kruggeler, "Unreliable Drunkards," 92.
29. Kruggeler, "Unreliable Drunkards," 97–98.
30. AGN, H-4 1715, Lima, Matrícula de Patentes, 118–120 (1833).
31. In a very different historical setting, Linda Colley argues for the importance of war in generating nationalist sentiment in eighteenth-century Britain. Colley points to the susceptibility of urban artisans to the propaganda that accompanies war efforts: "The urban artisan, because he had been

acculturated, because he was more easily reached by propaganda and recruiting parties, and because, crucially, he was not tied to the land, could be a more useful citizen in time of war than the solitary ploughman." Colley, *Britons* (New Haven, CT: Yale University Press, 1992), 300.

32. The "detal" indicates that his last name was unknown.

33. AHM, Carpeta 1, Leg. 3, Doc. 76, Sayan (1821).

34. AHM, Carpeta 4, Leg. 7, Doc. 10, Lima (1823).

35. The list of members of the First Battalion of the Infantry Regiment of the Militia of the City of Arequipa "Primera de Granaderos" lists a number of artisans, including silversmiths, carpenters, and tailors. AHM—Legajo Especial—Donaciones Particulares—Leg. 1, Doc. 8—Virreinato—6–16 (1783–87).

36. Johnson, "Artisans," in *Cities,* Hoberman and Socolow, 246.

37. Gootenberg, *Silver and Guano,* 50.

38. The law creating the National Guard indicated that the initiative came from the civic militias seeking greater privileges within the national setting: "acceding to the wishes of the civic corps to call themselves national guard and to have special privileges (*fuero*)." Juán Oviedo, comp., *Colección de leyes, decretos y órdenes publicadas en el Perú desde el año de 1821 hasta 31 de diciembre de 1859,* vol. 13 (Lima: F. Bailly, 1865), 250.

39. Ibid., 286.

40. Ibid., vol. 13, 299.

41. Ibid., vol. 13, 283–84.

42. Kruggeler, "Unreliable Drunkards," 104.

43. Article 166 of the 1828 constitution established "freedom of industry." See Juan Vicente Ugarte del Pino, *Historia de las constituciones del Perú* (Lima: Editorial Andina, 1978), 250.

44. AHML, Gremios, Caja 2, Doc. 25 (1825).

45. Romero, *Historia económica,* 267.

46. Ibid., 328.

47. Gootenberg, *Silver and Guano,* 51.

48. Gootenberg, "Artisans and Merchants," 81.

49. Ibid., 82.

50. AHML, Gremios, Caja 2, Doc. 29 (1836).

51. Ibid.

52. AHML, Gremios, Caja 1, Doc. 16, October 19 (1821).

53. Flores Galindo, *Ciudad sumergida,* 22.

54. Francisco Quiroz, "Gremios y sociedad," (1992), 24, manuscript in author's possession.

55. Some also served sentences in shoemaker workshops. Flores Galindo, *Ciudad sumergida,* 130.

56. Flores Galindo, *Ciudad sumergida,* 130.

57. For a discussion of the transition in methods of punishment and establishment of a modern penitentiary system see Carlos Aguirre, "The Lima Penitentiary and the Modernization of Criminal Justice in Nineteenth-Century Peru," in *The Birth of the Penitentiary in Latin America,* eds. Ricardo Salvatore and Carlos Aguirre (Austin: University of Texas Press, 1996), 44–77.

58. Quiroz, "Gremios y sociedad," 23.

59. Ibid., 24.

60. Jorge Basadre, *Historia de la República del Perú,* vol. 3 (Lima: Editorial Universitaria, 1968), 184.

61. *El Comercio,* May 25, 1839.

62. Quiroz, "Gremios y sociedad," 37.

63. AHML, Gremios, Caja 2, Doc. 41 (1830).

64. Ibid.

65. Quiroz, *Gremios, Razas,* 102.

66. AHML, Gremios, Caja 2, Doc. 42 (1830).

67. Ibid.

68. AMHL, Gremios, Caja 2, Doc. 41 (1830).

69. Gootenberg, "Artisans and Merchants," 131.

70. James Sheehan, *German History 1770–1866* (Oxford: Oxford University Press, 1989), 589.

71. For a full discussion of this episode see Gootenberg, "Artisans and Merchants," 176–85. Gootenberg also reproduces the full text of the speech on pp. 280–85.

72. It is significant that artisans should have been represented by cigar makers. Cigar shops (*cigarrerías*) were important places of social interaction in Lima.

73. *El Comercio,* October 17, 1849.

74. Successive Peruvian constitutions had made literacy a citizenship requirement but had extended the vote to the country's Indian population for limited periods under the assumption that during those periods, Indians would be integrated into a national education system. For example, the 1839 constitution gave the vote to illiterate Indians and mestizos in areas without schools until the year 1844. Basadre, *Historia República,* vol. 3, 89.

75. *El Comercio,* October 17, 1849.

76. Ibid.

77. Gootenberg, "Social Origins," 349.

78. Quiroz, *Protesta artesanos,* 27.

79. Jorge Basadre, *Introducción bases documentales,* vol.1, 198–99.

80. Basadre underlines the political nature of the crowd activity. Jorge Basadre, *La multitud, la ciudad y el campo en la historia del Perú* (Lima: Mosca Azul, 1980), 178.

81. Basadre, "El Perú," in *Perú en cifras,* 640.

82. Gootenberg, "Social Origins," 342.

83. Natalia Sobervilla, "The Influence of the European 1848 Revolutions in Peru," in *The European Revolutions of 1848 and the Americas,* ed. Guy Thomson (London: Institute of Latin American Studies, 2002), 203.

84. Quiroz, *Protesta artesanos,* 90.

85. Gootenberg, *Imagining Development,* 134.

86. *El Nacional,* March 14, 1867.

87. Quiroz, *Protesta artesanos,* Doc. 1 (transcribed by author from AGN O.L. 411–1469 [1858]).

88. Ibid., 94.

89. *El Comercio,* December 26, 1858.

90. Ibid., December 21, 1858.

91. Ibid., December 26, 1858.

92. *El Comercio,* December 22, 1858. The development of a working-class identity is discussed at length in chapter 5.

93. *Documento parlamentario. dictamen de la Comision de Hacienda de la Camara de Diputados sobre las representaciones de los gremios de Lima y Callao* (Lima: Tipografía de Aurelio Alfaro y Compañía, 1859), 4.

94. Ibid., 19.

95. E. J. Hobsbawn, *The Age of Capital 1848–1875* (New York: Vintage, 1996).

96. See chapter 1.

97. Safford, "Politics, Ideology, and Society," 96.

98. Gootenberg, *Imagining Development,* 135.

99. Jose Siméon Tejeda, *Libertad de Industria* (Lima: Ediciones Hora del Hombre, 1947), 42.

100. Ibid., 62.

101. José Silva Santisteban, *Breves reflexiones sobre los sucesos ocrurridos en Lima y el Callao con motivo de la importación de artefactos* (Lima: Imprenta calle de Jesus Nazareno, 1859), 6.

102. Ibid., 25.

103. Ibid., 7.

104. Ibid., 6.

105. Trazegnies, *Idea del derecho,* 100. Silva Santisteban did not follow the ideas of Heinecke (considered a second-rate philosopher in Germany), who had a strong influence in Latin America and developed a legal theory that incorporated some modern rationalist principles but continued to present

the traditional argument that the law had divine sanction and therefore was not based on utilitarian principles. Trazegnies, *Idea del derecho,* 77–78.

106. Silva Santisteban, *Breves reflexiones,* 15.

107. Ibid., 14.

108. Ibid., 22. This statement would need to be verified by examining the earnings of Lima's population during the guano boom. Evidently the so-called plutocracy or new elite that emerged during this period and derived its wealth from guano was able to consume luxury goods. While Silva Santisteban's statement strikes me as an exaggeration, government employment did increase notably during this period, and it remains to be determined whether government wages could have sustained consumption of certain luxury goods on the part of the middle sectors.

109. Ibid., 41.

110. Ibid.

111. Silva Santisteban, *Breves reflexiones,* 30.

112. The chocolate makers' guild listed Field, who would become a prominent candy producer still prominent to this day in Peru.

113. *El Comercio,* January 14, 1873.

114. AHML, Gremios (1887).

115. The word *guild,* "gremio," has survived in Peruvian political culture until the present. While it no longer has an institutional basis, it continues to be used informally. Industrialists, for example, are referred to as the "gremio de industriales."

116. AHML, Sindicaturas (1877). Particularly documents on shoemakers and bookbinders (these documents were not yet cataloged when I conducted my research in 1998).

Chapter 3

1. Sarmiento was president of Argentina from 1868 to 1874.

2. *El Comercio,* December 10, 1864.

3. For a study of the liberal cultural project in late-nineteenth-century and early-twentieth-century Mexico, see French, *Peaceful and Working People,* 63–86.

4. Silva Santisteban, *Breves reflexiones,* 41.

5. Gootenberg, *Imagining Development,* 38– 57, 130– 81.

6. For a study of national identity and notions of progress in Mexico as presented at the World Fairs between 1889 and 1929, see Mauricio Tenorio-Trillo, *Mexico at the World's Fairs: Crafting a Modern Nation* (Berkeley: University of California Press, 1996).

7. Aguirre, "Lima Penitentiary," 59.

8. French, *Peaceful and Working People,* 64. My analysis suggests that while there were obvious elements of social control in the educational process (Latin American historiography has emphasized this aspect of the liberal project), education also offered artisans a means of social mobility. For a view of education as empowering the popular classes, see David Holtby, "Education in Porfirian Mexico: The Role of Schools in the Coming of the Revolution," *Red River Valley Historical Journal of World History* 4, no. 1 (fall 1979): 31–51.

9. Louis James, ed., *Print and the People, 1819–1851* (London: Allen Lane, 1976), 20.

10. Sábato, *Política en las calles,* 13.

11. Safford, "Politics, Ideology, and Society," 53.

12. Ugarte del Pino, *Historia,* 165.

13. Eve-Marie Fell, "La construcción de la sociedad peruana: Estado y educación en el siglo XIX," in *America Latina: del estado colonial al estado nación,* ed. Antonio Annino et al. (Milano, Italy: Franco Angeli, 1987), 810.

14. Ibid., 811.

15. See chapter 1 for a discussion of Bourbon reforms in relation to artisans.

16. Basadre, *Historia República,* vol. 5, 8.

17. *El Comercio,* December 26, 1858.

18. Ibid., December 21, 1858.

19. Ibid., January 7, 1873.

20. BN, D3543 (1876).

21. *El Comercio,* December 10, 1864.

22. Ibid.

23. Ibid. The reference is to the 1824 battle of Ayacucho that brought an end to Spanish rule in Peru.

24. Ibid. The initial government allocation of 295,000 was supplemented with another 163,000 and then with a third, smaller sum.

25. *Reglamento de la Escuela de Artes y Oficios* (Lima: Imprenta del Estado, 1871), 40.

26. The department is the administrative unit into which Peru was subdivided following independence from Spain, following the French model.

27. *El Comercio,* December 13, 1864.

28. Ibid., December 10, 1864.

29. Gootenberg, *Imagining Development,* 151–52.

30. *El Comercio,* January 27, 1872.

31. See Michel Foucault, *Discipline and Punish: The Birth of the Prison* (New York: Vintage, 1979).

32. *Reglamento Artes y Oficios,* 34.

33. Ibid., 51.

34. Ibid., 21.

35. Ibid., 63.

36. Ibid., 22.

37. Ibid., 42.

38. A good example of such divergence can be found in Mario Vargas Llosa's fictional account of the military Leoncio Prado School, where students succeeded in avoiding the vigilance they were supposed to live under. See Mario Vargas Llosa, *La ciudad y los perros* (Barcelona: Editorial Seix Barral, 1965).

39. *El Nacional,* March 2, 1867.

40. See *El Comercio,* December 4, 1873, and *La Opinión Nacional,* December 1, 1877.

41. *La Patria,* July 1, 1872.

42. *El Nacional,* June 7, 1866.

43. *El Comercio,* April 16, 1873.

44. Ibid.

45. *La Opinión Nacional,* January 21, 1877.

46. *El Comercio,* April 17, 1873.

47. *La Opinion Nacional,* January 31, 1877.

48. BN, Manuscritos D3545 (1872). For an earlier request for delayed funds see also BN, Correspondencia de Manuel Mendiburu al Ministro de Estado, February 13, 1871.

49. *La Opinion Nacional,* January 31, 1877.

50. Ibid.

51. Personal communication, Megan Paulet, February 1, 1998.

52. Basadre, *Historia República,* vol. 7, 78.

53. Basadre deems these reforms to have been a failure. Ibid., 79.

54. *El Comercio,* January 7, 1873.

55. AHML, Instrucción (1873).

56. *El Comercio,* January 7, 1873.

57. Ibid.

58. Ibid.

59. Ibid.

60. Ibid.

61. McEvoy, *Proyecto nacional,* 188.

62. AHML, Instrucción (1873–74).

63. Ibid.

64. AHML, Instrucción (1873).

65. Ibid.

66. *Presupuesto del Concejo Provincial de Lima: Que deberá rejir del 1ero de julio de 1876 a 30 de junio de 1878* (Lima: Imprenta del Estado, 1877).

67. *Boletin Municipal* (September 5, 1874).

68. Ibid. (August 29, 1874).

69. Pedro M. Cabello, *Guía del Perú para el año de 1859* (Lima: Imprenta Masías, 1859), 302.

70. *El Hijo del Pueblo,* March 26, 1864.

71. Ibid., May 5, 1864.

72. Mariano Bolognesi was the brother of the now famous Francisco Bolognesi, hero of the War of the Pacific.

73. Ibid., March 1, 1875.

74. *El Comercio,* July 31, 1873.

75. *El Siglo,* November 1, 1874; ibid., August 1, 1875; ibid., July 1, 1876.

76. An earlier initiative in Lima on the part of José Granda to teach industrial design to artisans occurred in 1867 with the short-lived and unsuccessful Academia de Dibujo Industrial Para los Artesanos de Lima. See Natalia Majluf, "Entre pasatiempo y herramienta artesanal: aspectos de la enseñanza del dibujo en el diecinueve." *Sequilao* 2, no. 3 (May–July, 1993): 32–42.

77. *El Siglo,* June 1, 1876.

78. *El Comercio,* January 31, 1874.

79. *El Siglo,* September 1, 1875.

80. Ibid., October 1, 1875, and September 1, 1875.

81. Ibid., March 1, 1875.

82. Rolland Paulston, *Society, Schools and Progress in Peru* (Oxford: Pergamon, 1971), 45.

83. Frederick Pike, *The Modern History of Peru* (London: Weidenfeld and Nicolson, 1967), 136.

84. *El Siglo,* September 1, 1875.

85. *El Siglo,* March 1, 1875.

86. Ibid.

87. Ibid., April 1, 1875. Pablo Macera discusses the linguistic reforms that accompanied the arrival of enlightened ideas in eighteenth-century Peru. Baroque language was to be replaced by a simpler and more direct form of expression. See Macera, *Trabajos de historia,* vol. 2 (Lima: INC, 1977).

88. *El Siglo,* April 1, 1875.

89. Ibid.

90. Ibid.

91. The Beneficencia was a secular charitable organization.

92. Specifically "Títulos de la deuda pública, cédulas hipotecarias u otros valores señalados," Basadre, *Historia República,* vol. 6, 213–14.

93. Basadre, *Historia República,* vol. 6, 213–14.

94. *El Siglo,* April 1, 1875.
95. For a full account of Cisneros and other thinkers promoting industrialism, see Gootenberg, *Imagining Development.*
96. *El Comercio,* August 5, 1869.
97. The penitentiary had been inaugurated in 1862 and was yet another mark of progress for Lima's elites. See Aguirre, "Lima Penitentiary," 44–77.
98. *Hacienda* refers to large landed estates in Latin America whose history dates to the sixteenth century.
99. *El Comercio,* August 5, 1869.
100. Ibid., August 16, 1869.
101. Ibid., August 5, 1869.
102. Chapter 4 discusses the Sociedad de Artesanos at length.
103. *El Comercio,* August 16, 1869.
104. Ibid.
105. AHML, Sindicaturas (1878) (uncataloged box).
106. *El Comercio,* August 6, 1869. "Los trabajos que hoy han exhibido / Los plomeros mas célebres de Lima, / A nuestra exposicion dan un partido / Y logran ellos especial estima.... Renombre eterno para el feliz obrero / Que llena su misión sobre la tierra. / Tributando a trabajo verdadero / Todo el afán que el corazón encierra. El trabajo será el gran veneno / Que destruirá el disturbio, que aterra / Y hace del Perú un pueblo esclavo, / Sujeto á la ambición del que es mas bravo. Kemish y Melson, cual los primeros, / Que aman el trabajo y lo veneran, / Amigos del Perú los mas sinceros / Un grato porvenir para él esperan; / Los dias de la patria placenteros...."
107. Ibid., October 5, 1872. The article claimed that it was Manuel Atanasio Fuentes who had the idea of building the Palacio de la Exposición.
108. Basadre, *Historia República,* vol. 6, 231.
109. *Reglamento de la Exposición Nacional del Perú* (Lima: Imprenta del Estado, 1870), 3.
110. Ibid.
111. Basadre, *Historia República,* vol. 6, 314.
112. *La Patria,* July 1, 1872.
113. *El Comercio,* October 5, 1872.
114. *La Patria,* July 1, 1872. In his inaugural speech, Manuel Atanasio Fuentes, who played an important role in organizing the event, congratulated the representative in France, Luis E. Albertini, for having procured the materials needed for the building despite the problems posed by the Franco-Prussian War.
115. *El Comercio,* October 5, 1872.

116. For a more detailed description see Basadre, *Historia República*, vol. 6, 289–92.
117. *El Comercio*, October 5, 1872.
118. This artisan mutual aid society will be discussed in chapter 4.
119. *El Comercio*, December 30, 1873.
120. *La Patria*, July 5, 1872.
121. *Reglamento Artes y Oficios*, 45.

Chapter 4

1. *El Comercio*, September 29, 1864.
2. Trinidad Manuel Perez, *La industria y el poder* (Lima: Imprenta Liberal de "El Correo del Peru," 1875), 5.
3. Sheehan, *German Liberalism*, 26.
4. Giesecke, *Masas urbanas*, 140.
5. Gootenberg, *Imagining Development*, 143.
6. Temoche Benites, *Cofradías, gremios*, 78.
7. Fernando Armas Asin, *Liberales, protestantes y masones: modernidad y tolerancia religiosa. Perú, siglo XIX* (Lima: Centro Bartolomé de las Casas and Pontificia Universidad Católica del Perú, 1998), 86.
8. Romero, *Sociedad*.
9. Sobrevilla, "Influence 1848 Peru."
10. *Reglamento de la Sociedad Fraternal de Artesanos* (Lima: Imprenta del Universo, 1876), 21.
11. A similar formal rejection of politics can be found among Chilean mutual aid societies following the episodes of political unrest of the 1850s. In his detailed study of Chilean popular politics during the nineteenth century, Sergio Grez points to the fact that such claims of lack of political activity did not always correspond to reality. See Grez, *De la "regeneración del pueblo" a la huelga general. Génesis y evolución histórica del movimiento popular en Chile (1810–1890)* (Santiago: Biblioteca Nacional de Chile, 1997), 485.
12. Kruggeler claims that Cusco artisans were not as politically involved as their Lima counterparts. See Kruggeler, "Unreliable Drunkards," 166.
13. Pike, *Modern History*, 104.
14. Voters had to be twenty-one years or older and had to know how to read and write or be the master of a workshop or own property or pay taxes. See Jorge Basadre, *Elecciones y centralismo en el Perú* (Lima: Centro de Investigación de la Universidad del Pacífico, 1980), 23.
15. The 1866 census indicates literacy rates as high as 80 percent.
16. Peloso, *Liberals*, 187.

17. Charles Walker, "Montoneros, bandoleros, malhechores: criminalidad y política en las primeras décadas republicanas," in *Bandoleros, abigeos y montoneros: criminalidad y violencia en el Perú, siglos XVIII-XX*, eds. Carlos Aguirre and Charles Walker (Lima: Instituto de Apoyo Agrario, 1990), 114.

18. Ibid., 205.

19. Ibid., 187.

20. Peloso, "Liberals," 204.

21. For an extensive study of the 1850 election, including the role of artisans, see José Frank Ragas Rojas, "Ciudadania, cultura política y representación en el Perú: la campaña electoral de 1850." Bachelor's thesis, Pontificia Universidad Católica del Perú, 2003.

22. Basadre, *Bases Documentales*, vol. 1, 273.

23. Ibid., 192.

24. Manuel Atanasio Fuentes, *Aletazos del Murciélago*, 2nd ed. (Paris, 1866), quoted in Basadre, *Historia República*,131.

25. Juan Espinosa, *Diccionario para el pueblo* (Lima: Imprenta del Pueblo, 1855), 414–15.

26. Sábato, *Política en las calles*, 120.

27. McEvoy, *Utopía republicana*, 68.

28. McEvoy, *Proyecto nacional*, 258.

29. Safford, "Politics, Ideology, and Society," 95.

30. Ibid.

31. The distaste with traditional political practices bears strong parallels to the unsuccessful modern-day campaign of Mario Vargas Llosa for the presidency of Peru in 1990. A neoliberal, Vargas Llosa attempted to distance himself from patronage politics only to find that many of his supporters turned to his political organization in search of patronage ties. See Vargas Llosa, *Un pez en el agua* (Barcelona: Seix Barral, 1993), 162.

32. McEvoy, *Utopía republicana*, 76.

33. Ibid., 69.

34. McEvoy, *Proyecto nacional*, 266–67.

35. McEvoy includes the full list of names of "artisans and day-laborers" who attended the meeting. McEvoy, *Proyecto nacional*, 335–43.

36. Efraín Kristal, *The Andes Viewed from the City* (New York: Peter Lang, 1987), 69.

37. McEvoy, *Utopía republicana*, 74.

38. As Jeffrey Klaiber points out, there was an inconsistency between Vigil's defense of separation of powers and his call for the national state to supervise Church affairs. See Jeffrey Klaiber, *Religion and Revolution in Peru, 1824–1976* (Notre Dame, IN: University of Notre Dame Press, 1977), 14.

39. Such short-lived ideological newspapers were a common feature of nineteenth-century political life.

40. Gootenberg, *Imagining Development*, 141.

41. Gonzalo Portocarrero, "Conservadurismo, liberalismo y democracia en el Perú del siglo XIX," in *Pensamiento político peruano*, ed. Alberto Adrianzén (Lima: DESCO, 1987), 96.

42. Carlos Forment, "La sociedad civil en el Perú del siglo XIX," in *Ciudadanía política*, Sábato, 216.

43. Francisco de Paula González Vigil, *Importancia y utilidad de las asociaciones/Importancia de la educación popular* (Lima: Ediciones Hora del Hombre, 1948), 19.

44. Ibid., 32.

45. I hypothesize that given his training as a priest, he might fit into what Jeffrey Klaiber has referred to as an unexplored corporatist tradition of thought in nineteenth-century Peru. See Klaiber, "Independencia y ciudadanía," in *Pensamiento político peruano*, ed. Alberto Adrianzén (Lima: DESCO, 1987), 78.

46. Vigil, *Importancia asociaciones*, 22.

47. Ibid., 27.

48. Vigil, *Importancia asociaciones*, 25.

49. Tejeda, *Libertad de la industria*, 62. See the discussion of Simeón Tejeda in chapter 2.

50. On the new forms of sociability distinguishing Spanish American modernity during the early nineteenth century see Guerra, *Modernidad e Independencias*, 86–91. The most detailed study of these associations establishes a comparison with Mexico and equates such associations with the rise of a democratic polity in Latin America. See Carlos Forment, *Democracy in Latin America, 1760–1900*. Vol. 1, *Civic Selfhood and Public Life in Mexico and Peru* (Chicago: University of Chicago Press, 2003).

51. Carlos Illades, *Hacia la república del trabajo: la organización artesanal en la ciudad de México, 1853–1876* (Mexico: El Colegio de México, 1996), 86.

52. Brenda Harriman, "Los británicos en el Perú," in *Primer seminario sobre poblaciones inmigrantes* (Lima: Concitec, 1988), 152–53.

53. Pilar García Jordán, *Iglesia y poder en el Perú contemporaneo, 1821–1919* (Cusco: Centro Bartolomé de las Casas, 1991), 204.

54. *El Heraldo*, no. 294, June 18, 1855. *El Heraldo de Lima* (1854–56), founded by Luis Benjamín Cisneros and Toribio Pacheco, defended the conservative Echenique and attacked Castilla.

55. *La Zamacueca Política*, June 8, 1859.

56. Gootenberg, *Imagining Development*, 144–46.

57. Temoche Benites, *Cofradías, gremios*, 80.

58. Shane Hunt, "Growth and Guano in Nineteenth-Century Peru," in *The Latin American Economies,* ed. Roberto Cortés-Conde and Shane Hunt (New York: Holmes and Meier, 1985), 285.

59. Crossick makes the point that illness, unemployment, or sudden death could throw an artisan family into destitute poverty. Crossick, *Artisan Elite,* 174.

60. The rules went into great detail about the various possibilities of illness. If a member of the society who was receiving the twelve monthly soles for disability should become ill, the society made provisions for an additional fifty centavos per day. See *Reglamento Sociedad Fraternal,* 9.

61. Shane Hunt, "Growth and Guano," 292.

62. ASFA, Actas de las Sesiones de los Jueves, November 20, 1871, 71.

63. The link between artisan societies and citizen formation has parallels in revolutionary France. See Lynn Hunt, *Politics, Culture and Class in the French Revolution* (Berkeley: University of California, 1984), 72.

64. *Reglamento Sociedad Fraternal Artesanos,* 5.

65. Francisco García Calderón, *Diccionario de la legislación peruana,* vol. 1 (Paris, 1879), 172.

66. According to my analysis of the most numerous trades listed in the census of the city of Lima for 1866 (shoemakers, carpenters, tailors), 34 percent of the artisans belonging to these trades were listed as "zambo" (of indigenous and African heritage), 25 percent as "white," 16 percent as Indian, 13 percent as "mestizo" (mixed race), 6 percent as "black," and 6 percent as other, mixed ethnicities.

67. "Verás al dia siguiente / Muchos artesanos negros, / Chinos, zambos y mulatos, / Churpacos y otros pelos. Que si acaso los ocupan, / Para avíos piden luego, / Y ántes de acabar la obra, / Ya han recibido el dinero. / La que se la vende á otro, / Dejando sin ella al dueño, / Y si le pones demanda, / Te da cada mes un peso." Simón Ayanque, *Lima por dentro y fuera, obra jocosa y divertida* (Paris: A. Mezin, 1854), 144–45.

68. *El Artesano,* June 15, 1873.

69. Clemens Markham, *The War Between Peru and Chile* (London: Sampson Low, Martson, Searle, and Rivington, 1882), 86.

70. *El Obrero,* June 5, 1875.

71. Espinosa, *Diccionario pueblo,* 66.

72. AGN, Juzgado de Cofradías, Leg. 26, Cuaderno 358 (1835).

73. Olinda Celestino and Albert Meyers note in reference to the Andean city of Jauja during the early twentieth century that the "Sociedad de Artesanos" included members of cofradías. Celestino and Meyers, *Cofradías,* 215.

74. AGN, Juzgado de Cofradías, Leg. 31 (1848).

75. The title of this newspaper means "The Worker."

76. *El Obrero,* April 3, 1875.

77. The feast takes place on January 1.

78. AGN, Juzgado de Cofradías, Leg. 31 (1848).

79. The rules for the Sociedad Fraternal de Artesanos state: "This Society recognizes as its patron saint San Francisco Solano, whose fiesta is to be celebrated the first Sunday in January." *Reglamento Sociedad Fraternal Artesanos*, 5.

80. "Swearing in" is my translation of the term *sacramentación*, which evidently has more religious connotations than the term I have chosen. *Reglamento Sociedad Fraternal Artesanos*, 6.

81. AHML, Gremios (1870).

82. *El Comercio*, August 12, 1869.

83. For a study of Francisco Laso's painting in the social context of the nineteenth century, see Natalia Majluf, "The Creation of the Image of the Indian in 19th Century Peru: The Paintings of Francisco Laso (1823–1869)" (PhD thesis, University of Texas–Austin, 1995).

84. Jorge Basadre, *Bases Documentales*, vol. 1, 413.

85. Hilda Sábato, *La política en las calles*, 61.

86. ASFA, Libro de Actas Juntas Generales 1870–1893, pp. 91–92 (Sesión 28 mayo, 1872).

87. Ibid., p.182 (Sesión 21 mayo, 1876).

88. The availability of this meeting place points to the fact that the Sociedad enjoyed a prominent social standing.

89. *El Comercio*, December 14, 1872.

90. Basadre, *Historia República*, vol. 5, 99.

91. *El Nacional*, September 23, 1867.

92. *El Comercio*, November 11, 1873.

93. *El Comercio*, June 7, 1873.

94. For discussion of how these symbols become part of official revolutionary celebrations, see Hunt, *Politics, Culture and Class*, 59.

95. The importance of artisan participation in civic festivals is underlined by Sean Wilentz in his study of New York artisans. Wilentz, *Chants Democratic*, 90.

96. *El Nacional*, July 14, 1866.

97. *El Nacional*, July 31, 1866.

98. *El Artesano*, May 15, 1873.

99. The 1839 *Reglamento de Policía* specifies that artisans are to contribute to putting out fires. "It specifically mentions the obligation of carpenters, blacksmiths, masons and water carriers to come with the instruments of their trade and help the police intendant and his assistants to extinguish fires; shopkeepers and tavern owners must have a hook, a crowbar, a ladder and two leather buckets available for these cases." Basadre, *Historia República*, 317.

100. McEvoy, *Utopía republicana*, 87.

101. Giesecke, *Masas urbanas*, 100.

Chapter 5

1. *El Comercio*, November 27, 1872.

2. Ibid.

3. Here I draw on the concept of "languages of class" used by Gareth Stedman Jones. Stedman Jones's concept is highly relevant to my argument, as he argues that conceptions of class were not necessarily formulated only in the economic sphere; a class identity could be forged in the context of political struggles. See Stedman Jones, *Languages of Class: Studies in English Working Class History, 1832–1982* (Cambridge: Cambridge University Press, 1983). A more recent call for a return to examining the issue of class, a category that has received less attention with the decline of Marxist paradigms in the 1980s, can be found in Geoff Eley and Keith Nield, "Farewell to the Working Class?" *International Labor and Working-Class History* no. 57 (spring 2000): 1–30, and Barbara Weinstein, "Where Do New Ideas (About Class) Come From?" *International Labor and Working-Class History,* no. 57 (spring 2000): 53–59.

4. Historian Jorge Basadre has referred to this as the beginnings of a "proletarian press." The centrality of artisans leads me to refer to it as the "artisan press."

5. The titles *El Artesano* and *El Obrero,* with their direct reference to a social group, stand out among other newspapers, which were either politically partisan and aimed at attacking a given political group or took a more "balanced position," such as *La Patria, La Republica,* or *El Comercio,* or were aimed at spreading education to "the people," such as *El Hijo del Pueblo.* Peru's eminent historian Jorge Basadre refers to these newspapers, *El Artesano* and *El Obrero,* as the beginnings of a working-class or proletarian press. According to Gootenberg: "Repoliticized workers soon forged their own intellectual organs, such as *El Artesano* (1873) and, revealing of the transition in consciousness, José Enrique del Campo's *El Obrero* (1875–77), linked to the printers and the Sociedad de Artesanos." Gootenberg, *Imagining Development,* 154.

6. On the political role of newspapers during the period see Basadre, *Historia República,* vol. 6, 391.

7. Miriam Halpern Pereira, "Artesãos, operários e o liberalismo—dos privilégios corporativos para o direito au trabalho (1820–1840)," in *Ler Historia* 14 (1988): 42.

8. Walker, *Smoldering Ashes,* 175.

9. For a study of the liberal influence on the Mexican workers' press during the early twentieth century, see Diaz, "Satiric Penny."

10. Espinosa, *Diccionario para el pueblo,* 156.

11. Carmen McEvoy has written extensively on the Civilista concern with "creating citizens" for the republic. See McEvoy, *Utopía republicana,* 55– 120.

12. I distinguish "artisan liberalism" from the "popular liberalism" of Florencia Mallon's recent study of the relationship between peasant and national politics in Mexico and Peru during the nineteenth century. Mallon analyzes the conception of the liberal nation among peasants and argues for the development of a liberal discourse that challenged the hegemonic liberalism of elites. Artisan liberalism, on the other hand, was not set in direct opposition to elite liberalism. While artisans challenged some aspects of liberalism, they also borrowed strongly from prevailing liberal ideas. The work I have referred to is Mallon, *Peasant and Nation.*

13. Sewell, *Work and Revolution in France,* 199.

14. A similar term was used in Mexico: *empleomanía.* See Charles Hale, *Mexican Liberalism in the Age of Mora* (New Haven, CT: Yale University Press, 1968).

15. Pike, *Modern History,* 134.

16. Basadre, *Historia República,* vol. 7, 66–67.

17. Field remained an important Peruvian confectioner until the 1990s, when the company was purchased first by Nabisco and then by Kraft. (I thank the members of the listserve Markham Prom XXXII for this information.)

18. AHML, Gremios (1870). The larger scale of production associated with factories was not an entirely new trend. As Francisco Quiroz has demonstrated, many artisans during the late-colonial period had already begun to work in the context of larger workshops. See Quiroz, "Artesanos y manufactureros."

19. Jose Harris, *Private Lives, Public Spirit: Britain, 1870–1914* (London: Penguin, 1994).

20. Pease would later become a prominent name in Peru, for example, historian Franklin Pease (1939–1999) and his brother, politician Henry Pease (1944–).

21. *El Nacional,* May 12, 1866.

22. This topic, the role of women in the production process in nineteenth-century Peru, needs to be further explored. I have found scattered references, but since my work involves mainly examining public political discourse, which precluded women, I have not focused on the subject of women.

23. *El Nacional,* November 26, 1867. Given the quality of workmanship and extrapolating from present-day trends, Peruvian artisans could probably easily imitate new European styles of such goods as clothing and furniture. Therefore, despite the changes in taste and the influx of imported goods,

national artisans probably found a market for their goods among sectors of the elite and middle sectors.

24. Jorge Dulanto Pinillos, *Cuatro biografías* (Lima: Compañía de Impresiones y Publicidad Editores, 1938), 109.

25. Ibid., 123.

26. Pablo Macera, "El periodismo en la independencia," in *Trabajos de historia,* vol. 2, 326. For a discussion of the importance of the press in shaping a reading public see also John Hartley, *Popular Reality: Journalism, Modernity, Popular Culture* (London: Arnold, 1996).

27. Basadre, *Historia República,* vol. 5, 392.

28. This also included the publication of erudite works such as Mariano Felipe Paz Soldán's *Diccionario geográfico estadístico del Perú* in 1877. Paz Soldán also directed a periodical titled *La Revista Peruana.*

29. *El Obrero,* May 8, 1875.

30. *El Artesano,* May 15, 1873.

31. Ibid., August 1, 1873. The author's initials are M. F.

32. Walker, *Smoldering Ashes,* 174.

33. See Natalie Zemon Davis, "Printing and the People," in *Society and Culture in Early Modern France* (Stanford: Stanford University Press, 1975), 189–226.

34. Jeffrey Brooks, *When Russia Learned to Read: Literacy and Popular Literature, 1861–1917* (Princeton: Princeton University Press, 1985), 34.

35. Ibid., 34.

36. *El Artesano,* March 15, 1873.

37. I was able to consult only the incomplete collections available at the Biblioteca Nacional (*El Artesano,* March–December, 1873, and *El Obrero,* March 1875–January 1876, with significant gaps). I rely on Basadre for the dates of the entire run of *El Obrero.* I think that Basadre's claim that *El Artesano* ran until 1879 needs to be confirmed, given the fact that the December 1 issue claims to be the last one, given that *El Obrero* does not mention *El Artesano,* as would seem likely, and given that Ignacio Manco y Ayllón (the editor of *El Artesano*) is to be found writing for *El Obrero* in 1875. For dates of these newspapers, see Basadre, *Bases Documentales,* vol. 1, 413.

38. *El Artesano,* March 15, 1873.

39. Basadre, *Historia República,* vol. 7, 72. While I agree with the general sense of the remark, I disagree with the unproblematic notions of class, as explained in my introduction.

40. The biographical information on del Campo comes from Basadre, *Historia República,* vol. 7, 71–72.

41. BN, D2632, 1868.

42. *El Obrero,* May 22, 1875.

43. *El Artesano,* May 1, 1873.

44. Ibid. The article is signed only with the initials M. B.
45. Ibid.
46. *El Hijo del Pueblo,* March 26, 1864.
47. *El Artesano,* June 16, 1873.
48. Ibid., March 15, 1873.
49. Ibid., July 15, 1873.
50. *El Artesano,* September 15, 1873.
51. Ibid., April 15, 1873.
52. Ibid., May 1, 1873.
53. *El Nacional,* March 14, 1867.
54. *El Hijo del Pueblo,* February 27, 1864.
55. *El Artesano,* March 15, 1873.
56. *El Obrero,* March 27, 1875.
57. *El Artesano,* May 15, 1873.
58. Ibid.
59. Ibid.
60. Ibid., October 1, 1873.
61. *El Obrero,* June 5, 1876.
62. Ibid., March 15, 1873.
63. Ibid., July 1, 1873.
64. Ibid., June 16, 1873.
65. *El Artesano,* May 15, 1873.
66. See discussion of this issue in chapter 2.
67. *El Comercio,* November 27, 1872.
68. *El Artesano,* October 1, 1873.
69. Halpern Pereira has noted the centrality of work for liberalism in Brazil. Halpern Pereira, "Artesãos, operários e o liberalismo," 41.
70. See McEvoy, *Utopía republicana,* p.86.
71. Manuel Pardo, "Discurso de aceptación de la candidatura presidencial," in *El Comercio,* April 24, 1871, cited by McEvoy, *Utopía republicana,* 86.
72. *El Artesano,* April 15, 1873.
73. Ibid.
74. Ibid.
75. Ibid.
76. Ibid.
77. Ibid., August 1, 1873. *Esto me hace comprender / Que en este mundo malvado, / Para ser asesinado / Es mejor ser coronel / No vale un grano de aniz / La vida de un artesano; / La del militar peruano/ Vale todo un Potosí.* In the last quoted line, Potosí refers to the wealthy silver mines of colonial times.
78. Ibid.
79. Ibid.

80. Ibid., May 1, 1873.

81. Ibid., March 15, 1873.

82. *El Artesano*, March 15, 1873. The notion of the suffering artisan is a clear precedent to a phenomenon noted by David Parker for early-twentieth-century Peru: the notion that the middle class was the one that most suffered. See Parker, *The Idea of the Middle Class.*

83. *El Artesano*, October 1, 1873.

84. Ibid.

85. For more on artisan pride see ibid., October 15, 1873.

86. Ronald Schultz, *The Republic of Labor: Philadelphia Artisans and the Politics of Class, 1720–1830* (New York: Oxford University Press, 1993), 4–5.

87. *El Artesano*, July 1, 1873.

88. The subtitle may have begun with an earlier issue, but a gap exists in the only available collection of *El Obrero* held at the National Library, between no. 15 (June 26, 1875) and no. 44 (January 15, 1876).

89. *El Obrero*, March 20, 1875.

90. Ibid., March 27, 1875.

91. Ibid., May 8, 1875.

92. Ibid., June 26, 1875.

93. Ibid., April 10, 1875.

94. Ibid., May 8, 1875.

95. Ibid., March 27, 1875.

96. Ibid. For a full discussion of this artisan lecture, see chapter 3.

97. *El Artesano*, November 17, 1873.

98. *El Obrero*, March 27, 1875.

99. *El Artesano*, September 1, 1873.

100. Reflecting the problems with the liberal/conservative dichotomy in Latin American politics, historian Frederick Pike pointed to Piérola's strong economic liberalism. He characterizes Piérola in the following terms: "More extreme in his classical economic liberalism than even Castilla, the naïve Piérola of 1869 in many ways resembled the romantic liberals of the José Simeón Tejeda school who sincerely believed that the unregulated structure of pure economic individualism would usher in an ideal human existence." Pike, *Modern History*, 123.

101. *El Obrero*, April 3, 1875.

102. Ibid., April 3, 1875.

103. For various accounts of state regulation of popular culture in Mexico see William Beezley et al., eds., *Rituals of Rule, Rituals of Resistance* (Wilmington, DL: Scholarly Resources, 1994).

104. *El Obrero*, March 27, 1875.

105. Hugo Gavarito Amézaga, *El Perú liberal: partidos e ideas politicas de la ilustración a la república aristocrática* (Lima: Ediciones El Virrey, 1989), 200.
106. *El Obrero,* May 15, 1875.
107. Ibid., June 12, 1875.
108. Ibid., April 10, 1875.
109. Ibid., May 1, 1875.
110. Ibid.
111. Ibid., May 8, 1875.

Conclusion

1. Safford, "Politics, Ideology and Society," 94.
2. *El Comercio,* October 17, 1849.
3. Ibid., November 27, 1872.

Bibliography

Archives

Archivo Arzobispal de Lima

Archivo de la Beneficencia de Lima

Archivo Denegri Luna

Archivo General de la Nación (AGN)

Archivo Histórico Militar (AHM)

Archivo Histórico Municipal de Lima (AHML)

Archivo del Museo Nacional de Historia y Antropología

Archivo de la Sociedad Fraternal de Artesanos (ASFA)

Biblioteca del Instituto Riva Aguero, Pontificia Universidad Católica del Perú

Biblioteca Nacional del Perú (BN)

Newspapers

El Artesano (1873)

El Comercio (1845–79)

El Heraldo de Lima (1854–56)

El Hijo del Pueblo (1864 and 1868)

El Nacional (1869–71)

El Obrero (1875)

La Patria (1870–73)

El Siglo (1875–76)

La Zamacueca Política (1859)

Published primary works

Ayanque, Simón. *Lima por dentro y fuera: Obra jocosa y divertida.*
Paris: A. Mezin, 1854.

Basadre y Chocano, Modesto. *Diez años de historia política del Perú (1834–1844).*
Lima: Editorial Huascarán, 1953.

Cabello, Pedro M. *Guía del Perú para el año de 1859.* Lima: Imprenta Masías, 1859.

Cisneros, Luis Benjamín. *Obras completas,* vol. 3. Lima: Librería e
Imprenta Gil, 1931.

*Documento parlamentario. Dictamen de la Comisión de Hacienda de la Camara de
Diputados sobre las representaciones de los gremios de Lima y Callao.* Lima:
Tipografía de Aurelio Alfaro y Compañía, 1859.

Echenique, José Rufino. *Memorias para la historia del Perú (1808–1878).* 2 vols.
Lima: Editorial Huascarán, 1952.

Espinosa, Juan. *Diccionario para el pueblo.* Lima: Imprenta del Pueblo, 1855.

Fuentes, Manuel Atanasio. *Lima, apuntes históricos, descriptivos, estadísticos y de
costumbres.* Paris: Librería de Firmin Didot hermanos, hijos y Ca., 1867.

González Vigil, Francisco de Paula. *Importancia y utilidad de las
asociaciones/Importancia de la educación popular.* Lima: Ediciones
Hora del Hombre, 1948.

Markham, Clemens, *The War Between Peru and Chile, 1879–1882.* London:
Sampson Low, Marston, Searle, and Rivington, 1882.

Mugaburu, Josephe de, and Francisco de Mugaburu. *Diario de Lima (1640–1694),*
vol. 6. Lima: Imprenta y Librería Sanmarti y Ca., 1917.

Oviedo, Juan., comp. *Colección de leyes, decretos y órdenes publicadas en el Perú
desde el año de 1821 hasta 31 de diciembre de 1859,* vol.13. Lima: F. Bailly, 1865.

Palma, Ricardo. *Recuerdos de España precedidos por la bohemia de mi tiempo.*
Lima: Imprenta La Industria, 1899.

Perez, Trinidad Manuel. *La industria y el poder.* Lima: Imprenta Liberal de
"El Correo del Peru," 1875.

*Presupuesto del Concejo Provincial de Lima: Que deberá rijir del 1ero de julio de 1876
a 30 de junio de 1878.* Lima: Imprenta del Estado, 1877.

Radiguet, Max. *Lima y la sociedad peruana.* Lima: Biblioteca Nacional
del Perú, 1971.

Reglamento de la Escuela de Artes y Oficios. Lima: Imprenta del Estado, 1871.

Reglamento de la exposición nacional del Perú. Lima : Imprenta del Estado, 1870

Reglamento de la Sociedad Fraternal de Artesanos. Lima: Imprenta del
Universo, 1876.

Sarmiento, Domingo Faustino. *Facundo.* Madrid : Alianza Editorial, 1988.

Silva Santisteban, José. *Breves reflexiones sobre los sucesos ocurridos en Lima y el Callao con motivo de la importación de artefactos.* Lima: Imprenta calle de Jesús Nazareno, 1859.

Tavara, Santiago. *Historia de los partidos.* Lima: Editorial Huascarán, 1951.

Tejeda, Simeón. *Libertad de industria.* Lima: Ediciones Horas del Hombre, 1947.

Secondary works

Adrianzén, Alberto, ed. *Pensamiento político peruano.* Lima: DESCO, 1987.

Aguila Peralta, Alicia del. *Callejones y mansiones: espacios de opinión pública y redes sociales y políticas en la Lima del 900.* Lima: Pontificia Universidad Católica, 1997.

Aguirre, Carlos, "The Lima Penitentiary and the Modernization of Criminal Justice in Nineteenth-Century Peru," in *The Birth of the Penitentiary in Latin America,* eds. Ricardo Salvatore and Carlos Aguirre. Austin: University of Texas Press, 1996, 44–77.

Aguirre, Carlos, and Charles Walker, eds. *Bandoleros, abigeos y montoneros: criminalidad y violencia en el Perú, siglos XVIII–XX.* Lima: Instituto de Apoyo Agrario, 1990.

Alba, Victor. *Politics and the Labor Movement in Latin America.* Stanford: Stanford University Press, 1968.

Aljovín, Cristobal. *Caudillos y constituciones Perú: 1821–1845.* Lima: Pontificia Universidad Católica y Fondo de Cultura Económica, 2000.

Annino, Antonio, ed. *Historia de las elecciones en Iberoamérica, siglo XIX.* Buenos Aires: Fondo de Cultura Economica, 1995.

Annino, Antonio, et al., eds. *América Latina: del estado colonial al estado nación.* Milano, Italy : Franco Angeli, 1987.

Armas Asin, Fernando. *Liberales, protestantes y masones: modernidad y tolerancia religiosa. Perú, siglo XIX.* Lima: Centro Bartolomé de las Casas and Pontificia Universidad Católica del Perú, 1998.

Baker, Keith Michael. *Inventing the French Revolution.* Cambridge: Cambridge University Press, 1990.

Basadre, Jorge. *Elecciones y centralismo en el Perú: Apuntes para un esquema histórico.* Lima: Universidad del Pacífico, 1980.

———. *Historia de la República del Peru,* 6th ed., vols. 1–7. Lima: Editorial Universitaria, 1968.

———. *Introducción a las bases documentales para la historia de la República del Perú con algunas refleciones,* vol. 1. Lima: Ediciones PLV, 1971.

————. *La multitud, la ciudad y el campo en la historia del Perú con un colofón sobre el país profundo*. Lima: Ediciones Treintaitrés y Mosca Azul Editores, 1980.

————. "El Perú republicano," in *El Peru en cifras, 1944–1945*, ed. Dario Sainte Maries. Lima: Empresa Gráfica Scheuchs SA, 1945.

————. *Perú: problema y posibilidad y otros ensayos*. Caracas: Biblioteca Ayacucho, 1992.

————. "La riqueza territorial y las actividades comerciales e industriales en los primeros años de la República." *Mercurio Peruano*, Año X, vol. XVII (1928): 15–31.

————. *Sultanismo, corrupción y dependencia en el Peru republicano*. Lima: Editorial Milla Bartres, 1981.

Beezley, William, et al., eds. *Rituals of Rule, Rituals of Resistance*. Wilmington, DL: Scholarly Resources, 1994.

————, and Colin MacLachlan. *Latin America: The Peoples and their History*. Fort Worth, TX: Harcourt Brace College Publishers, 2000.

Bendix, Reinhard. *Nation-Building and Citizenship: Studies of Our Changing Social Order*. Berkeley: University of California Press, 1964.

Blanchard, Peter. *The Origins of the Peruvian Labor Movement, 1883–1919*. Pittsburgh: University of Pittsburgh Press, 1982.

Bourricaud, François. *Power and Society in Contemporary Peru*. Trans. Paul Stevenson. New York: Praeger, 1970.

Bowser, Frederick. *The African Slave in Colonial Peru, 1524–1650*. Stanford: Stanford University Press, 1974.

Brooks, Jeffrey. *When Russia Learned to Read: Literacy and Popular Literature, 1861–1917*. Princeton: Princeton University Press, 1985.

Burkholder, Mark, and Lyman Johnson. *Colonial Latin America*. Oxford: Oxford University Press, 1998.

Bushnell, David, and Neill Macaulay. *The Emergence of Latin America in the Nineteenth Century*. 2nd ed. New York: Oxford University Press, 1994.

Cardoso, Fernando Henrique, and Enzo Faletto. *Dependency and Development in Latin America*. Berkeley and Los Angeles: University of California Press, 1979.

Carrera Stampa, Manuel. *Los gremios mexicanos*. Mexico: EDIAPSA, 1954.

Casanovas, Joan. *Bread or Bullets! Urban Labor and Spanish Colonialism in Cuba, 1850–1898*. Pittsburgh: University of Pittsburgh Press, 1998.

Castro Gutierrez, Felipe. *La extinción de la artesanía gremial*. Mexico: Universidad Nacional Autónoma de México, 1986.

Celestino, Olinda, and Albert Meyers. *Las cofradías en el Perú: región central*. Frankfurt/Main: Verlag Klaus DieterVervuert, 1981.

Chambers, Sarah. *From Subjects to Citizens: Humor, Gender, and Politics in Arequipa, Peru 1780–1854.* University Park: Pennsylvania State University Press, 1999.

Colley, Linda. *Britons.* New Haven, CT: Yale University Press, 1992.

Crossick, Geoffrey, ed. *The Artisan and the European Town, 1500–1900.* Hants, England: Scolar Press, 1997.

———. *An Artisan Elite in Victorian Society: Kentish London, 1840–1880.* London: Croom Helm, 1978.

Curcio-Nagy, Linda. "Giants and Gypsies: Corpus Christi in Colonial Mexico City," in *Rituals of Rule, Rituals of Resistance,* ed. William Beezley et al. Wilmington, DL: Scholarly Resources, 1994, 1–26.

Davis, Natalie Zemon. *Society and Culture in Early Modern France.* Stanford: Stanford University Press, 1975.

Descola, Jean. *Daily Life in Colonial Peru, 1710–1820.* Translated by Michael Heron. New York: Macmillan, 1968.

Diaz, Maria Elena. "The Satiric Penny Press for Workers in Mexico, 1900–1910: A Case Study in the Politicisation of Popular Culture." *Journal of Latin American Studies,* vol. 22, part 3 (October 1990): 497–525.

di Tella, Torcuato. "The Dangerous Classes in Early Nineteenth Century Mexico." *Journal of Latin American Studies* 5, no. 1 (May 1973): 79–105.

Drinot, Paulo. "After the Nueva Historia: Recent Trends in Peruvian Historiography." *European Review of Latin American and Caribbean Studies,* no. 68 (April 2000): 65–76.

Dulanto Pinillos, Jorge. *Cuatro Biografías.* Lima: Compañía de Impresiones y Publicidad Editores, 1938.

Eley, Geoff, and Keith Nield. "Farewell to the Working Class?" *International Labor and Working-Class History* 57 (spring 2000): 1–30.

Estenssoro, Juan Carlos. *Musica y sociedad coloniales, Lima 1680–1830.* Lima: Editorial Colmillo Blanco, 1989.

Foucault, Michel. *Discipline and Punish: The Birth of the Prison.* New York: Vintage, 1979.

Flores Galindo, Alberto. *La ciudad sumergida: aristocracia y plebe en Lima, 1760–1830.* 2nd ed. Lima: Editorial Horizonte, 1991.

Forment, Carlos. *Democracy in Latin America, 1760–1900.* Vol. 1, *Civic Selfhood and Public Life in Mexico and Peru.* Chicago: University of Chicago Press, 2003.

French, William. *A Peaceful and Working People: Manners, Morals and Class Formation in Northern Mexico.* Albuquerque: University of New Mexico Press, 1996.

García Ayluardo, Clara. "A World of Images: Cult, Ritual, and Society in Colonial Mexico City," in *Rituals of Rule, Rituals of Resistance,* eds. William Beezley et al. Wilmington: Scholarly Resources, 1994, 77–94.

García Calderón, Francisco. *Diccionario de la legislación peruana,* vol. 1. Paris, 1879.

———. *Le Pérou Contemporain.* Paris: Dujarric et Cie, Editeurs, 1907.

García Jordán, Pilar. *Iglesia y poder en el Perú contemporáneo, 1821–1919.* Cusco: Centro Bartolomé de las Casas, 1991.

Gargurevich, Juan. *Historia de la prensa peruana, 1594–1990.* Lima: La Voz Ediciones, 1991.

Gavarito Amézaga, Hugo. *El Perú liberal: partidos e ideas politicas de la ilustración a la república aristocrática.* Lima: Ediciones El Virrey, 1989.

Giesecke, Margarita. *Masas urbanas y rebelion en la historia, golpe de estado: Lima 1872.* Lima: Centro de Divulgación de Historia Popular, 1978.

Gootenberg, Paul. *Between Silver and Guano.* Princeton: Princeton University Press, 1989.

———. *Imagining Development.* Berkeley: University of California Press, 1993.

———. "The Social Origins of Protectionism and Free-Trade in Nineteenth-Century Lima." *Journal of Latin American Studies* 14, no. 2 (1982): 329–58.

Green, David R. *From Artisans to Paupers: Economic Change and Poverty in London, 1790–1870.* Hants, England: Scolar Press, 1995.

Grez, Sergio. *De la "regeneración del pueblo" a la huelga general. Génesis y evolución histórica del movimiento popular en Chile (1810–1890).* Santiago: Biblioteca Nacional de Chile, 1997.

Guerra, Francois Xavier. *Modernidad e Independencias.* Madrid: Mapfre, 1992.

Haber, Stephen. *Industry and Underdevelopment: The Industrialization of Mexico, 1890–1914.* Stanford: Stanford University Press, 1989.

Habermas, Jürgen. *The Structural Transformation of the Public Sphere.* Translated by Thomas Burger. Cambridge, MA: MIT Press, 1989.

Hale, Charles. *Mexican Liberalism in the Age of Mora, 1821–1853.* New Haven, CT: Yale University Press,1968.

Harriman, Brenda. "Los británicos en el Perú," in *Primer seminario sobre poblaciones inmigrantes.* Lima: Concitec, 1988.

Harris, Jose. *Private Lives, Public Spirit: Britain, 1870–1914.* London: Penguin, 1994.

Harth-terré, Emilio, and Alberto Márquez Abanto. "Perspectiva social y económica del artesano virreinal en Lima." *Revista del Archivo Nacional del Perú,* vol. XXVI, no. 2, 1962.

Hartley, John. *Popular Reality: Journalism, Modernity, Popular Culture.* London: Arnold, 1996.

Herr, Richard. *The Eighteenth-Century Revolution in Spain.* Princeton: Princeton University Press, 1958.

Hobsbawm, E. J. *Worlds of Labour: Further Studies in the History of Labour.* London: Wiedenfeld and Nicolson, 1984.

———. *The Age of Capital: 1848–1875.* New York: Vintage, 1996.

Holtby, David. "Education in Porfirian Mexico: The Role of Schools in the Coming of the Revolution." *Red River Valley Historical Journal of World History* 4, no. 1 (fall 1979); 31–51.

Hunt, Lynn. *Politics, Culture and Class in the French Revolution.* Berkeley: University of California, 1984.

Hunt, Shane. "Growth and Guano in Nineteenth-Century Peru," in *The Latin American Economies: Growth and the Export Sector 1880–1930,* ed. Roberto Cortés Conde and Shane Hunt. New York: Holmes and Meier, 1985.

Ilades, Carlos. *Hacia la república del trabajo: la organización artesanal en la ciudad de México, 1853–1876.* Mexico: El Colegio de México y la Universidad Autónoma Metropolitana, 1996.

Jacobsen, Nils. *Mirages of Transition: The Peruvian Altiplano 1780–1930.* Berkeley: University of California Press, 1993.

James, Louis, ed. *Print and the People, 1819–1851.* London: Allen Lane, 1976.

Jimenez, Michael. "'Citizens of the Kingdom': Toward a Social History of Radical Christianity in Latin America." *International Labor and Working-Class History* no. 34 (fall 1988): 3–21.

Johnson, John. *Political Change in Latin America: The Emergence of the Middle Sectors.* Stanford: Stanford University Press, 1958.

Johnson, Lyman. "Artisans," in *Cities and Society in Colonial Latin America,* ed . Louisa Schell Hoberman and Susan Migden Socolow. Albuquerque: University of New Mexico Press, 1986, 227–50.

———. "The Entrepreneurial Reorganization of an Artisan Trade: The Bakers of Buenos Aires, 1770–1820." *The Americas* 37, no. 2 (October 1980): 139–60.

———. "The Silversmiths of Buenos Aires: A Case Study in the Failure of Corporate Social Organization." *Journal of Latin American Studies* 8, no 2. (1976): 181–213.

Johnson, Lyman, and Sonia Lipsett-Rivera, eds. *The Faces of Honor.* Albuquerque: University of New Mexico Press, 1998.

Jones, Gareth Stedman. *Languages of Class: Studies in English Working Class History, 1832–1982.* Cambridge: Cambridge University Press, 1983.

Joyce, Patrick, ed. *The Historical Meanings of Work.* Cambridge: Cambridge University Press, 1987.

Katznelson, Ira, and Aristide Zolberg, eds. *Working Class Formation: Nineteenth-Century Patterns in Western Europe and the United States.* Princeton: Princeton University Press, 1986.

Klaiber, Jeffrey. *Religion and Revolution in Peru, 1824–1976.* Notre Dame, IN: University of Notre Dame Press, 1977.

Kristal, Efraín. *The Andes Viewed from the City: Literacy and Political Discourse on the Indian in Peru 1848–1930.* New York: Peter Lang, 1987.

Laurie, Bruce. *Artisans into Workers: Labor in Nineteenth-Century America.* New York: Hill and Wang, 1989.

Levin, Johnathan. *The Export Economies: Their Pattern of Development in Historical Perspective.* Cambridge, MA: Harvard University Press, 1960.

Lockhart, James, and Stuart Schwartz, *Early Latin America.* Cambridge: Cambridge University Press, 1983.

Lynch, John. *The Spanish American Revolutions, 1808–1826.* New York: Norton, 1973.

Macera, Pablo. *Trabajos de historia,* vol. 2. Lima: Instituto Nacional de Cultura, 1977.

Majluf, Natalia. "Entre pasatiempo y herramienta artesanal: aspectos de la enseñanza del dibujo en el diecinueve." *Sequilao* 2, no. 3 (May–July, 1993): 32–42.

Mallon, Florencia. *Peasant and Nation: The Making of Postcolonial Mexico and Peru.* Berkeley: University of California Press, 1995.

Mann, Michael. *The Sources of Social Power.* Vol. II: *The Rise of Classes and Nation-States, 1760–1914.* Cambridge: Cambridge University Press, 1993.

Maravall, José Antonio. *Culture of the Baroque: Analysis of a Historical Structure.* Minneapolis: University of Minnesota Press, 1986.

McEvoy, Carmen. *Un proyecto nacional en el siglo XIX: Manuel Pardo y su visión del Perú.* Lima: Pontificia Universidad Católica del Perú, 1994.

———. *La utopía republicana: Ideales y realidades en la formación de la cultura política peruana (1871–1919).* Lima: Pontificia Universidad Católica del Perú, 1997.

Moore, John Preston. *The Cabildo in Peru under the Bourbons.* Durham, NC: Duke University Press, 1966.

Morse, Richard. *New World Soundings.* Baltimore: Johns Hopkins University Press, 1989.

Mücke, Ulrich. "Elections and Political Participation in Nineteenth-Century Peru: The 1871–72 Presidential Campaign." *Journal of Latin American Studies* 2, no. 33 (May 2001): 311–46.

———. "Political Culture in Nineteenth-century Peru: The Rise of the Partido Civil." Translated by Katya Andrusz. Pittsburgh: University of Pittsburgh Press, 2004.

Murilo de Carvalho, José. *Os bestializados o Rio de Janeiro e a república que não foi,* 3rd ed. São Paulo: Editora Schwarcz Ltda, 1998.

Olton, Charles S. *Artisans for Independence: Philadelphia Mechanics and the American Revolution.* Syracuse: Syracuse University Press, 1975.

O'Phelan, Scarlett. *Rebellions and Revolts in Eighteenth-Century Peru and Upper Peru.* Cologne: Bohlau Verlag, 1985.

———, ed. *El Perú en el siglo XVIII (La era borbónica).* Lima: Instituto Riva Aguero de la Pontificia Universidad Católica, 1999.

Panfichi, Aldo H., and Felipe Portocarrero, eds. *Mundos Interiores: Lima 1850–1950.* Lima: Universidad del Pacífico, 1995.

Parker, David. *The Idea of the Middle Class: White-Collar Workers and Peruvian Society, 1900–1950.* University Park: Pennsylvania State University Press, 1998.

Paulston, Rolland. *Society, Schools and Progress in Peru.* Oxford: Pergamon, 1971.

Peloso, Vincent, and Barbara Tenenbaum, eds. *Liberals, Politics and Power: State Formation in Nineteenth-Century Latin America.* Athens: University of Georgia Press, 1996.

Pérez-Mallaína Bueno, Pablo Emilio. "Profesiones y oficios en la Lima de 1850." *Anuario de Estudios Americanos* XXXVII (1980): 191–233.

Pike, Frederick. *The Modern History of Peru.* London: Weidenfeld and Nicolson, 1967.

Prothero, Iorwerth. *Artisans and Politics in Early Nineteenth-Century London: John Gast and His Times.* Kent: Dawson and Son, 1979.

Quiroz, Francisco. *Gremios, razas y libertad de industria: Lima colonial.* Lima: Universidad Nacional Mayor de San Marcos, 1995.

———. *La protesta de los artesanos Lima-Callao, 1858.* Lima: Universidad Nacional Mayor de San Marcos, 1988.

Reddy, William. *The Rise of Market Culture: The Textile Trade and French Society, 1750–1900.* Cambridge: Cambridge University Press, 1984.

Romero, Emilio. *Historia económica del Perú.* Buenos Aires: Editorial Sudamericana, 1949.

Romero, L. A. *La sociedad de la igualdad: los artesanos de Santiago de Chile y sus primeras experiencias políticas, 1820–1851.* Buenos Aires: Editorial del Instituto Torcuato di Tella, 1978.

Sábato, Hilda. *La política en las calles: entre el voto y la movilización, Buenos Aires, 1862–1880.* Buenos Aires: Editorial Sudamericana, 1998.

————, ed. *Ciudadanía política y formación de las naciones: perspectivas históricas de América Latina.* Mexico: El Colegio de Mexico y Fondo de Cultura Ecónomica, 1999.

Safford, Frank. "Politics, Ideology and Society," in *Spanish America After Independence, c.1820–c.1870,* ed. Leslie Bethell. Cambridge: Cambridge University Press, 1987, 48–122.

Samayoa Guevara, Héctor Humberto. *Los gremios de artesanos en la Ciudad de Guatemala.* Guatemala: Editorial Universitaria, 1962.

Sarrailh, Jean. *L'Espagne éclairée.* Paris: Imprimerie Nationale, 1954.

Schultz, Ronald. *The Republic of Labor: Philadelphia Artisans and the Politics of Class, 1720–1830.* New York: Oxford University Press, 1993.

Sewell, William. *Work and Revolution in France: The Language of Labor from the Old Regime to 1848.* Cambridge: Cambridge University Press, 1980.

Sheehan, James. *German History 1770–1866.* Oxford: Oxford University Press, 1989.

————. *German Liberalism in the Nineteenth-Century.* Atlantic Highlands, NJ: Humanities Press, 1995.

Sobrevilla Perea, Natalia. "The Influence of the European 1848 Revolutions in Peru," in *The European Revolutions of 1848 and the Americas,* ed. Guy Thomson. London: Institute of Latin American Studies, 2002.

Sonenscher, Michael. *Work and Wages: Natural Law, Politics and the Eighteenth-Century French Trades.* Cambridge: Cambridge University Press, 1989.

Sowell, David. *The Early Colombian Labor Movement.* Philadelphia: Temple University Press, 1992.

Spalding, Hobart A., Jr. *Organized Labor in Latin America: Historical Case Studies of Workers in Dependent Societies.* New York: New York University Press, 1977.

Spalding, Karen. *Huarochirí: An Andean Society under Inca and Spanish Rule.* Stanford: Stanford University Press, 1984.

Telenta de Vértiz, Elizabeth, and Roberto Vértiz Cabrejos. *Pedro Ruiz Gallo: Una vida consagrada al servicio del Perú: Biografía ilustrada y documentada.* Lima: Editorial Libertad, 1994.

Temoche Benites, Ricardo. *Cofradías, gremios, mutuales y sindicatos en el Perú.* Lima: Impresora Escuela Nueva, 1987.

Tenorio-Trillo, Mauricio. *Mexico at the World's Fairs: Crafting a Modern Nation.* Berkeley: University of California Press, 1996.

Thompson, E. P. *The Making of the English Working Class.* New York: Vintage, 1966.

Thurner, Mark. *From Two Republics to One Divided: Contradictions of Postcolonial Nationmaking in Andean Peru*. Durham, NC: Duke University Press, 1997.

Trazegnies, Fernando de. *La idea del derecho en el Perú republicano del siglo XIX*. Lima: Pontificia Universidad Católica, 1992.

Ugarte del Pino, Juan Vicente. *Historia de las constituciones del Perú*. Lima: Editorial Andina, 1978.

Valcarcel, Carlos Daniel. *Breve historia de la educación en el Perú*. Lima: Editorial Educación, 1975.

Vargas Llosa, Mario. *La ciudad y los perros*. Barcelona: Editorial Seix Barral, 1965.

———. *Un pez en el agua*. Barcelona: Seix Barral, 1993.

———. "Questions of Conquest: What Columbus Wrought, and What He Did Not." *Harper's* (December 1990): 43–53.

Vargas Ugarte, Ruben. *Ensayo de un diccionario de artífices de la América meridional*, 2nd ed. Burgos: Imprenta de Aldecoa, 1968.

Wagley, Charles. *The Latin American Tradition: Essays on the Unity and the Diversity of Latin American Culture*. New York: Columbia University Press, 1968.

Walker, Charles. *Smoldering Ashes: Cuzco and the Creation of Republican Peru, 1780–1840*. Durham, NC: Duke University Press, 1999.

Wallach Scott, Joan. *The Glassworkers of Carmaux: French Craftsmen and Political Action in a Nineteenth-Century City*. Cambridge, MA: Harvard University Press, 1974.

Weinstein, Barbara. "Where Do New Ideas (About Class) Come From?" *International Labor and Working-Class History* 57 (spring 2000): 53–59.

Wilentz, Sean. *Chants Democratic: New York City and the Rise of the American Working Class, 1788–1850*. New York: Oxford University Press, 1984.

Dissertations and Theses

Aljovín, Cristobal. "Representative Government in Peru: Fiction and Reality, 1821–1845." PhD diss., University of Chicago, 1996.

Gootenberg, Paul. "Artisans and Merchants: The Making of an Open Economy in Lima, Peru, 1830 to 1860." MPhil thesis, Oxford University, 1981.

Kruggeler, Thomas. "Unreliable Drunkards or Honorable Citizens? Artisans in Search of Their Place in the Cusco Society (1825–1930)." PhD diss., University of Illinois at Urbana-Champagne, 1993.

Majluf, Natalia. "The Creation of the Image of the Indian in 19th Century Peru: The Paintings of Francisco Laso (1823–1869)." PhD thesis, University of Texas–Austin, 1995.

Myers, Jorge. "Languages of Politics: A Study of Republican Discourse in Argentina from 1820 to 1852." PhD diss., Stanford University, 1997.

Naro, Nancy. "The 1848 Praieira Revolt in Brazil." PhD diss., University of Chicago, 1981.

Quiroz, Francisco. "Artesanos y manufactureros en Lima colonial." Master's thesis, Pontificia Universidad Católica del Perú, 1998.

Ragas Rojas, José Frank. "Cuidadania, cultura política y representación en el Perú: la campaña electoral de 1850." Bachelor's thesis, Pontificia Universidad Católica del Perú, 2003.

Warren, Richard Andrew. "Vagrants and Citizens: Politics and the Poor in Mexico City, 1808–1836." PhD diss., University of Chicago, 1994.

Index

About the Book and Author

Crafting the Republic
Lima's Artisans and Nation-Building in Peru, 1821-1879

Iñigo García-Bryce

This clearly written, cogently argued assessment of social and political mobilization in nineteenth-century Peru focuses on 5,000 Lima artisans, 70 percent of whom were black, Indian, or mestizo. García-Bryce traces the evolution of these guild artisans into class-conscious workers. His discussion gives special attention to how artisans' declining economic success meant not only a loss of income but undercut gains in social status. It is in this interplay of economics and race that García-Bryce's analysis of the origins of class identity is most revealing.

The fate of Lima's artisans, the most numerous of whom were shoemakers, tailors, and carpenters, is discussed against the backdrop of nineteenth-century Liberalism, which sought to align everyone to the "greater good" of the state while sidestepping demands from special interest groups such as craft workers. Indeed, following the abolition of guilds in 1862, the artisans fully subscribed to the modernization promised by the liberal elites. But when in the 1870s it became clear the state could not deliver on its promises, working-class identity began to emerge, especially fostered by a newly emergent group of artisans, the printers.

"This is an elegantly written social history that contributes to our understanding of modern Peru and also participates in debates about labor and urban history."

—Charles Walker, associate professor of history,
University of California, Davis

❧

Iñigo García-Bryce is an assistant professor of Latin American history at New Mexico State University, Las Cruces.